Reading
Organization
Theory

Albert J. Mills' research activities centre on the impact of organization upon people, focusing on organizational change and human liberation. These lifelong concerns were formulated on the shop-floor of British industry and through involvement in the movements for social change that predominated in the 1960s. Mills' early images of organization – images of frustration, of sexually segregated work, of power disparities, of conflict – were experienced through a series of unskilled jobs and given broader meaning through campaigns for peace, women's liberation, environmental survival and social change. In his early twenties, Mills went on to full-time study at Ruskin College, Oxford, and then on to the universities of Durham, Sheffield and Southern California.

To date, Mills has taught management in the U.K., U.S., Canada, Holland, Hungary, Macedonia, Slovenia and Kuwait. He writes a bi-weekly column for *Ekopres,* a Macedonian business magazine. In addition to a series of journal articles, he is the co-author (with Steve Murgatroyd) of *Organizational Rules* (Open University Press, 1991) and the co-editor (with Peta Tancred) of *Gendering Organizational Analysis* (Sage, 1992). Mills is Associate Professor in the Management Department and the Associate Dean of the Faculty of Commerce at Saint Mary's University, Halifax, Nova Scotia.

Tony Simmons has pursued an undistinguished career at Athabasca University, where he spends much of his time writing correspondence courses in sociology for distance education students, and teaching special needs students in prisons, reservations and other outreach locations. He is presently working on two other books, one an anthology of classical sociological theory, the other a manual of urban terrorist tactics for use against neo-conservative provincial governments and government bureaucracies. Tony Simmons currently lives in Edmonton with his cat, Reilly, where he continues in a struggle to align his theory with his practice.

Reading Organization Theory

ALBERT J. MILLS AND TONY SIMMONS

Garamond Press

Printed and bound in Canada.

A publication of Garamond Press

Copy Editors: Melodie Mayson and Ted Richmond
Cover design and Illustrations: Margaret Anderson
Typesetting and Layout: Robin Brass Studio

Garamond Press,
77 Mowat Ave., Suite 403
Toronto, On.
M6K 3E3

Canadian Cataloguing in Publication Data

Mills, Albert J. , 1945–
        Reading organization theory

Includes bibliographical references and index.
ISBN 0-920059-07-4

1. Organizational sociology.   I. Simmons, Anthony M.
(Anthony Michael) , 1945–   .   II. Title .

HM131 . M55 1994   302 . 3 ' 5   C94-932063-3

Contents

ACKNOWLEDGMENTS xi

CHAPTER 1

DEVELOPING A CRITICAL APPROACH TO ORGANIZATIONAL STUDY 1

Alice in Organization Land 1

INTRODUCTION 2

✓ ORGANIZATIONAL STUDY AND THE NEGLECT OF CLASS, GENDER,
AND RACE/ETHNICITY 3

WHY STUDY ORGANIZATIONS?: GETTING INTERESTED 5

The Organizational World 5

✓ OUTLINING A CRITICAL APPROACH 9

Comprehension: The Many Faces
of Organizational Analysis 10

Reading: Deconstructing the Text 13

Taken-for-granted Assumptions 14

Silences, Exclusions, and Deletions 15

Examples 16

Asides 17

Illustrations 17

Acting: The Praxis of Research 18

Writing: Reaching Out and Authorizing 21

KEY TERMS 23

REVIEW QUESTIONS 23

EXERCISE 1.1 25

FURTHER READING 26

END NOTES 27

CHAPTER 2

UNDERSTANDING BUREAUCRACIES: THE AGE OF THE ORGANIZATIONAL GIANTS 29

"The Dark Side" 29

INTRODUCTION 30

LIVING IN A BUREAUCRATIC WONDERLAND 32

WHAT IS BUREAUCRACY? 34

THE BIRTH OF BUREAUCRACY IN CLASSICAL ORGANIZATION
    THEORY 36

THE BUREAUCRATIC IMAGE: THE ORGANIZATION AS MACHINE 40

DEBATING THE BUREAUCRACY: DILEMMAS OF MODERN
    ORGANIZATION THEORY. 41

    Rigidity 43

    Goal Displacement 44

    Impersonality 45

    Empire-building and Self-perpetuation 45

    Resistance to Change 46

    Secrecy 46

    Anti-democratic 47

STANDING IN THE SHADOWS: BUREAUCRACIES AND
    MINORITY GROUPS 48

KEY TERMS 52

REVIEW QUESTIONS 52

EXERCISE 2.1 53

FURTHER READING 54

END NOTES 54

CHAPTER 3

CALLING THE SHOTS: HOW ORGANIZATION THEORY RELATES TO MANAGERS 57

INTRODUCTION 57

THE VISIBLE HAND: BIG BUSINESS AND THE MANAGERIAL
    REVOLUTION 61

READING BETWEEN THE LINES: MANAGEMENT THEORY AND
    CLASS STRUGGLE 68

THE PERIODIZATION OF THEORY AND THE ILLUSION OF PROGRESS:
    THE CASE OF SCIENTIFIC MANAGEMENT 70

MANAGEMENT IN PRACTICE: WHAT MANAGERS REALLY DO 77

KEY TERMS 83

REVIEW QUESTIONS 84

EXERCISE 3.1 85

FURTHER READING 89

END NOTES 89

CHAPTER 4

CREATING THE PSYCHIC PRISON 95

Work and Identity – An Interview With Sharon Webb 95

INTRODUCTION 96

PSYCHIC PHENOMENA AND ORGANIZATIONAL BEHAVIOUR 98

IMAGES OF THE PSYCHIC PRISON 101

    Critical Theory 102

    Humanist 107

    Marxist 110

    Post-Modernist 113

    Psychoanalysis 115

    Feminist 118

SUMMARY 122

KEY TERMS 122

REVIEW QUESTIONS 123

EXERCISE 4.1 124

FURTHER READING 127

END NOTES 127

CHAPTER 5

SEX AND ORGANIZATIONAL ANALYSIS 131

In/digestion at a Quebec Hospital 131

INTRODUCTION 132

SEX AND ORGANIZATIONAL LIFE 133

✓ SEX AND ACADEMIA 136

SEX AND ORGANIZATIONAL RESEARCH 138

ISSUES IN SEX AND ORGANIZATIONAL RESEARCH 142

Equity Issues 142

Barriers to change 143

Sex, Power, and Authority issues 146

Identity Issues 148

Research Issues 148

KEY TERMS 149

REVIEW QUESTIONS 149

EXERCISE 5.1 151

FURTHER READING 152

END NOTES 152

CHAPTER 6

OUT OF SIGHT, OUT OF MIND: RACE, ETHNICITY AND ORGANIZATION THEORY

OUT OF SIGHT, OUT OF MIND: RACE, ETHNICITY AND
ORGANIZATION THEORY 155

*October 20th, 1983. Proceedings of the Special Committee on the Participation
of Visible Minorities in Canadian Society.* 155

INTRODUCTION: ETHNIC AND RACIAL INEQUALITY IN CANADA 157

THE POLITICALIZATION OF RACE AND ETHNIC RELATIONS 160

The Evolution of Government Policy 161

Academic Theory 163

Public Reaction and Debate 166

RACE AND ETHNIC RELATIONS IN ORGANIZATIONAL THEORY 169

The Silence of Organizational Theory 169

The Influence of American Assimilation Theory 173

THE ETHNICITY PARADIGM 175

The Ethnicity Paradigm and Canadian Research 178

Beyond the Ethnicity Paradigm 180

WHAT DOES THE FUTURE HOLD? 184

KEY TERMS 187

REVIEW QUESTIONS 187

EXERCISE 6.1 188

FURTHER READING 190

END NOTES 191

CHAPTER 7

KNOWLEDGE AND POWER IN ORGANIZATION THEORY: THE ORGANIZATIONAL WORLD AND THE MANAGERIAL PARADIGM 195

INTRODUCTION 195

FROM PARADIGM TO DISCOURSE: UNDERSTANDING THE
   MANAGERIALIST DOMINANCE OF OT. 196

INSIDE THE MANAGERIALIST VIEW OF REALITY 200

WHAT IS TO BE DONE? THE CHALLENGE AND LIMITATION OF
   RADICAL THEORIES OF ORGANIZATION... 201

END NOTES 208

GLOSSARY OF TERMS 209

BIBLIOGRAPHY 227

INDEX 245

ACKNOWLEDGMENTS

Books are deceptive. They carry but three sets of names – those of the author or authors, the book title, and the publisher. Hidden from view, buried deep in the text, is the contribution of many other people whose energy, intellectual stimulation, and tireless efforts were no less important in bringing the book into being. For our part, we would like to thank Carol Agócs, Peta Tancred and Jerry White for a wealth of useful and encouraging comments on earlier drafts of the book; Carol Schafer for being there at the right time; and Peter Saunders of Garamond Press for his continued commitment to the book.

Individually, we would like to thank the following people:

Albert: For me, this book owes much to several people. I thank Val Delorme not only for providing secretarial assistance but for her strong and fast friendship over the years; Steve Schafer for library assistance above and beyond the call of duty; Stewart Clegg for his intellectual comradeship and for his encouraging remarks on an earlier draft of the book; Terry Morrison for believing in the project when others doubted; and my colleagues old and new – Peter Chiaramonte, Jean Hatfield, Dave Hooper, Paul Iles, Andy Khan, Richard Marsden, Glenn Morgan, Jules Pisacarne, and Liz Shorrocks – whose intellectual exchanges over the years have somehow found their way into the text. A special thanks to Julie Kautz Mills, my partner of twelve years, whose encouragement, support, intellectual comment, and a host of direct and indirect assistance have made my contribution both possible and readable.

We would like to thank Margaret Anderson whose wonderful drawings have helped to simplify and make clear a number of otherwise complex ideas.

Tony:
For Sybil: who believed
For Albert: who waited
For Irene: who understood

CHAPTER 1

Developing a Critical Approach to Organizational Study

This chapter discusses the need for a critical approach to organizational study and outlines the main elements of a critical approach. The chapter examines competing views (or paradigms) within organizational analysis, and explains how to deconstruct organizational texts, how to develop a reflexive research agenda, and how to "reach out and authorize" the reader in the process of writing-up research findings.

Alice in Organization Land

Once upon a time there was a girl called Alice. Alice, with her parents, had recently emigrated from Underdeveloped Land to the United States of Industrialization where she lived in one of the poorer neighbourhoods of a major city.

One day something miraculous happened. Alice was walking just outside the city limits when she tripped and fell down a large hole. The fall seemed endless but when she finally reached the bottom she was confronted by a strange looking man, with wire rimmed glasses, a blackboard and a large, voluminous book. "Hello little girl," he said, emphasizing the word girl, "welcome to Organization Land." As Alice stared in amazement the man opened the book, placed it on the floor and invited her to step into it. Reaching out his hand the man reassured Alice with these words, "A Willy Wonka world of chocolate this is not, but a land of reality made up of many wondrous things." Alice took a deep breath and stepped into the book and what she saw was truly amazing. She had stepped into a world where no one talked of class, race, ethnic background, or gender.

Everything was so white, so sanitized, so comfortable, so male that after a bit the whiteness became too overbearing and no one seemed to understand Alice. At first she thought that people had trouble hearing her but then it began to dawn on her that no one even noticed her. Then suddenly she heard it. It was faint at first but the sound began to grow, "Girl, girl, girl," and as the noise grew louder it sounded increasingly menacing, Alice began to feel constrained, she could hardly breathe, she wanted to yell. Finally, she was able to close her eyes and let out a loud scream. As she opened her eyes she found her mother leaning over her bed "Oh mummy," she cried, "I had a bad dream. I don't ever want to go to Organization Land." "My poor child," said the mother trying to comfort her, "it wasn't a dream."

INTRODUCTION

This book explains and develops a critical approach to understanding organizations. It is aimed primarily at the student of organization across the various subdivisions, which the field has been subjected to over the years. It is not our intention to reinforce the existing fragmentation of the field into organization theory (OT), organizational behaviour (OB), and the sociology of organizations. We do not accept that organizational structure and behaviour can be understood without reference to one another. Nor do we accept that organizations can be simply understood as reflections of the broader society in which they are located or as social entities in their own right. It is our contention that organizations need to be understood as the outcome of several levels of abstraction that includes internal and external factors, structural and behavioural factors and various combinations of each factor. To that end the book's title is a reference to the theory of organization (in the broadest sense) rather than the more disciplinary and narrow organization theory.

This book is not a substitute for mainstream texts. It is assumed that the reader will either be familiar with, or in the process of studying, mainstream accounts of organization. Instead, this book will challenge the reader to think about many of the assumptions involved in his/her course of study. The objective of the book is to introduce the reader to five key areas of understanding:

(i) A critical analysis of mainstream studies of organization (that is, from Taylorism through to current theories of organizational culture).

ii) An awareness that there are several, competing approaches to organizational analysis.

iii) The notion that issues of class, gender and race/ethnicity are essential features of organizational analysis.

iv) The viewpoint that organizations are historically constructed entities.

v) Ways of developing a critical approach to organizational analysis.

ORGANIZATIONAL STUDY AND THE NEGLECT OF CLASS, GENDER, AND RACE/ETHNICITY

The story of Alice in Organization Land is not a fairy tale. Pick up any of the large organization theory (OT) or organizational behaviour (OB) texts, turn to the index and try to find any reference to race, ethnicity, class, or gender. Chances are that you will find little or nothing. Yet the issues are not trivial. The workforce of the major industrial nations consists of large numbers of female workers, and people from different ethnic backgrounds. In Canada a Royal Commission on "Equality in Employment,"[1] reporting in 1984, listed fourteen major "selected ethnic groups" which included "British, French, other European, Indo-Pakistani, Indo-Chinese, Japanese, Korean, Chinese, Pacific Islands, Black, Native People, and Central/South American." The Commission went on to state that there was evidence of widespread "systemic discrimination" against "native people, and visible minorities" as well as "disabled persons" and women, and added that:

> It is not fair that many people in these groups have restricted employment opportunities, limited access to decision-making processes that critically affect them, little public visibility as contributing Canadians, and a circumscribed range of options generally (p.1).

It is hard to believe that issues of this kind – even after the public scrutiny of a Royal Commission in Canada and employment equity legislation in the U.S., Britain, and Canada – have remained largely unspoken within OT and OB texts.

It is only recently that business educators have begun to come to terms with the issues. At the start of 1990 the U.S. Commission on Admission to Graduate Management Education named race and gender as two of the most pressing issues that business schools in the U.S. need to account for in their programs. Commenting on the study, William Ouchi – one of the Commission members – pointed out the lunacy of existing approaches to management education:

> [An MBA class] has to be a heterogeneous group. For example, if you were in Southern California in the year 2000, you could not call yourself a sensible person if you weren't fully committed to a diverse, multi-cultural workplace with full representation of Latinos, Blacks, Asian-Pacifics, and women. The way we currently approach that problem is to say that our entering students have to be able to do algebra II and calculus, and then do everything we can to compose a student body that will be sufficiently diverse from among those

who have sufficient mathematics. Well, that's absolutely nuts. The world isn't saying, "Give us people who can do math, and then do the best you can to make them adequately diverse." The world is saying, "Your mission is to see that people of all races and both genders have equal access to the fruits of this society and to participation in the business community." (Selections, Interview, Spring 1990: 38)

To continue our experiment, turn back to one of the organizational texts and now attempt to find references to the impact of organizations on the lives of people. Again you will find next to nothing despite the fact that the effects of organizational life have been linked to a lack of self-esteem (Leonard, 1984), sexual harassment (DiTomaso, 1989), a sense of powerlessness (Kanter, 1977), a segregated work life (Fox and Fox, 1987), pay inequities (Conklin and Bergman, 1989), racism (Wallis, 1989), stress (Lowe and Northcott, 1986), and physical injury[2]; the list goes on and on.

As a final experiment look through the text and try to assess how much of it deals with experiences with which you are familiar. If your experiences are anything like ours you will have little to note down. It is hardly surprising that studies of organization strike so many students as boring and outside their interests and experiences. Many students are soon likely to feel that organizations are something that people serve rather than the other way around. If you are as Alice you might run away, give up, or simply keep going just to obtain the credits. But do not despair. When organizational analysis is approached from a fresh and critical approach, you will find that it is one of the most important areas of study that you will ever undertake.

The aim of this book is not to turn anyone away from the study of organizations. On the contrary, through an exploration of class, gender, race/ethnicity and the impact of organizations on social and psychic life we hope to stimulate a renewed interest in organizational analysis. To that end, the book encourages you to think for yourself and to provide information and ideas to help you find your own way. Above all else, the book sets out to provide you with the tools of analysis rather than simply an alternative view of organizations. The content does, of course, reflect our version of reality – our way of viewing organizations, but its purpose is to engage in dialogue with existing theories of organization in a way which will challenge you to think about organizations and how to study them.

In this chapter our central objective is to challenge you to think about the character of mainstream organizational analysis, to expose you to a number of alternative approaches, and to start you thinking about how you might begin to develop a critical approach. First we want to inspire an interest in the study of organizations.

WHY STUDY ORGANIZATIONS?: GETTING INTERESTED

Welcome to the world of high-risk technologies. You may have noticed that they seem to be multiplying, and it is true. As our technology expands, as our wars multiply, and as we invade more and more of nature, we create systems – organizations, and the organization of organizations – that increase the risks for operators, passengers, innocent bystanders, and for future generations. [These systems include] nuclear power plants, chemical plants, aircraft and air traffic control, ships, dams, nuclear weapons, space missions, and genetic engineering. Most of these risky enterprises have catastrophic potential, the ability to take the lives of hundreds of people in one blow, or to shorten or cripple the lives of thousands or millions more. Every year there are more such systems. That is the bad news. The good news is that if we can understand the nature of risky enterprises better, we may be able to reduce or even remove these dangers (Charles Perrow 1984: 3).

We live in a time dominated by organizations. Organizations permeate nearly everything we do. They shape the way we live, the way we think, the way we are valued and the way we value ourselves. They offer opportunities for social improvement but they also threaten our very existence. In short, we cannot afford to ignore organizations.

The Organizational World

Because of a reliance by organizations on petroleum products the twentieth century has been called the "oil century," and its last quarter has been characterized as an era of "oil crisis" (Halberstam, 1986). This characterization ignores that organizational arrangements preceded oil, that in order for oil to be extracted and utilized there had to be large-scale organizations to make it happen. The organization is the real symbol of the twentieth century, and the last quarter is more appropriately characterized as an era of organizational crisis. The importance of both oil and organization was highlighted during the Gulf War in 1991. It can be argued that the issue of access to oil was a central feature of the war, but we should also note that the resolution of this issue through armed conflict signalled a major failure in the character of existing organizations. The United Nations, for example, was unable to prevent war; and the

Parliament of Canada could not maintain its commitment to peacekeeping activities.

Organizations are not new, they have been a part of human social development from as far back as we know. Indeed, as early as 600 BC there was in Greek society an association with characteristics which are similar to those found in modern corporations (Hatton, 1990). Before the Industrial Revolution, in the mid-eighteenth century, the development of organizations to deal with specific tasks was restricted to relatively few areas of social endeavour — such as religion (churches), wars and taxation (armies), scholarly communities (universities), trade and colonization (merchant and craft guilds, and trading companies). But the organized bodies typical of the time, such as universities or merchant guilds, rarely dealt with large numbers of the population. Where organizations touched the lives of many people they did so in an irregular fashion, for example, as in the collection of taxes or the raising of an army.

All that was to change with the onset of the Industrial Revolution and the widespread development of manufactories, which brought people together under one roof for purposes of production. The new factory organizations generated a host of other new organizations to deal with the distribution, sale, and regulation of goods. Political parties developed to protect the interests of different classes of people associated with the new means of production, and within the factories trade unions began to develop as workers saw a need to defend and improve their economic conditions.

Bound up with the proliferation of organizations came a new type of thinking — organizational thinking. Increasingly, an array of social problems and activities began to be dealt with through the development of organizations. The principles of factory organization were used to deal with other aspects of social life:

> Schools, hospitals, prisons, government bureaucracies, and other organizations thus took on many of the characteristics of the factory — its division of labour, its hierarchical structure and its metallic impersonality. Even in the arts we find some of the principles of the factory. Instead of working for a patron, as was customary during the long reign of agricultural civilization, musicians, artists, composers, and writers relied on the mercies of the marketplace. More and more they turned out 'products' for anonymous consumers. (Alvin Toffler 1981: 45)

This situation has developed to the present day where we can hardly think of an aspect of our life without thinking about an organizational answer. Whether we are going to work or school, taking in a movie, getting a Big Mac, listening to a concert, or attending a hockey game we are involved with one organization or another.

The modern organizational world and capitalism have developed hand in hand. At its simplest, capitalism involves three major features that have become embodied within modern principles of organizations – i) ownership and control of organizations lies with very few persons, ii) production is for profit, with products offered for sale in competitive, market situations and iii) productive tasks are carried out by employees who rely on work as their only or major source of income. This has resulted in a number of organizational dynamics that centre on issues of control. For those in charge of the organization, competition creates pressures to control costs. Production for a market, where you can never ultimately tell whether enough people will buy your products, creates pressures to control uncertainties. And the fact that the employees who are hired to do the work are mainly interested in the wages they will receive for the job creates pressures to control organizational behaviour. This has helped to shape organizations as hierarchical arrangements, where decision-making is top down, and broken into departments, with various posts created to control employees (e.g., supervisors, personnel departments) and the market (e.g., marketing departments). Interpersonal relationships within organizations are largely impersonal, manipulative, mistrustful, and mediated by money.

The soul-destroying aspects of organizational life were long ago captured in the works of the founding group of sociologists – Emile Durkheim, Karl Marx and Max Weber. For Durkheim modern organization brought with it the destruction of a sense of community which resulted in the increasing atomization of individuals to the point where they felt unable to relate to others and the broader society. In a similar vein Marx saw organizations as alienating and soul destroying, preventing individuals from realizing their full human and social potential. Weber predicted an ever increasing bureaucratization of life to the point where people's lives would be drab, impersonal and soulless. He called this "the iron cage of bureaucracy." Both Durkheim and Marx were optimistic in believing that it was possible to transform the organizational world. Durkheim believed that over time organizational arrangement could create a new sense of community but only if organizations were limited in size (to a few hundred persons), and only if workplace relationships were organized along more democratic lines. Marx's optimism rested on the assumption that capitalist forms of organization would – through revolution – be replaced by socialist forms which, in turn, would encourage a "withering away" of organizational arrangements as we know them. Weber, on the other hand, was extremely pessimistic, confident that the inevitable spread of bureaucracy would be hastened not hindered by the rise of socialism.

Durkheim's vision was ill-placed in the twentieth century world of large-scale organization. But in 1917 the Russian Revolution breathed new life into Marx's dream of a classless society. When this revolution gave rise to the founding of the Soviet Union in 1922, the new socialist state served as a model to many people seeking an alternative to capitalism. Around the world people argued, and fought, over this model for the next seventy years. But then the fall of the Berlin Wall and the collapse of communist governments in Eastern Europe and the Soviet Union confirmed that these states had been no more than a realization of Weber's worst fears of bureaucracy.

The ending of decades of Communist rule in Eastern Europe has been hailed as a victory for capitalism, "the end of history" (Fukuyama, 1989). But this interpretation is a travesty of reality. Rather than being a victory for capitalism, these stunning political events represent a clarification of the fundamental crisis in humankind's ability to organize. The rigid state bureaucracies of the East were marked by economic shortages, widespread environmental devastation and a political rot that led to their collapse. But the capitalist states of the West remain characterized by poverty, social inequities, mass unemployment, lingering recession, environmental crisis, and growing support for authoritarian political solutions. Capitalism today is only successful in the sense that capitalist organizations continue to thrive. To see capitalism as somehow victorious is to ignore the thousands of businesses that go bankrupt each year[3], the corruption and greed at various levels of government and business[4], the dubious government aid to companies[5],

> In terms of pollution the last few years alone have been disastrous. In 1989 the U.S. Environmental Protection Agency revealed a list of 75,000 firms that emit toxic wastes. A similar list for Ontario included 20,250 companies. In that same province a major fire, in 1990, threatened the health of the people of Hagersville when a poorly cared-for tire dump caught alight: the fire released close to 5.5. million gallons of oil – half as much as the tanker Exxon Valdez spilled into Alaskan waters in March, 1989 (Jenish 1990). The previous year a fire in a PCB storage warehouse in St.Basile-le-Grand, Quebec led to the evacuation of the town.
> The Westray Mine (Plymouth, Nova Scotia) disaster of May 1992 exemplifies several concurrent problems including dubious Provincial government aid, charges of criminal negligence, social and environmental disaster in the form of an explosion which caused the death of 26 miners and the closure of the mine.

continuous class conflict[6], and various industry-related social and environmental disasters[7].

The situation looks bleak, but that is the bad news. The good news, as Charles Perrow rightly says, is that we may be able to do something about it. To take an active interest in the study of organization is an important starting point but begin with a healthy scepticism. Healthy, in this case, means not being discouraged or overwhelmed by what seems a daunting task. Remember these three things, i) always dare to dream; without a vision we will succumb to the darkness, ii) there are examples of alternative modes of organizing, we need to search them out and iii) never be afraid to think small. The big picture consists of many images, and it may be that effecting a small change will contribute to overall change. Scepticism means being prepared to question the value of organizing as a way of dealing with social problems: it means accepting the possibility that an absence of a (formally constituted) organization may be the alternative to a given way of organizing.

NOW TURN TO EXERCISE 1.1 AT THE END OF THE CHAPTER

OUTLINING A CRITICAL APPROACH

Healthy scepticism is the basis of a critical approach to organizational analysis, but what is a critical approach? There is no one correct answer to this question. Definitions, like beauty, are often in the eye of the beholder. Our definition is a framework, rather than a prescription, to guide you through the rest of our analysis and discussion. We define a critical approach as one that takes as its starting point a concern to understand and change the way that organizational arrangements impact on people. In contrast to mainstream organizational analysis that concerns itself with the efficient use of people for formal organizational ends, a critical approach sets out to uncover the ways in which organizational ends can be detrimental to people.

Through an examination of two contrasting definitions of organizational behaviour we can see the difference between a mainstream and a critical approach. The first quotation is from a mainstream text.

> Organizational behaviour ... is a field of study that investigates the impact that individuals, groups, and structure have on behaviour within organizations, for the purpose of applying such knowledge toward improving an organization's effectiveness. (Robbins, 1989, p.5).

Note how the author's definition of organizational behaviour is constructed around concern with organizational effectiveness. Implicit in this approach is support for the status quo; existing patterns of organizational ownership and control go unchallenged. Now look at the second quotation taken from a critical approach

> People in organizations are frequently treated in organization theory as either sources of social psychological 'problems' or as embodiments of individual needs and dispositions. We eschew this perspective ... in favour of one which stresses the reality of structural divisions in society: notably sexual and class divisions. These are not only of major importance in their own right but are also significantly interrelated. As practices they are in large part reproduced by organizations, particularly in their recruitment strategies and work design. (Clegg and Dunkerley, 1980, p.6).

In this second quotation the authors' central concern is the impact of organizations on the lives of people, specifically, the relationship between organizations and discrimination. Implicit within this approach is the need for social and organizational change. Unlike the first author who talks about people in an undifferentiated way, these authors talk about people's location within sex and class differentiated groups. Indeed, a hallmark of a critical approach is a focus on organizational disparities of power and opportunity and how this affects women, persons of colour, aboriginal peoples, and/or the working class.

A focus on redressing organizational disparities of power and opportunity is only the starting point of a critical approach. At least four main elements are involved in the process of critical organizational analysis. These processes, which are basic to any school work, are comprehension, reading, writing, and acting.

Comprehension: The Many Faces of Organizational Analysis

The first thing to know about any theory of organization is that it is rooted in a particular set of assumptions and way of looking at the world. Reading through many of the books labelled 'Organization Theory' or 'Organizational Behaviour' you would hardly have noticed that fact; with minor differences, they reflect a similar view of organizations that is based on the notion of fact or universal truth. But these textbooks can not claim to have captured any kind of universal truth. Rather, they market a dominant interpretation of organizational theory, a particular version of reality.

Historically, as we discuss at length in chapter three, the fields of OT and

OB developed out of a set of scholarly pursuits which were specifically de-signed to assist the development of capitalist enterprises. Scientific Manage-ment, for example, is a strand of OT which arose out of the needs of employ-ers to increase their employees' efficiency. Similarly, the Human Relations strand of OB developed out of the specific concerns of the Western Electric company to improve productivity at their Hawthorne Works in Chicago. This led to the development of organizational disciplines that were managerialist in nature, that is, that take the defined needs of those in charge of organizations as the starting point for the development of research foci and projects. Harold Gram (1986), for example, writes that the contents of the book – *An Introduc-tion to Management* – were selected to answer two major questions:

> What are the characteristics of the variables which affect how, when, where, and why managers perform their jobs in Canada? What theories and practica-ble techniques do managers need to manage effectively and efficiently and to succeed in a managerial career? (p.v)

The focus here is in on managerial success through efficiency.

The development of OT and OB was also shaped by the backgrounds of those involved, including ergonomics, engineering, and industrial psychology. This contributed to a "real world" approach to life, that is, reality was what you felt through the five senses. This "real world" approach proved acceptable both to the business and the academic worlds which the new disciplines were trying to work within. Evidence of a 'scientific' approach to study helped to ease the pathway to academic acceptance and legitimacy and, in turn, offered comfort and legitimacy to managerial pursuits and demands (Rose, 1975).

Managerialist approaches to organizations have developed into a strong and dominant orthodoxy and alternative ways of viewing organizations have, as a result, been treated as deviant and non-legitimate theories of organization (Burrell and Morgan, 1979).

A number of radical approaches to organization have been developed in the last two decades – including actionalist, radical, and feminist approaches (Mills and Murgatroyd, 1991). Briefly, the actionalist (or interpretive) approach has as its focus explanation of how organization is created and maintained.

This approach assumes that, far from being concrete, people create and ne-gotiate sets of understandings about the world that they then act on. An organi-zation, thus, is 'an expressive form, a manifestation of human consciousness that is to be understood and analyzed not mainly in economic or material terms, but in terms of its expressive, ideational, and symbolic aspects'. This shapes a very different research agenda, namely, 'the exploration of the phenomenon of organization as subjective experience and to investigate the patterns that make organized action possible' (Smircich, 1983:347-8). This approach is similar to the orthodox approach in that it is concerned with documenting rather than challenging the status quo of existing organizational power arrangements. It differs from the orthodox approach, however, in focusing on human understandings and negotiation as the creators of organizational reality, and away from the narrow preoccupation with efficiency. The project is more sociological, more concerned with explaining the creation of order within organizations rather than justifying and strengthening it.

The radical approach, on the other hand, takes as its starting point a concern to understand and change the alienating and/or exploitative effects of organizations on people.

This approach covers a range of perspectives – from radical structuralist to radical humanist (Burrell and Morgan, 1979) – which reflect a major schism in the radical left political groups of the 1960s and 1970s. While both ends of the radical spectrum view organizations as spheres of domination, and are prepared to challenge managerialism head on, structuralists have been concerned with the exploitative character of organizations as "modes of production" or class systems, while humanists have focused on organizations as processes of ideological domination. In terms of methodology, structuralists are akin to the orthodox approach in taking a realist view of life, but humanists are akin to the interpretive approach in focusing on human subjectivity in the creation of meaning. Radical humanists differ with the interpretive approach by emphasizing that the negotiation of meaning takes place in the context of given power relationships, so that the views of the few dominate.

In more recent years we have seen the development of feminist organizational analysis which takes as its focus the impact of organizational arrangements on women – seeking to address issues of gender-based discrimination. This approach also includes a range of perspectives from the orthodox to the radical: those akin to the orthodox approach accept the underlying managerialist assumptions but seek to include more women in the process of management; feminist interpretive perspectives seek to add in to the picture women's understandings of reality; and radical feminist perspectives seek to change the character of organizational arrangements to end the domination of women by men. Feminist organizational analysis is not simply a female clone or revision of male-developed approaches; it stands as a vibrant new approach on its own. This is especially true in the face of the demise of the old, political left and the continued development of the women's movement.

What is currently missing from organizational analysis are approaches centred on the experiences of people of colour and aboriginal peoples: organizational analysis is still a 'white game'; this is beginning to change with the work of Ella Bell (1989), Stella Nkomo (1988), Marta Calas (1988), Joy Mighty (1991) and others but much has yet to be done to incorporate a genuinely anti-racist perspective into organizational theory.

By understanding that there are competing views of organizations, rooted in different assumptions and world-views, we can resist accepting as given any particular focus, set of concerns, or 'evidence'. It also probes us to examine our own underlying assumptions as we approach the task of critical organizational analysis. Reviewing the various approaches to organizational analysis we include as critical any approach — radical, feminist, people of colour centred — which focuses on organizational change as a means of addressing human oppression.

Reading: Deconstructing the Text

Shulamit Reinharz (1988) argues that most scholarly writing is "embedded" within a dominant perspective which is capitalist in orientation, as well as patriarchal, homophobic, racist, and ageist; that is, it reflects the thinking of dominant, white, heterosexual, males in society: thus, she continues, we need "to treat scientific writing not only as a source of information as defined by the author, but also as a text revealing something about the author" (p.168).

By reading not only the content but the underlying assumptions beneath the surface of any text we can uncover the author's value system and way of looking at the world. This will put us in a much better position to evaluate the book and its contents.

Reinharz indicates a number of ways of approaching the task of deconstruction, that is, of attempting to uncover the underlying assumptions of a work:

> Although the passive voice of much scientific writing hides the author's voice
> to a large extent, clues can sometimes be found in introductions, conclusions,
> and asides (ibid.).

Reinharz suggests that the task of uncovering hidden assumptions involves a thorough examination of texts,

> not in terms of their major arguments, but rather in terms of their asides, illustrations and examples. [Looking] not at what the authors thought needed explaining, but at what they thought did not – that is, their taken-for-granted assumptions. [This] is a first strategy ... – facing the preconceptions squarely. Examples writers use reveal the images with which they think and build their arguments. The examples writers offer can be likened to Thematic Apperception Test pictures used by psychologists to trigger their subjects' way of looking at the world [p.163].

Using Reinharz' guide to deconstruction we are able to get to the bottom of any given OB or OT text and uncover the hidden assumptions involved. To see how this works in practice we will begin with an examination of taken-for-granted assumptions.

Taken-for-granted Assumptions

Here is an excerpt from an OT text by Richard Daft (1989: p.9) which, in a section titled "What is an Organization?", relates the importance of organizations to the everyday life of the reader:

> We know organizations are there because they touch us every day. Indeed, they are so common we take them for granted. We hardly notice that we are born in a hospital, have our birth records registered in a government agency, are educated in schools and universities, are raised on food produced on corporate farms, are treated by doctors engaged in joint practice, buy a house built by a construction company and sold by a real-estate agency, borrow money from a bank, turn to police and fire departments when trouble erupts, use moving companies to change jobs, receive an array of benefits from government agencies, spend forty hours a week working in an organization, and are even laid to rest by a church and undertaker.

At one level this statement is a fairly innocuous listing of areas of social life which can be related to organizations. It is constructed to show us how organizations impinge on various aspects of our lives. Yet, when we look further into the statement it would seem that its purpose is to convince us of the importance of organization theory rather than the significance of organizations in the lives of people; the overwhelming majority of the text is devoted to the attainment of organizational effectiveness and efficiency.

If we examine the list closer we find that there are a number of taken-for-granted examples that are somehow meant to be generic and appropriate to all readers. But the fact is that people do not all stand in the same relationship to organizations; many people are not fortunate enough to receive a university education, to buy a house, borrow money from a bank, or be engaged in full-time paid employment; some people prefer to have their children born and educated at home; some people are more likely to be the subject of police attention, and some people will spend more time resisting organizational control rather than being in control of organizations.

Daft's statement completely ignores the reality of disparities based on class, ethnicity and gender. If we consider only the issue of gender, for example, Daft's list fails to note that it is females who bear children, while the doctors involved in the delivery are usually males; and that males are much more likely than females to receive a university education and become a university professor. Furthermore, the task of buying of groceries is usually done by women, while it is mainly males who own and manage corporate farms, construction firms and real-estate agencies, and who build houses and manage banks and government agencies. The staff of police and fire departments are mainly male; the professions of the priesthood and undertaking are almost exclusively male. Generally, full-time employment remains more characteristic of males than females.

Silences, Exclusions, and Deletions

On issues of race/ethnicity, gender and class Daft is not alone in ignoring the issues: look through most organizational behaviour or theory texts and you will find little or nothing on those issues, nor will you find much attention paid to addressing the potential negative impact of organizations on the lives, communities, and environments of people. Take, for example, texts by Gary Johns (1988), Richard Daft (1989), and Stephen Robbins (1989). Not only are these three of the more widely read texts in the field but they are among the best of their kind. Yet, on the issue of the impact of organization on people's lives they are all silent. There are no references to race and ethnicity, and discussion of class is limited to cursory references to trade unions. Daft is the better of the three in that he touches on sources of "worker-management conflict", but this brief reference is not expanded upon, and, as with the other two texts, issues of power, control, and ownership are left out.

In all three texts treatment of gender is minimal and trivial. The Robbins

text is the better of the three in this regard – devoting 5 of its 599 pages to issues of "sex characteristics", and "sex-role stereotypes". The Daft text is as
much of interest for what it omits as for what it states. The 1989 (Third) edition of the text makes only one reference to gender. On page 429 the first of
twelve "discussion questions" asks,

> 1. One form of management tyranny occurs when male senior managers try
> to exploit sexual favours from female subordinates. These women experience
> extreme pressure because their jobs depend upon the recommendation of the
> managers, and they often need the jobs to support their families. Based upon
> the discussion in this chapter, what advice would you give to a woman to help
> her block the abuse of power by her manager?

As important as this question is the text in no way prepares the student to
make any assessment of the problem of gender, or more specifically sexual harassment, within organizations. The text is completely silent on issues of sex and
sexuality. And it makes almost no reference to women. Of eight cases used in
the chapter not one woman is mentioned; every reference to a manager or
executive is to a man. The single reference to a woman anywhere in the chapter is to a female secretary who "blew the whistle" on her male boss's corrupt
financial dealings. Daft's earlier, 1986, text did include the "Bendix Case"
which details the use of sexual innuendo to get a female executive fired from
her position but this has been dropped from the 1989 edition: it would seem
that on the issue of sex discrimination the Daft text has taken a step backwards!

Examples

The Johns text exemplifies the way gender is minimized in OB/OT texts.
Ninety-one pages into the text we find three pages that focus upon "sex stereotypes," in which it is argued that,

> Women are severely underrepresented in managerial and administrative jobs.
> There is evidence that sex stereotypes are partially responsible for this state of
> affairs, discouraging women from business careers and blocking their ascent to
> managerial positions (p.91).

But later on Johns completely ignores his own point when he approvingly
focuses on the work of "Wardrobe engineer" John T. Molloy, who argues that
the clothing worn by organizational members sends clear signals about their
competence, seriousness, and affects their ability to be promoted:

For [that] reason, Molloy strongly vetoes sweaters for women executives. Molloy stresses that proper clothing will not make up for a lack of ambition, intelligence, and savvy. Rather, he argues that the wrong clothing will prevent these qualities from being detected. To this end, he prescribes detailed "business uniforms," the men's built around a conservative suit and the women's around a skirted suit and blouse (p.368).

This advice reinforces the very sex stereotypes that Johns had referred to earlier!

Asides

The Johns text ends with an equally mixed message because of the asides used. In a small section devoted to "Women and Mentors" we are told that women's career development is inhibited due to the difficulty they face in establishing a mentor relationship; a problem that stems from the fact that those best placed to be mentors – senior staff – are usually men. The text suggests that the problem may be primarily "interpersonal," in part due to women themselves, whose "preoccupation with young children lasts for at least a small period of their adult lifetime," and, in part, due to men who lack experience in dealing with a woman "in some role other than daughter, wife, or lover" (p.641). This type of aside reinforces stereotypical notions of women as primary child carers, and encourages the idea that sex discrimination is rooted in purely interpersonal relationships. As much as some men may have difficulty in relating to women there is considerable evidence that the problem is much more deep rooted in the very way that we structure and think about organizations, a point we shall be exploring in depth in chapter five.

Illustrations

Finally, we can tell a lot about assumptions by the types of illustrations that a text uses. The Johns text makes use of photographs and cartoons to illustrate an idea. In none of the seven photographs and eighteen cartoons are people of colour evident, and only one photograph depicts a group of working-class people – female secretaries. The great bulk of the photographs and cartoons depict white males in positions of power. Only one photograph is used to discuss women as executives and only then to advise them to "dress for success." Women only appear in five of the cartoons, and in only one is the woman shown as holding a professional position.

Regardless of intentions, silences, asides, examples, taken-for-granted assumptions, and illustrations serve to reinforce stereotypical notions about the respective worth and place of people in organizations depending on their colour, gender, and class origins. By deconstructing the text we can learn something about the character and application of a particular approach to the study of organizations.

Acting: The Praxis of Research

Understanding the different theoretical perspectives and underlying assumptions of various approaches to the study of organizations is one part of developing a critical perspective, developing your own research strategy is the other part.

As we saw earlier in the chapter, much of OT research has developed out of management concerns with efficiency and effectiveness. Management research develops out of direct and indirect responses to perceived management needs. In the first case, research develops in response to specific management needs, as in the case of Western Electric and their Hawthorne Works. In the second case, research aims at answering broad management concerns, for example, motivation, leadership, organizational structure. This type of research usually builds on existing theories and attempts to validate or improve on them, to contribute to improved management practice.

Critical organizational research, on the other hand, is mainly concerned with those who are less powerful or devoid of power within organization. This preoccupation leads researchers to identify and address those elements which create, or magnify, inequality and discrimination within the organization. Thus the critical theorist is interested in exposing disparities of power, inequities, degradation, and any other factors which inhibit human growth, dignity, and potential. Critical research often arises out the researcher's own experiences with or as a member of a disaffected group – women, people of colour, the working class.

Here are two contrasting examples of research agendas. The first is a management theorist – Edgar Schein, and the second is by a critical theorist – Ivan Illich.

In his book *Organizational Culture and Leadership* Schein (1985) is eager to distinguish his "clinical" approach from that of an "ethnographic" one. According to Schein, ethnographers, "for intellectual and scientific reasons," bring to the situation "a set of concepts or models that motivated the research in the first place." The groups being studied "are often willing to participate but usually have no particular stake in the intellectual issues that may have motivated the study" (p.21):

> In contrast, a "clinical perspective" is one where the group members are clients who have their own interests as the prime motivator for the involvement of the "outsider," often labelled "consultant" ... in this context.... Consultants also bring with them their models and concepts for obtaining and analyzing information, but the function of those models is to provide insight into how the client can be helped ... I believe that this clinical perspective provides a useful counterpoint to the pure ethnographic perspective, because the clinician learns things that are different from what an ethnographer learns. Clients are motivated to reveal certain things when they are paying for help that may not come out if they are only "willing" to be studied. (Schein, 1985, pp.21-22)

Schein's ingenious use of the term "client" masks the fact that organizational clients will invariably be management, but the "groups" being studied will almost certainly be employees.

Ivan Illich's interest in organizations was inspired by a different set of concerns – neither clinical nor ethnographic. Illich experienced the oppressive nature of organizations as a child in his native Austria. Anti-Semitic laws forced him – as "a half-Jew" – to flee the country at the age of 15; although his father was Catholic his mother was Jewish. After the Second World War, now a Catholic priest, Illich came to the United States and, instead of taking up his theological studies at Princeton University, asked to be assigned to a Puerto Rican parish of New York. Illich had become instantly interested in the plight of the Puerto Ricans and in the next few years worked tirelessly to improve their lot.

His interest in the Puerto Rican people led him to an appointment, in 1956, as the vice-rector of the Catholic University at Ponce in Puerto Rico. That appointment led to involvement on the school board that governed the island's entire educational establishment and here "he was exposed to a new and puzzling vocabulary with terms like 'development,' 'human resources,' 'man-power planning'" (David Caley, 1988, p.4). Illich came to the conclusion that "planning" was a "new species of the sin presumption":

> The idea of planning as presumption, or pride, as a way of defending ourselves against surprise and against dependence on others would be central to Illich's later analyses of all modern systems (Caley, op cit., p.4).

The more Illich was exposed to the school system the more doubts were raised in his mind. Here he explains to David Caley (1988, pp.4–5) the process which led him to write Deschooling Society

> [It] was quite evident that after ten years of intensive [...] development of the school system in the country which at that moment was a showcase for development ... around the world, in Puerto Rico, schooling was so arranged that half of the students who came from the poorer families had a one in three chance to finish five years of elementary education, which were compulsory. Nobody faced the fact that schooling served, at least in Puerto Rico, to compound the native poverty of that half of children with a new interiorized sense of guilt for not having made it. I therefore came to the conclusion that schools inevitably are a system to produce dropouts, to produce more dropouts than successes, because since the school is open to 16 years, 18 years, 19 years of schooling, it never closes the door on anyone. It produces a few successes and a majority of failures. School really acts as a lottery system in which those who don't make it don't just lose what they had paid in, but for all their life they are stigmatized as inferior.... Schooling I increasingly came to see as the ritual of a society committed to progress and development, creating certain myths which are a requirement for a consumer society.

We can see from this statement that Illich's research was fuelled by an involvement with the poor and a general concern for what institutions can do to people. It led Illich to advocate a non-organizational alternative to school-based education. In the book *Deschooling Society,* Illich argued that education should be an open process of learning involving everyone, and that the establishment of schools had led to a narrow institutionalization of education in which rules and regulations, control and discipline were more important than knowledge and learning.

Illich's approach in many ways summarizes the development of critical research – involvement, concern, reflection, action. The foci for many critical researchers arise out of their own experiences, out of involvement with disaffected groups or in struggles to cause change in people's lives. Concern to address the issues that are thrown up in acts of resistance and protest has helped to clarify research foci for many critical researchers. In this way critical research addresses issues that people are confronted with. The act of writing then becomes a process of reflection and guidance for further action and involvement; this in turn will generate answers to the questions asked, raise new questions, encourage new research. This process we call praxis – the translation of experiences into ideas, the testing out of those ideas through new experiences, and further reflection on the new experiences. This is the essence of a critical approach.

Writing: Reaching Out and Authorizing

The process of critical research involves a classic irony. It takes place in the context of traditional organizational forms – often with a need to satisfy values rooted in the very organizational problems that the researcher sets out to analyze and review. Grants are usually awarded only to those who appear to be "playing the game," to be operating within the same broad assumptions that inform those in charge of research moneys. For example, a large U.S. corporate-funding body was reluctant to fund a major study of black women in the workplace unless the study included white women. To get the grant the researchers were forced to alter their research plan. In another case, a U.S. federal funding agency refused to fund a conference on feminism and organizational science unless the conference included "prominent," (white) male management theorists from a list provided by the agency.

Organizational constraints play an ever more stringent role when it comes to "disseminating" or writing-up the results of research. Usually the researcher has to find an "approved" academic journal or conference, through which to publish the results. Academic journals in particular but also books contain assumptions about authorship. The writer is expected to adopt an "objective," and "detached" style of writing. In reading the work the reader is in a passive role in which s/he is being talked to by the expert – the author. In effect, the reader is "de-authorized".

This process has obvious implications for the critical writer. The content of the work – which sets out to review inequities – is undermined by a form that helps to recreate inequities. Critical researchers have found various ways around this. In some cases research has been undertaken for groups, such as feminist organizations and trade unions, who usually expect the results to be disseminated in the form of reports and articles in the organization's own press or newsletters and in other cases research has been disseminated through the presses of environmentalists, feminists, socialists, other radical groups and even the columns of the national press. These avenues are important for reaching out to those for whom and with whom the critical researcher is working.

For the critical researcher in the academic world, whose existence often depends on "academic publication," some efforts have been made to establish independent journals, such as Feminist Review, that publish radical material.

There has also been less successful attempts to resist the pressure to publish in prescribed journals. In recent years efforts have been made to address the issue of "authority" in publishing, that is, to write in a way that attempts to author-ize and include the reader. This style of writing is still rare but includes an ef-fort by the writer to share something of his- or herself with the reader, to share their doubts about some of the things they are writing about, to avoid "speak-ing" in a way that indicates a one-way relationship of authority-reader, to raise questions rather than simply to provide answers.

To write in a way that authorizes those reading a work is far from easy but is surely an important consideration in reporting critical research findings and ideas. For an example of this style of writing you may wish to look at Jane Flax (1990) who attempts to resolve many of the problems of authorship by sharing much about her struggles and concerns in writing the book – including the tragic death of her husband. She writes in the form of "conversations," that is, counterposing different views on theories rather than attempting to determine the "truth" in each. In this way those reading the book are involved in the process of making up their own mind. She reminds us that she is,

> not a neutral participant in or a disinterested facilitator of these dialogues. At least three purposes motivate their evocation: a desire to grasp certain aspects of the texture of social life in the contemporary West; a fascination with ques-tions of knowledge, gender, subjectivity, and power and their interrelations; a wish to explore how theories might be written in postmodernist voices – nonauthoritarian, open-ended, and process-oriented.... The conversational form of the book represents my attempt ... to (find) one way (among many possible ways) to continue theoretical writing while abandoning the "truth" enunciating or adjudicating modes feminists and postmodernists so powerfully and appropriately call into question. (Flax, pp.3-4)

The book ends appropriately enough with "No Conclusions," a chapter devoted to raising as many doubts about the process of knowledge as the issues in focus.

> A fundamental and unresolved question pervading this book is how to justify – or even frame – theoretical and narrative choices (including my own) with-out recourse to "truth" or domination[...] I do not find it helpful to think about this question in terms of a search for "less false" representations[....] Rather I would argue it is both necessary and difficult to displace truth/falsity with problems of meaning(s)... It is also possible that such yearning for mean-ing itself reflects experiences in this culture and outmoded ways of thinking.

Perhaps it is better only to analyze desires for meaning and to learn to live without grounds (Flax, pp.222-3).

Like Flax, we are not neutral or disinterested parties. The object of this book is not to replace one set of claims to universal truth with another, but rather to encourage a questioning of the basis of claims to truth within different elements of organizational theory.

KEY TERMS

The following are a list of key terms used in the chapter. The review questions below are designed to strengthen your understanding of the terms. Many of the terms are defined in the text of the chapter. The definitions of those in italics can be found in the glossary of terms at the end of the book.

gender	race	ethnicity
class	critical approach	managerialist
actionalist approach	radical structuralist	feminist
radical humanist	deconstruction	praxis
authorize		

REVIEW QUESTIONS

The following questions are designed to strengthen your understanding of the chapter, and to encourage you to develop a broader knowledge of critical writing on organizations. Write short notes in answer to each question. The assignments are designed to allow you to reflect on what you have read so far. The further study questions, marked "FS", are designed to help you to extend your knowledge and understanding through long-term study and extra reading.

Q1. Briefly define each of the following terms, and say how each can be relevant to an understanding of how organizations operate:
>   class
>   gender
>   race
>   ethnicity
>   praxis

Assignment: Now turn to the glossary at the end of the book and compare your definitions.

Q2. What is meant by a "critical approach to organization study"?

Assignment: Write down five key factors which would define a "critical" approach and say how that would differ from a mainstream OB or OT approach.

[FS: read a chapter or article from the non-fictional lists on pages 26-27. Note how the author(s) defines his/her approach and compare it with the definition outlined in chapter 1 of this book].

Q3. Briefly define each of the following approaches:
managerialist
actionalist
radical humanist
radical structuralist
feminist

Assignment: Write short notes on each approach and compare and contrast any two – stating what the major differences and similarities are.

[FS: read any one of the following chapters or articles, and then (a) attempt to assess which approach is being taken, and (b) detail the problems involved in attempting to classify research into given "approaches."

Rosabeth Moss Kanter (1977) *Men & Women of the Corporation,* Chapter 8. New York: Basic Books.

Gibson Burrell (1984) "Sex and Organizational Analysis," *Organization Studies,* 5(2): 97-118.

Gareth Morgan (1986) *Images of Organization,* Chapter 5. London: Sage.

Smircich, Linda (1985) 'Is the Concept of Culture a Paradigm for Understanding Organizations and Ourselves?' in P.J. Frost, et al (Eds) *Organizational Culture,* pp.55-72. Beverly Hills, CA.: Sage.]

Q4. Outline a people of colour approach to the study of organizations.

Assignment: In developing a people of colour approach what key factors would be most relevant? List and discuss at least five factors.

[FS: Read one of the articles from the 1990, Volume 11, issue of the Journal of Organizational Behaviour and, (a) note down five factors which, in your opinion, marks the approach as people of colour centred, and then, (b) compare this article with the article or chapter that you read for question 3. How do the approaches differ? What are the main factors which distinguish one approach from the other?]

Q5. What is meant by the term "deconstruction" and how is it applicable to reading organizational and management theory?

Assignment: From any mainstream organization or management text, analyze some of the pages, chosen at random, and state (a) what you think is absent or silent, b) what the taken-for-granted assumptions are, and c) what kinds of message do you get from the illustrations, asides, and/or examples utilized.

Q6. What is the use of studying organizations?

Assignment: Choose a current news item and state how an understanding of organizations might help to address the problem in question.

EXERCISE 1.1

This exercise is designed to make you think about the significance of organizations to the lives of people generally and to your life in particular. Do the tasks individually and then discuss your findings in small groups.

A. Down one side of a sheet of paper:

    1. List the top ten things which you most enjoy doing.

    2. List the top ten things which you least enjoy doing.

    3. List the ten most significant things that you have done this week.

B. Now, against each item in all of your three lists:

    1. Indicate whether the activity directly, indirectly, or not at all, involves an organization of some kind.

EXAMPLE:-

THINGS I ENJOY DOING

Activity	Organizational Link		
	Direct	*Indirect*	*None*
Going to the movies	–	Y	–
Singing	Y	Y	Y
Reading	–	Y	Y

In small groups discuss your lists. Come up with a composite list of a number of activities which are directly or indirectly linked to organizations; detail the problems which you had in deciding under which category (indirect, direct, or none) to put each item; what conclusions do you draw from this exercise?

C. Using the same list ask older family members (that is, someone at least a generation older than you) what things they preferred, disliked, and usually did when they were your age. Check back with your lists. Do you notice any difference? What do you conclude – are we becoming more or less organizational in our activities?

D. Keep a one day diary of your activities and thoughts: note down as many things that happen to you, indicate whether you feel it had any direct, indirect or no connection to an organization; note down any other observations or thoughts that occur to you about the relationship between people and organizations.

In a week's time discuss activity C and D in a small group, and determine the following things: a) what percentage of people's activities are associated with organizations? b) are some people less 'organizational' than others? c) what can we learn from the fact that many of our activities have numerous organizational connections? d) do people's organizational associations differ according to their race/ethnicity, class or gender? What does that tell us about organizations?

FURTHER READING

Here are selected readings. They provide further insights into some of the key points that we have been making, and to encourage creative thinking. Read any or all at your leisure.

On the impact of organization upon our ways of thinking and of living:
Alvin Toffler, THE THIRD WAVE. Glasgow: Pan (1981).
Gareth Morgan, IMAGES OF ORGANIZATION, Chapter 1 (1986).

Literary Images of Organizational impact:
Franz Kafka, THE TRIAL.
Arthur Miller, DEATH OF A SALESMAN, and ALL MY SONS
George Orwell, 1984
John Le Carré, THE SPY WHO CAME IN FROM THE COLD
Margaret Atwood, THE HANDMAID'S TALE

The non-organizational alternative:
Ivan Illich, DESCHOOLING SOCIETY★.

An overview of competing approaches:
Gibson Burrell & Gareth Morgan (1979) SOCIOLOGICAL PARADIGMS AND OR-GANIZATIONAL ANALYSIS
W.G. Astley & A.H. Van de Ven (1983) CENTRAL PERSPECTIVES AND DEBATES IN ORGANIZATIONAL THEORY
Albert. J. Mills & Stephen. J. Murgatroyd (1991) ORGANIZATIONAL RULES

On feminist approaches:
J. Hearn, D.L. Sheppard, P. Tancred-Sheriff, & G. Burrell [eds] (1989) THE SEXUALITY OF ORGANIZATION.
A.J. Mills & P. Tancred [eds] (1992) GENDERING ORGANIZATIONAL ANALYSIS.

On people of colour:
JOURNAL OF ORGANIZATIONAL BEHAVIOR, Vol.11, 1990.
A.J. Mills & P. Tancred [Eds] 1992. See especially Chapter 11 by Marta Calas and Chapter 13 by Ella Bell and Stella Nkomo.

On developing a critical methodology

Shulamit Reinharz (1988) FEMINIST DISTRUST: PROBLEMS OF CONTENT IN SOCIOLOGICAL WORK.

Marta Calas (1992) RE-WRITING GENDER INTO ORGANIZATIONAL THEORIZING

E.L. Bell, T. Denton, & S.M. Nkomo (1992) WOMEN OF COLOR IN MANAGEMENT

L. Stanley & S. Wise (1983) BREAKING OUT: FEMINIST CONSCIOUSNESS AND FEMINIST RESEARCH

S.L. Kirby and K. McKenna (1989) EXPERIENCE, RESEARCH & SOCIAL CHANGE

P. Feyeraband (1978) AGAINST METHOD

G. Morgan [ed] (1983) BEYOND METHOD

J. Irvine, I. Miles & J. Evans (1979) DEMYSTIFYING SOCIAL STATISTICS

On case analysis.

A. Mikalachki, D.R. Mikalachki, and R.Burke (1992) GENDER ISSUES IN MANAGEMENT

END NOTES

1. More commonly referred to as 'The Abella Commission' after its chair, Judge Rosalie Silberman Abella.

2. Approximately one million Canadians are injured each year in work-related accidents. Statistics Canada (1989) Work Injuries 1986-88.

3. In Canada between 1991 and 1992 business bankruptcies rose from 13,496 up to 14,317, a percentage increase of 6.1% with total liabilities rising from $6,170,251,000 up to $7,374,212,000 (Statistics Canada, Market Research Handbook, 1993-1994, p.28, Table 1-13, Business Bankruptcies by Province 1991 and 1992; Statistics Canada, Yearbook 1994, p.592, Table 19.16, "Bankruptcies".

4. The 1980s was an era of scandals and included insider trading on the U.S. stock exchanges and corrupt junk bond deals (e.g., respectively, the Ivan Boesky and Mike Milken cases); conflict of interest cases at Federal (Jim Wright in the U.S.; Sinclair Stevens in Canada) and Provincial levels of government (including the Starr case in Ontario; and the Van der Zalm case in B.C.); and dubious business practices (e.g., the collapse of the Alberta-based Principal Group in

1987 which deprived 67,000 people of their investment).

5. For example, Gainers Meats of Edmonton, Alberta have received extensive grants and loans from the governments of Alberta and Saskatchewan. In 1987 the company opened a plant in North Battleford, Saskatchewan and received $825,000 in incentives, including $125,000 in a straight industrial grant, from the town (Pugh 1987a). The Province provided a $21 million loan of which Gainers only had to repay $11 million (Pugh 1987b).

6. By the beginning of the 1990s Statistics Canada was recording 3-3.5 million "person-days lost" per year due to work stoppages.

7. The closing of companies, such as the Sydney Steel Works or National Sea Products, can mean economic disaster for small communities. The closure of the National Sea Products plant in Canso (N.S.) in 1990 meant the end of the town's only industry. In the period December 1989 to June 1992 unemployment in Canada rose from 7.7% to 11.6%.

8. Rose (1975) provides a fascinating history of management thought and the links with capitalist development and interests.

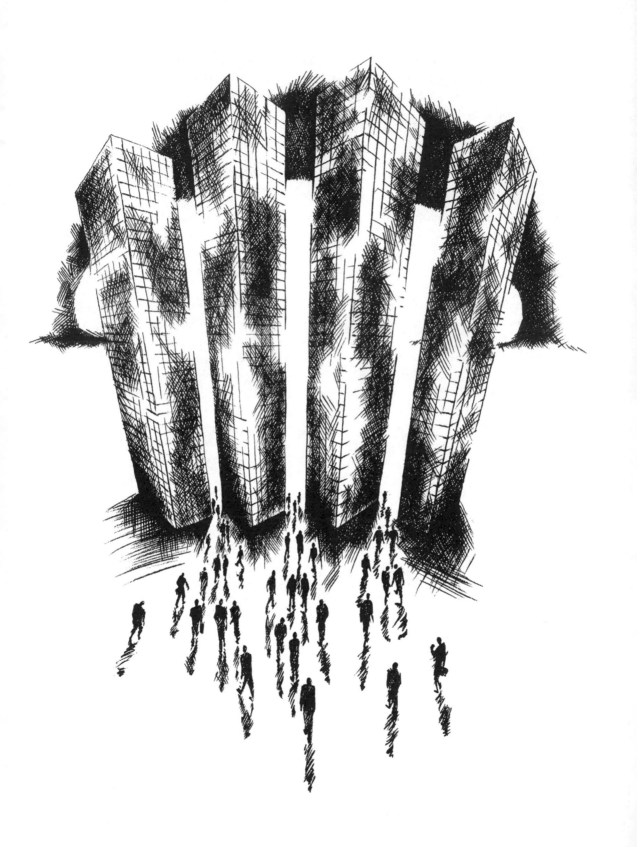

CHAPTER 2

Understanding Bureaucracies: The Age of the Organizational Giants

This chapter examines the character of the bureaucratic phenomenon and its implications for understanding the nature of modern organization. By way of an historical framework, the reader is encouraged to analyze the relationship between social thought, social divisions, and organizational structure. The objective is to provide the reader with a basic vocabulary of organizational analysis (viz rationalization, bureaucracy, centralization, hierarchy, etc.) while challenging him/her to think about the impact of bureaucracy upon social structure (the way we organize), organizational outcomes (efficiency), and social life (our sense of self, identity, public/private divisions)

"The Dark Side"

There is a dark side to living in Newfoundland which the average employed person knows nothing about. The welfare recipient, or the applicant is the one who knows about it: he knows less than civil treatment from civil servants, gets the feeling that he is a criminal-minded scrounger and is not sure whether he should walk in like a man and demand his rights or should crawl in on his hands and knees and beg for mercy.

Most welfare recipients live in fear and dread of the welfare officer. They look on him as the all powerful lord who can give or take away. A frown from the welfare officer is almost the same as a death sentence and few people are brave enough to risk the wrath of these lords of welfare.

At most welfare offices the recipient is treated with less respect than the mat on the floor (...) in most areas the welfare officer is lord and master of all he surveys and those who seek his time and attention must put up with his whims, his quirks of personality and any mean or vicious streak that may be included in his character. Most of the people who deal with him treat him with fear rather than respect. They have learned from experience that to make an enemy of the welfare officer is unhealthy and unwise (...) Arming civil servants with too much power can be dangerous (...). Evening Telegraph, 1973 (St. Johns, Newfoundland).[1]

INTRODUCTION

For many members of our society, bureaucracies – especially government bureaucracies – are objects of resentment, and even of fear. As the quotation above shows, even a lawful and commonplace activity such as applying for welfare assistance, can become an intimidating and demoralizing experience for those who make these applications. For in this bureaucratic world, welfare officials and welfare applicants, (or recipients), meet each other on very unequal terms: the former possesses all the power and authority while the latter possesses none. It is a world in which bureaucrats exercise very real power over the lives of their clients, and where the final word of these officials often acquires the force of law. Because of this political inequality, welfare applicants often find that they must humble themselves before officials, and tolerate violations of their privacy and self-respect which would be unthinkable in any other social situation.

Of course, the welfare department is not the only bureaucracy where the lines of authority are clearly drawn between bureaucrat and client, or where the lives of individuals may be deeply affected by the decisions of bureaucratic officials. Other bureaucracies in our society may exercise powers which are far greater than those of the welfare bureaucracy.

The Department of Indian and Northern Development, for example, has traditionally administered and controlled all aspects of the lives of registered Indians in Canada. It has exercised the power to confer or to withhold registered Indian status, to disburse treaty payments, and to provide funding for local bands. In earlier times, Indian agents, as officials of the Indian Affairs bureaucracy, also exercised the power to grant voting rights, to ship Indian children off to residential schools, to keep alcohol off the reserves, and even to authorize the travel of Indians away from the reserves. Looking back on the colonial aspects of Indian policy in Canada, many of us would be tempted to say that the traditional power that the Indian Affairs bureaucracy exercised over Indian people was nothing less than totalitarian in its scope and application (Ponting, 1986; Ponting, 1980; Weaver, 1981)

Similarly, the Department of Immigration, as another government bureaucracy, has also exercised tremendous power over the lives of individuals. This has included the power to issue or withhold admission rights to individuals at ports-of-entry, the power to facilitate family reunion and the power to issue and enforce deportation orders. Consequently, resentment and fear of this bureaucracy has not been uncommon among those immigrants who have experienced first-hand the arbitrary use, or even abuse, of power at the hands of immigration officials.[2]

Whether we use the dramatic examples of Welfare, Immigration, or Indian Affairs or whether we use the more benign examples of Revenue and Taxation, or Motor Vehicles Branch of provincial departments of transportation, there is no doubt that bureaucracies wield considerable power in our society. They are now a weighty force within society. And although most of our examples have been drawn from government bureaucracies, it should not be forgotten that private sector bureaucracies have the power to make decisions which may make or break our lives in different ways. One has only to think about the power which banks and insurance companies exercise over our financial lives; or the power exercised by large corporations such as Canadian Pacific, General Motors, Imperial Oil, or Stelco over the livelihoods of hundreds of thousands of Canadian workers. There is no escape from the power of bureaucracies in the modern world. For as one observer has suggested:

> Bureaucracy is like sin — we all know something about it, but only those who practice it enjoy it. Ordinary people tend to be against both, and experts on the subject tend to become obsessed, so that some see bureaucracy everywhere as fanatical clerics see sin up every back alley. If you hold that all sex is sin, you simply mean you wish you had never been born; if you believe all bureaucracies are degenerate you are simply registering a protest against modern society. (Quoted from Brian Chapman, "Facts of Organized Life", *Manchester Guardian Weekly*, Jan. 26, 1961)

In this chapter, we shall look at some of the different images of bureaucracy which have appeared at various times in the writings of both popular and scholarly authors. Bureaucracies have been lambasted and lampooned, but they have also been celebrated and idealized. Some writers have seen them as dark and sinister forces carrying the seeds of totalitarianism and oppression. Other writers have seen them as models of rationality and efficiency which characterize the evolution of modern organizations. But whether they are viewed as forces of light or forces of darkness, most images of bureaucracy have, until recently, told us little or nothing about the role of gender, ethnicity or class in modern organizations. Most of the work on organization and bureaucracy has remained strangely silent in these important areas. Part of the task of this chapter is to speak to these traditional silences of organizational theory.

But in order to begin our discussion, let us start by looking at the impact that large organizations have had on the lives of all of us, not only in this country, but all over the world.

LIVING IN A BUREAUCRATIC WONDERLAND

Modern organizations are an inescapable part of our everyday experience. Whether we live in crowded cities or in outlying rural parts of the country, all of us remain dependent upon organizations for most aspects of our lives. Many of us belong to a number of different organizations such as trade unions, chambers of commerce, political parties, churches, ethnic organizations, school boards, hunting and fishing societies, or provincial motor associations. Membership in these organizations helps to give our lives meaning and purpose.

We don't have to join organizations, however, in order for them to exercise a pervasive influence over our lives. We depend upon organizations for the production and distribution of essential goods and services, for our information, communication and transportation, indeed, for all activities which require the cooperation of groups and individuals in our society. Only an imaginary Robinson Crusoe, isolated and entirely self-sufficient, could remain independent of the pervasive web spun by organizations in the modern world.

Today, the role of large organizations in our society, in both the public and private sectors of our society has increasingly come into question. And while it is generally accepted that the efficiencies of these large organizations have made possible the unprecedented economic and technological development of the twentieth century, there is a growing popular awareness that the tremendous power and influence wielded by these organizations may already be threatening some of our basic social and political values, especially those of individual liberty and political democracy.

Although the nightmare visions of George Orwell (1949) and Aldous Huxley (1950) have, so far, failed to materialize in our society, the disturbing growth in the control which centralized bureaucratic organizations exercise over our lives leaves little cause for complacency. Most of us are unaware of how much information about our personal finances, taxes, travel, politics, hospital records, telephone calls and citizenship status is routinely collected and shared among the giant corporations and public bureaucracies in our society. Indeed, the ability of modern organizations to collect and store essential information on individuals has led one recent writer to refer to these modern trends as "friendly fascism" (Gross, 1980). Whether we like it or not, most of us now live in societies in which many aspects of our lives are controlled by large organizations.[3]

Large organizations have played an important part in the development of both capitalist and socialist societies. In our own society, we have all seen the trend towards the growth of big business on a national and international level.

In recent years we have seen the takeover of Wardair by PWA; Texaco by Imperial Oil; Molson Brewery by Carling-O'Keefe; and recently (1993) the takeover of Woodwards by the Hudson Bay Co.

Basically the difference between monopoly and oligopoly is one of form rather than outcome – monopoly is the dominance of the market by a single firm while oligopoly is dominance of the market by a small group of firms. Either form means little choice for consumers. An obvious example is the automobile industry. Fifty years ago there was still a variety of U.S. auto manufacturers, including Studebaker, Packard, Nash and Hudson. Today only the big three remain: General Motors, Chrysler and Ford.

Sometimes the growth of big business is accomplished through swallowing up competitors through corporate takeovers or through other amalgamations. When this happens, we often begin to talk about the development of monopolies, or even oligopolies, in certain industries where a few large corporations have become dominant. Many consumer advocates, and even some economists, have warned that when a few big businesses take control of an industry, competition becomes a thing of the past. With the decline of real competition in the marketplace, the power that consumers once had to shop elsewhere is slowly lost, for where else can you go when one or two large companies run the only game in town? Even without fully realizing it, the traditional characterization of the 'free enterprise system' – as a system based on 'free and fair competition', has long been undermined by the growth of big business and its market dominance.

In the former socialist societies, large organizations played an even greater role in the political, economic and technological development of those societies. Large state-run organizations were used by socialist governments to rapidly industrialize underdeveloped regions of the world, sometimes bringing impressive material achievements to those societies. At the same time, the large state-run organizations in many of the former socialist countries also helped to build up harsh police states and oppressive bureaucratic regimes. The crumbling of the Berlin Wall, and the fall of the Communist governments in Eastern Europe and the USSR have shown how hated these regimes were by the majority of people forced to live under them. In fact the popular hatred of the all-pervasive state bureaucracies was a key element in the crisis of these regimes.

Although the political problems of living in bureaucratic socialist societies are generally well known, until recently less attention has been paid to the economic inefficiencies and distortions of public policy created by over-centralized systems of directive planning. Only with the launching of the campaigns for *glasnost* and *perestroika* in the last years of the USSR, did some of the economic, social and environmental costs of bureaucratic organization begin to be openly debated.[4]

WHAT IS BUREAUCRACY?

Virtually all large organizations in the modern world are run as bureaucracies. These may be government-run bureaucracies such as Revenue Canada or the Department of Indian and Northern Development, corporate bureaucracies such as the Hudson Bay Company or the Ford Motor Company, or even non-governmental bureaucracies such as the Roman Catholic Church or Alcoholics Anonymous. What all these institutions have in common is that they are run according to bureaucratic principles of organization.

When most people hear the term "bureaucracy", they are likely to think of all the bad experiences they have had with large organizations, especially with government agencies. Trying to collect an unemployment cheque from a Canada Employment and Immigration Centre, filling in tax returns for Revenue Canada, nominating relatives for immigration to Canada: most of us have had some frustrating and time-wasting experiences with government bureaucracies. It's hardly surprising then, that for many people the term "bureaucracy" conjures up images of 'red tape' – lost files, unanswered letters, forms in triplicate, unsympathetic officials, and general hassles with authority. More than anything else, the term "bureaucracy", for many people has come to mean inefficiency.

Within mainstream organization theory, however, the term, "bureaucracy", has a more technical and a more neutral meaning. It refers to the way in which an institution is organized irrespective of whether it is a government agency or a private business. Part of the meaning of the term, "bureaucracy", can be seen from its roots in 'bureau' (a writing desk, or an office), and 'cracy' (a form of government). A shorthand definition of bureaucracy could well be: 'government by the paper-pushers', as well as 'government by office holders'.

When mainstream theorists talk about bureaucracy what they have in mind is a large and complex formal organization, which is organized through an elaborate division of labour, under an hierarchical structure of authority, and which operates according to explicit rules and procedures. While this is a rather general definition, it shows how theorists are mainly concerned with the principles of organization which characterize bureaucracies. Bureaucratic organization has developed as something of an enigma in the modern world. On the one hand, bureaucracies have suffered from a bad press, with many people associating bureaucracy with inefficiencies, i.e, their own personal experiences of less than full service. Yet, on the other hand, we have witnessed a tremendous growth in the development of bureaucratic organization due to the fact that managers have associated bureaucracy with organizational efficiency, i.e., in this case, the ability to process a large number of organizational factors, within a relatively short time. The high degree of routinization, specialization, formalization, and standardization that can be obtained through bureaucratic organization has allowed managers to achieve certain tasks in ways that reduce duplication (each person has a specific function to perform), training and orientation (each person learns a standard and formal way of doing things), costs (the cheapening of jobs by breaking them down into routine elements), time (routinization and standardization assists people to undertake their tasks in a simple and quick way), and control (bureaucratic rules and regulations replace the need for a series of overseers and supervisors). As we shall see later, these 'efficiencies' are often achieved at great human costs to employees. The dilemma is that without bureaucracies the processing of a number of services would make life more difficult and cumbersome for many of us.

An every day example of a bureaucracy is the Motor Vehicles Branch run by provincial governments. These offices are streamlined for processing large numbers of people and large amounts of information on a routine basis. Although hundreds of applications are made every day to register motor vehicles, for most of us, this transaction only takes a few minutes to complete. When it comes to the mass processing of people and information, bureaucracies are often the most efficient organizations for the job.

This is not to deny that some people do experience problems when dealing with bureaucracies – especially with government bureaucracies. But when we think of the large numbers of people, and the enormous amounts of information which are processed every day in an efficient and routine manner by most government bureaucracies, the problem cases may be seen as exceptions to the general trend of efficiency within these organizations. We shall return to the problems of bureaucracy later in this chapter.

NOW TURN TO EXERCISE 2.1 AT THE END OF THE CHAPTER

THE BIRTH OF BUREAUCRACY IN CLASSICAL ORGANIZATION THEORY

The growth of large bureaucracies in the modern world first attracted the attention of several prominent European social thinkers during the nineteenth and early twentieth centuries. Karl Marx, Max Weber and Robert Michels were all keenly aware that in modern industrial societies, there had been a rapid growth in the size and complexity of organizations. At the same time, however, each of these social thinkers had his own views about the future of bureaucratic organizations in modern society.

Karl Marx believed that the growth of bureaucracy in government and the civil service was directly related to the rise of the capitalist state. The real purpose of the state and its bureaucracy, he believed, was to defend the economic interests of the capitalist ruling class against the attempt of other social classes – especially the working class – to seize political power. For Marx, then, the state bureaucracy, including the bureaucrats who worked as part of it, was seen as an essential part of the system of capitalist domination which would disappear after the overthrow of capitalism and the victory of socialism. Marx expected that the state bureaucracy would diminish and eventually disappear from socialist society because the working class would take over direct control of its own political and economic institutions. Bureaucracy, for Marx, was a sign that workers were alienated from the centres of economic and political power which were being run by the capitalist class in its own interests. With the introduction of socialism and the advent of a democratic working-class government, Marx believed that the working class would run its own affairs directly, and thus the need for bureaucracy would disappear.[5]

Other Marxists such as Lenin also believed that the growth of bureaucracy in modern society was a temporary and transitional phase which would come to an end with the victory of socialism. In fact, Lenin predicted that eventually, under communism, there would be a "withering away of the state", or, in other words, the gradual disappearance of the bureaucratic institutions of government. When we look back today, however, at the development of socialism in the USSR and in Eastern Europe, it is clear that Marx' and Lenin's forecasts were unrealistically optimistic and even utopian in their expectations.

If the Marxists were overly optimistic about the eventual disappearance of bureaucracy, Max Weber was decidedly more pessimistic in his outlook. He believed that the growth of large bureaucracies in the modern world was part of a general historical trend towards greater rationalization – by which he meant the tendency for people to evaluate events, circumstances, and other people in calculative terms, the logic of mean-ends in which people weigh up and value things according to a perceived balance of what they put in against what they can get out of a situation. For Weber, this found its supreme expression in the development of organizational forms, bureaucracies, in which the logic of calculability is translated into its organizational form- efficiency, i.e., the drive to achieve the maximal ends with the least expenditure of time and energy. This drive for efficiency, in turn, according to Weber, reinforces the process of rationalization. As we shall see later, Weber's concept of 'rationality' has since been challenged as reflecting male-associated values.

Max Weber believed that in the modern world – characterized by the logic of rationality – all organizations are under constant pressure to become more and more efficient. This is true not simply for business enterprises or governments, but for all organizations in society including churches, universities, political parties, the armed forces, dating services, as well as the local McDonald's.[6] In a culture of rationalization no organization remains untouched by the constant pressures for greater efficiency.

Weber suggested that most organizations adapt to the pressures for greater efficiency by introducing bureaucratic principles of organization. The bureaucracy is the hallmark of efficiency in modern society and is the best example of an organization based on what Weber calls the "rational-legal" type of authority".

In addition to analyzing the bureaucracy in terms of efficiency, Weber was also interested in it as an institution of authority. Unlike other types of authority which are based either on traditional, hereditary institutions like the monarchy, the nobility and the church, or on the personal authority of charismatic individuals like religious prophets or political leaders, the bureaucracy is based on the institutions of rational-legal authority. This latter type of authority, according to Weber, is distinguished by its use of impersonal rules of administration, and by the fact that authority is linked to office held rather than to the person of the office holder. The bureaucracy, more than any other institution, epitomizes this rational-legal form of authority.

According to Weber, the modern bureaucracy is based on a set of organizational principles which distinguish it from more traditional forms of organization. Taken together, these principles provide a complete description of an hypothetical bureaucracy, or what Weber calls "an ideal-type", although he concedes that it is unlikely that any actual bureaucracy in the real world would follow all of these principles.

Weber's ideal type of bureaucracy is an hypothetical model, or a template, which can be used to study actual organizations in the real world. When examining modern organizations, we can always see how closely they correspond to, or depart from, the general principles of bureaucratic organization outlined in Weber's hypothetical model.

Weber suggested that the modern bureaucracy was run according to a general set of principles which distinguished it from earlier, or pre-modern, organizations. He outlined six general principles of bureaucratic organization.

1. EACH OFFICE IN A BUREAUCRACY HAS A CLEARLY DEFINED SPHERE OF COMPETENCE AND BUREAUCRATIC OFFICIALS ARE ONLY SUBJECT TO AUTHORITY WITH RESPECT TO THEIR OFFICIAL OBLIGATIONS.

In other words, all bureaucracies are organized around a specialized division of labour. The work of a modern organization is divided among all its members, so that each member performs a highly specialized task. Canada Post, for example, divides its work among letter carriers, mail sorters, counter clerks, supervisors and so on. Everyone becomes a cog in the organizational machine.

2. OFFICIALS IN A BUREAUCRACY ARE ORGANIZED IN A CLEARLY DEFINED HIERARCHY OF OFFICES.

In other words, besides having a specialized division of labour, bureaucracies also have a system of authority which flows downwards from the top of the organization. This is the official chain of command in which the highest officials in the organization have the most authority. All officials in the organization give orders to those immediately below them, and accept orders from those immediately above them. In other words, all bureaucracies are arranged in an elaborate pecking-order.

3. ADMINISTRATION IS BASED UPON WRITTEN DOCUMENTS. THE BODY OF OFFICIALS ENGAGED IN HANDLING THESE DOCUMENTS AND FILES, MAKE UP THE "BUREAU" OR "OFFICE".

In other words, bureaucracies are run according to an elaborate set of written rules and regulations. These may be manuals of technical instruction which have to be followed to the letter, as in the case when auto mechanics, or computer technicians, service and repair high technology equipment. Or there may be procedural or policy manuals used by government officials to process applications for unemployment benefits, accident compensation, immigrant visas, child allowances, and so on. Bureaucracies are notorious for their paperwork, and for following written rules and regulations to the letter. But it should be noted that written rules are designed for efficiency (everyone can learn the same rules), and for equity (everyone is treated according to the same rules). There are supposed to be no favourites in bureaucracies: everyone is treated the same.

4. ADMINISTRATION IS BASED UPON GENERAL RULES AND REGULATIONS WHICH ARE ENFORCED IN AN OBJECTIVE AND IMPERSONAL MANNER.

In other words, people who work for bureaucracies, whether for the Motor Vehicles Branch, or for the Hudson Bay Company, relate to each other primarily as office-holders and only secondarily as individuals. This means that people are defined first and foremost in terms of the jobs they do rather than who they are as people. People may come and people may go in a bureaucracy, but the jobs remain to be done as long as the organization survives. All of this results in the fact that people usually treat each other in a formal and impersonal manner because it is their jobs which bring them together rather than friendship, or common interests. Similarly, people who work in bureaucracies usually try to treat their clients, (members of the public), in a formal and impersonal manner – as "cases" rather than as unique individuals. If everyone is to be treated the same, then everyone will be treated impersonally.

5. CANDIDATES ARE APPOINTED ON THE BASIS OF TECHNICAL QUALIFICATIONS, BY EXAMINATIONS OR DIPLOMAS, CERTIFYING TECHNICAL TRAINING.

In other words, people who work for bureaucracies are normally hired because of their training, qualifications and experience for the job: their technical expertise. Most bureaucracies will claim to hire people on the basis of their knowledge and their skills, and not for their personal qualities. They claim as well that appointments and promotions are made on the basis of individual merit rather than social connections, political patronage or bribes.

6. OFFICES WITHIN A BUREAUCRACY ARE VIEWED AS PROFESSIONAL CAREERS. PROMOTION IS BASED UPON SENIORITY OR ACHIEVEMENT, OR BOTH.

In other words, bureaucracies offer their members the chance for long-term careers. With the proper training and experience, it is usually possible for staff to move up the rungs of the organizational ladder. Workers in a bureaucracy are heavily dependent upon the organization for their long-term employment. The bureaucracy may protect its job security through seniority rules, and may even open up new career paths to other positions within the organization.

For Max Weber, then, these six principles of organization typified the modern bureaucracy, and distinguished it from more traditional forms of organization found in pre-modern societies. This is not to suggest that Weber believed that all modern bureaucracies are organized according to each and everyone of these principles only that these principles are represented in the typical bureaucracy.

THE BUREAUCRATIC IMAGE: THE ORGANIZATION AS MACHINE

In constructing his classical ideal-type of bureaucracy, Weber gave birth to an image which has continued to dominate the field of organization studies. This is the image of the organization as a machine, made up of a set of mutually interdependent human parts which work together in a systematic and orderly way to achieve a number of formally defined goals.

Looking back at the history of Organization Theory, we can see just how compelling this image of organization has been. Indeed, no writer since the time of Max Weber has managed to escape its influence, and most have accepted its overall validity, even when they have quarrelled with its details. The image of the bureaucracy as an organizational machine has become established as a *leitmotif*, or dominant theme, of most traditions of Organization Theory. It is an image which emphasizes a number of mechanistic properties of the bureaucratic organization including, among other things:

- calculability
- rationality
- technical expertise
- knowledge
- impersonality
- uniformity

Underlying all of these different properties, however, it is the conception of efficiency which really defines the modern bureaucracy for Weber, and sets it apart from earlier forms of organization. But as several commentators have noted, Weber's conception of efficiency was derived from examples of the authoritarian institutions of his own time – particularly the modern army, and the Catholic Church.[7] It is for this reason, that Weber's notion of the ideal-typical bureaucracy rests on the embedded values of hierarchy, inequality, conformity, determinism and objectivity. For Weber, then, the notion of efficiency is understood within an authoritarian structure of social relations.

This has been the great appeal of Weber's work for subsequent generations of management theorists, and is part of the explanation for the remarkable longevity of Weber's image of bureaucracy. At the same time, however, the authoritarian assumptions of his ideal-type have also created problems for later theorists who have sometimes struggled to reconcile this mechanistic image of the formal structure of organizations with the reality of the informal network of social relations which is also a part of most organizations.

Most large organizations in modern societies are run along bureaucratic lines in order to achieve the goal of maximum efficiency. In the modern world, efficiency has become the name of the game: the universal standard which is used to measure the performance of all organizations – in both the public and the private sectors of the economy and society.

DEBATING THE BUREAUCRACY: DILEMMAS OF MODERN ORGANIZATION THEORY.

In Max Weber's writings, the image of the bureaucracy as a machine found its most eloquent expression, although other writers such as Frederick Winslow Taylor (1911), and Henri Fayol (1949) had already used this image in their own studies of organizations, several decades before Weber's work became known outside Germany.

For management theorists, viewing the organization as a machine implied that it could be redesigned (for greater efficiency and productivity), in much the same way as other machines which were stripped down and reassembled in the workshops. The appeal of the machine image to the early schools of Scientific, and of Universalistic, Management lay in the assumption that all aspects of the organization – especially its formal structure – were wholly amenable to managerial supervision and control. According to this image, individual workers were seen as just so many cogs in a machine who could be manipulated and replaced depending upon the operational needs of the organization. The machine image proved a powerful one in management circles, and its legacy may still be seen today in some aspects of organization theory, and in some updated versions of the policies of Scientific Management. Old theories never really die, it is only their advocates who slowly fade away.

During the 1930s and 1940s, these earlier management theories of organization began to lose ground to a new generation of organization theorists who owed more to sociology and social psychology than to engineering. Beginning with the Hawthorne Studies conducted by Elton Mayo (1933), and his associates, and followed shortly after by Chester Barnard's (1938) study of the executive, the image of the organization as a machine gradually gave way to that of the organization as an organism, and as a social system. The discovery of the influence of informal work groups, and the new emphasis on cooperative rather than authoritarian styles of management, paved the way for the Human Relations school of management studies. Although it was still motivated by the interests of effective management and organizational efficiency, the Human Relations school brought a new emphasis to bear on the importance of humane leadership, as well as cooperation and communication between management and workers. The iron fist had all but disappeared into the velvet glove.

The rise of the organism, and the decline of the machine, as alternative images of organization produced a new generation of behavioural studies of bureaucracy. Weber's image of the bureaucracy as a rational and efficient form of organization was successfully challenged throughout the decades of the 1930s, 1940s and 1950s by a number of writers who sought to demonstrate the dysfunctional, inefficient and irrational features of bureaucratic organizations. Writers like Robert Merton (1940), Alvin Gouldner (1954), Seymour Martin Lipset (1950), Philip Selznick (1949), Victor Thompson (1961), among others, undertook a series of studies of actual bureaucracies and found that, in many empirical cases, bureaucratic behaviour was often very different from that suggested by the traditional image.

Many of these studies showed that officials working within bureaucracies were not always motivated by the dispassionate and impersonal norms of bureaucratic behaviour suggested by Max Weber. Bureaucrats often had their own personal interests in mind, and their own professional axes to grind, all of which detracted from the rational and efficient running of the organization. At the same time, other studies demonstrated how the rationality and efficiency of a bureaucracy could also be impaired when officials became over-preoccupied with rigidly following the rules.

This debate over the effectiveness of the bureaucracy as a form of organization continued well into the 1960s, and has never really ended. It marked the point at which modern theorists of organization began to seriously question the ideal-typical model of bureaucracy in the light of what was being learned about actual bureaucratic organizations. What became clear from many of the empirical studies done during this period was that bureaucracies did not always live up to their textbook reputations as models of rationality and efficiency: like everything else, they had their advantages and disadvantages.

The up side of bureaucracy – its advantages as a form of organization – has been recognized since the time of Max Weber. Bureaucracies, which are run along objective and impersonal lines, and which are based upon a technical division of labour, are well adapted to meet the goals of maximum efficiency. When compared to pre-industrial bureaucracies (of ancient China, Egypt, Rome, South America, Medieval Europe, etc.), the modern bureaucracy has to a great – although not complete – extent, replaced traditional values which were based on personal, familial, ethnic or regional loyalties with the modern values of objectivity and efficiency. It was this transition from traditionalism to modernity that Max Weber described as the process of rationalization.

By the middle of the twentieth century, however, organization theorists had become familiar with many of the down sides of the bureaucracy – its limitations and shortcomings as a model of organization. Several major problems of bureaucracies came to light during this period.

Rigidity

Bureaucracies can sometimes appear inflexible and inefficient when dealing with unusual, exceptional or atypical cases. This is because bureaucracies are organized, first and foremost, to process large numbers of people, and large amounts of information, with the greatest possible efficiency. For most cases, the standard rules and regulations work well enough. However, what works well for the large majority of typical cases may not work well for a sizeable minority of exceptional or unusual cases. Thus, a passport applicant who is unable to produce a birth certificate, for example, may find the bureaucrats at the Passport Office unwilling and unable to process his/her application in a routine manner. There may be a considerable delay in resolving this type of problem. Or someone who has taken paternity leave may find the bureaucrats at the Canada Employment and Immigration Commission most unhelpful when applying for U.I. benefits if the normal rules cannot be easily applied. Similarly, anyone who, in the past, visited the old USSR as an individual tourist would have recognized that, for overseas visitors, hotel accommodations, restaurant reservations, concert bookings, guided tours and other activities were primarily oriented towards charter groups, rather than to individual tourists. In this respect, the Soviet tourist bureaucracy – Intourist – was very efficient in making arrangements for charter groups, but much less flexible and efficient when it came to accommodating the needs of individual tourists.

To a greater or lesser extent, most bureaucracies are streamlined to process large numbers of similar cases but are often less prepared to deal with unusual or idiosyncratic cases. Most of us can vividly recall the occasional 'hassles' we have had with bureaucracies, but we tend to forget the countless times they have provided us with (relatively) efficient routine service – as when mailing a letter, registering an automobile, or making an airline reservation.

Goal Displacement

In some bureaucracies, the goals of individual bureaucrats, or of the departments they work for, may become more important than the official goals of the organization. Robert Merton (1940) showed, for example, how the goal of obsessively following rules and regulations may become more important to the individual bureaucrat than the broader goals of the institution. Merton defined this as the problem of "bureaucratic ritualism", in which the means (of accomplishing goals) came to displace the goals themselves.

Most of us have probably experienced this problem in one form or another. Anyone who has waited patiently (and unsuccessfully) for service in a department store in which the store assistants appear more concerned with tidying their display units than with serving customers, has witnessed an example of goal displacement. Or again, anyone who has tried to register for university courses only to be told that class quotas have been filled, or that prerequisites are necessary, has probably felt that the broader goals of education are being displaced by the strict enforcement of bureaucratic rules and regulations.

Another American sociologist, Philip Selznick (1949) has also described how goal displacement in organizations may arise when the goals of particular departments, or sections, begin to override the official goals of the organization as a whole. In universities, for example, the loss of funds through government cutbacks may lead to the growing importance of external fund-raising as a central activity of the institution. Some departments within the university may begin to define their goals in entrepreneurial and business terms which may conflict with, or even partially displace, the more traditional academic goals of the university as an institution of higher learning.[8] Most large and complex formal organizations, whether located in the public or private sectors, are vulnerable to some degree of goal displacement.

Impersonality

Many people who work for bureaucracies, or who are clients of bureaucracies, find them to be impersonal and uncaring institutions.[9] The quotation which opens this chapter describes how welfare applicants, or recipients, are often humiliated and intimidated in their dealings with welfare officials. This may often be the case when people in difficult and emotionally-charged situations are dealt with in an insensitive bureaucratic manner. Sexual assault victims and immigrant applicants, among others, may also experience the impersonality of the bureaucracy. This problem may be further exacerbated when differences of ethnicity and gender are also involved. Ethnic and gender inequalities often combine to make bureaucracies very unpleasant places for immigrants, native people and women.[10]

Empire-building and Self-perpetuation

One of the most famous critics of bureaucracy was the popular author, C. Northcote Parkinson, who argued that bureaucrats have a vested interest in making work for themselves in order to justify hiring assistants and, thereby, increase their own statuses. He believed that this tendency towards empire-building was endemic to all bureaucracies. In a similar vein, Lawrence Peter – a one time professor at the University of British Columbia – argued that officials in bureaucracies are normally promoted beyond the level of their competence to do the job. These conclusions have become enshrined in popular folk wisdom as 'Parkinson's Law' (Parkinson, 1957) – which states that 'work expands in direct proportion to the needs of the office holder', and the 'Peter Principle' (Peter and Hull, 1969) – which states that 'people are promoted to the level of their incompetence'.

Most bureaucracies will continue to stay in business long after their basic goals have been achieved, and after their original usefulness has been outlived. A good example of this is NATO which is no longer concerned with the collective military security of the Western alliance since the collapse of commu-

nism in the USSR and the rest of Eastern Europe. Today, the goals of NATO
have been redefined as those of encouraging greater political and ideological
cooperation between the 'two Europes'.[11] Another example of a bureaucracy
which changed its goals to stay in business is the National Foundation for Infantile Paralysis (U.S.). It was originally established to fight poliomyelitis, but
today, it campaigns against arthritis.

Resistance to Change

Bureaucracies may also acquire a certain amount of institutional inertia which
make them unsympathetic, or even resistant, to change. In his study of the first
(social democratic) Cooperative Commonwealth Federation provincial government in Saskatchewan, Seymour Martin Lipset (1950a, 1950b) described
how upper class senior civil servants conspired to retard and to resist many of
the progressive reforms which were introduced by the new social democratic
government. Although the government had passed the new reforms, senior
civil servants were able to frustrate and obstruct their implementation.[12] Similarly, top civil servants in the United Kingdom also conspired to obstruct the
implementation of reforms passed by the postwar Labour government. More
recently, Warren Allmand has described the opposition he encountered from
top officials in his ministry when he attempted to introduce reforms into the
Department of Indian and Northern Development.[13]

Secrecy

Bureaucracies may also attempt to conceal information from the public domain. This is particularly true of government bureaucracies which may claim
that public disclosure of information is contrary to the interests of national security.[14] Thus, when the British civil servant, Clive Ponting, revealed that the
Argentine warship, the Admiral Belgrano, had been sunk outside of the Falk-
lands' war zone, he was prosecuted for a breach of the Official Secrets Act. The
Nixon administration similarly withheld information about its unauthorized
bombing raids into Cambodia by also invoking national security interests (cf.
Shawcross, 1979).

Private bureaucracies may also suppress information when disclosure is felt
to be inconvenient or embarrassing. During the oil shortage of the 1970s, for
example, U.S. oil companies were reluctant to supply information about current supplies, and about the amount of proven oil reserves.

Anti-democratic

Ever since the time of Max Weber, bureaucracy has been seen as incompatible with the ideals of democracy. This is because hierarchy remains the great organizing principle of bureaucracy, and stands opposed to the most basic assumptions of democracy. Weber, himself, was well aware of the authoritarian potential of bureaucracy and in his later life, wrote pessimistically about the "iron cage" of bureaucratic organization.

It was left to Robert Michels (1949), however, to more fully document the anti-democratic tendencies of modern bureaucracies. Michels concluded that all large bureaucratic organizations would eventually succumb to the "iron law of oligarchy". He meant by this that all large organizations – whether political parties, corporations, government bureaucracies, or even trade unions – would, sooner or later, fall under the domination of oligarchies, i.e., small ruling elites. He concluded that all bureaucracies were destined to undergo this concentration and centralization of power and authority at the top of their organizations.

These debates produced some important new theoretical and empirical insights, and showed that the classical textbook image of bureaucracy was unable to do justice to the range of complexity and variation which existed between actual organizations in the real world. Today, debates over the future of bureaucracy continue to preoccupy organization theorists. Some writers, like Warren Bennis (1966), have analysed bureaucracies as organizational dinosaurs and predicted that they are on their way to extinction. This view sees bureaucracies as basically rigid and inflexible organizations which performed efficiently when the demand for goods and services was unchanging, but are unable to adapt to the needs of a constantly changing marketplace. Bureaucracies, from this viewpoint, are good for standardization and predictability, but perform poorly in adapting for innovation. The current trend across Eastern Europe, in which many of the formerly all-powerful state bureaucracies are being dismantled, is consistent with this critique of bureaucracy.

This view has been challenged, however, by other writers such as Robert Miewald (1970) who maintains that the news of the death of bureaucracy has been greatly exaggerated. Bureaucracies, in his view, have already shown that they can be flexible and can adapt to new situations. Many bureaucracies have long ago dispensed with the older machine-like image of organization in favour of new images and structures which emphasize professionalism and collegiality rather than authority and supervision.[15] The development of quality circles in Japanese factories is only one example of how new forms of bureaucracy are no longer so heavily dependent upon hierarchy as a fundamental principle of organization.

At the same time, however, although these and other studies succeeded in disclosing some of the dysfunctions and problems which were never shown in the idealized textbook image of bureaucracy, most theorists and managers still remained committed to the most basic assumptions of the bureaucratic model of organization. Notwithstanding its blindness to some of the disadvantages of bureaucracy, the basic assumptions of the Weberian model continued to be accepted by most mainstream theorists within the field of organization studies:

> The Weberian structure has been built upon, rationalized, adjusted, twisted and modified for the past forty years, but its essential assumptions still govern the popular conception of organizations and administrators in our colleges and universities, the research that is undertaken in the field, the development activities that produce our most usable and used technologies, and the way we talk about our workplaces (Clark, 1985:51).

While these debates have illuminated many different aspects of bureaucracies, and have helped to advance our understanding of organizations, it is from its silences and its omissions that we are best able to define the present limits of modern organization theory. Among these silences have been the topics of power and inequality in bureaucracies which, until recently, have been largely neglected by modern organization theorists. This neglect has made it difficult to speak of other topics such as race, ethnicity, gender and class which are, of course, intimately connected with the issues of power and inequality. It is to address these silences that we now turn.

STANDING IN THE SHADOWS: BUREAUCRACIES AND MINORITY GROUPS

One of the most neglected areas in the study of bureaucracy has been the position of so-called minority groups within and in relation to these organizations. Standard accounts in Organization Theory have paid scant attention to the position of women, ethnic groups, or other minorities in terms of their relations to the majority group which runs most bureaucratic organizations. This neglect can be partly explained by the fact that many writers in the Organization Theory tradition subscribe to the prevailing image of bureaucracies as rational organizations which are administered by impersonal and objective rules and procedures. Under these conditions, there would appear to be little room for favouritism, nepotism, or other forms of non-rational evaluation – such as sexual or racial discrimination. For all intents and purposes, the bureaucracy functions as a meritocracy in which rewards are wholly determined by technical competence.

According to this image of the bureaucracy, the ethnicity or gender of those who work within bureaucracies is of minor concern compared to their formal and technical qualifications. People are supposedly judged on what they do within the organization, rather than who they are – in terms of their gender or ethnicity (or social class). Consequently, some writers have suggested that bureaucracies – because of their commitment to impersonal and objective norms – help to break down traditional status divisions between people, such as gender, ethnicity and class, and thereby contribute to a levelling of social differences. In fact, Max Weber, himself, advanced this argument in the course of his writings on bureaucracy:

> The development of bureaucracy greatly favours the levelling of social classes and this can be shown historically to be the normal tendency. Conversely, every process of social levelling creates a favourable situation for the development of bureaucracy for it tends to eliminate class privileges, which include the appropriation of authority as well as the occupation of offices on an honorary basis or as an avocation by virtue of wealth. This combination everywhere inevitably foreshadows the development of mass democracy (Weber, 1947:340).

Because of the general acceptance in mainstream Organization Theory of this heavily idealized image of the bureaucracy, very little attention has been paid to the experiences of minority people organized within a majority setting. Only now is this beginning to change, and those who have stood for a long time in the shadows of bureaucracy are at last becoming subjects of serious study.

Part of the impetus for the growing interest in, what may be called, "organizational minorities" comes from recent attempts by a newer generation of theorists to reintroduce the issues of power, authority, inequality, and conflict back into mainstream Organization Theory.[16] This theoretical reorientation, as much as anything else, has helped to focus attention on the inequalities of power and status which exist in bureaucracies, and on the experiences of those who suffer them.

One of the early consequences of studying organizational minorities has been to shatter the image of the impersonal and objective bureaucracy. It is clear from the experiences of many minority groups that bureaucracies have usually mirrored the prejudices of the larger society. In the United States, for example, Blacks were forbidden to carry the mail until 1865, because of their perceived threat to national security. It was not until 1869 that they were allowed to work in the federal bureaucracy.[17] Similarly, it was not until 1967 that outright discrimination against women in the federal bureaucracy was ended by a presidential executive order. This, and other evidence, of the historical and contemporary discrimination against women and other minority groups in the U.S. federal bureaucracy, has prompted one critic to completely disavow the "merit myth" which continues to underlie the traditional view of bureaucracy:

> The myth which makes public employment almost synonymous with "civil service", asserts that virtually all public servants have been chosen largely on the basis of merit, evidenced by objective written tests and other scientifically determined criteria, and that only the "best and brightest" survive this fair selection process to be appointed to and promoted within federal, state and local government jobs. The facts, however, are that most public employees today are not under a civil service or merit system, and that overt discrimination against racial-ethnic minorities and women, preferential treatment for others, and covert "scientific" techniques, have combined to produce an unrepresentative "meritless" bureaucracy (Kranz 1976: 204).

Indeed, as Kathy Ferguson (1984) has argued, the very character of bureaucratic rationality has served to operate as a set of principles against which women have been judged unfavourably as potential members of the bureaucracy. A 'discourse of bureaucracy' – with its stress on rationality, objectivity, and impersonality, developed alongside a 'discourse of domesticity' – which stressed emotionality, subjectivity, and familial values. Historically, bureaucratic principles, in contrast to domestic principles, became associated with males and maleness and served to exclude women (seen as having domestic and thus inappropriate characteristics) from the bureaucracies or to restrict them to the lower levels.[18]

Other writers have also rejected the idealized picture of the bureaucracy and have pointed to the persistent underrepresentation of women and ethnic minorities as evidence of institutionalized discrimination within these organizations. Indeed, as Gideon Sjborg (1983:276) laconically remarked:

> [...] one does not have to be a Marxist to recognize that bureaucracy is the single most important means for sustaining class differences in modern society.

Rosabeth Moss Kanter's (1977) now classic study of the private bureaucracy helped to draw attention to the inequitable distribution of power in the bureaucracy and its impact on the largely powerless women (and men). Kanter revealed how women more than men are concentrated at the lower rungs of the organization and have less opportunities than men to rise in the organization. She called this the "opportunity structure" which serves to signal to women (and some men) that they are not fully valued members of the organization.

In Canada, there has been no shortage of evidence to suggest that bureaucracies have often failed to uphold the universalistic standards envisaged by Max Weber. Examples of institutionalized discrimination in various forms have been uncovered in studies ranging from francophones in public sector and private sector bureaucracies (Beattie, 1975), women in work organizations (Abella, 1984), as well as immigrants and visible minorities in the labour market (Li, 1988; Bolaria and Li, 1985; Ramcharan, 1982). In fact, the degree of inequity which has been observed, in both public and private sector employment, between the dominant white, Anglo-saxon, middle-class male group and subordinate minority groups caused one authority to label the whole of Canadian society – and the institutions within in – as a "vertical mosaic" (Porter, 1965). In terms of women, Nicole Morgan's (1988) study of the Canadian Public Service provides a classic example of the inequities prevalent within bureaucratic organizations. Morgan details the fact that it took two world wars and various government decrees for women to gain entrance to the Canadian Public Service (women were only 30% of the service by 1939 and only 44% two decades later) and to develop into a stable part of the bureaucracy but that, in the process, they have been subjected to numerous discriminatory recruitment and promotion practices which were consolidated in the development of 'women's work' within the bureaucracy and the restriction of women to the lower levels of the hierarchy. Even today the ghettoisation of women's work continues as an aspect of the Canadian Public Service and few women have yet been recruited to the upper echelons. The response of government bureaucracy has been to deal with the issue in ways which have crystalized rather than challenged the problem: in the establishment of government positions and policies to deal with 'women's issues' the notion that there are specific gender areas or concerns within the bureaucracy has been strengthened (Grant and Tancred, 1992).

Most of these studies were completed by scholars outside of the discipline of Organization Theory, in such areas as sociology, history and political science. Only very recently have organization theorists begun to study the relations between majority and minority groups within an organizational setting. Of the few Canadian studies which presently exist in this area most have focused on gender relations in organizations[19] – an issue we look at in greater depth in chapter five. There has been very little done on ethnic relations within organizations[20] which is surprising, given the official ideology of multiculturalism in this country. It is to partly rectify this omission that we develop a more detailed discussion of ethnicity in chapter six.

KEY TERMS

authority	bureaucracy	calculability
division of labour	efficiency	formalization
hierarchy	impersonality	power
rational-legal authority	traditional authority	charismatic authority
rationality	routinization	specialization
standardization	uniformity	rigidity
goal displacement		

REVIEW QUESTIONS

Q1. Define bureaucracy.

Assignment: Now turn to the glossary at the end of the book and compare your definitions.

Q2. Briefly define each of the following terms, and say how each relates to the notion of bureaucracy:
hierarchy
standardization
formalization
specialization
impersonality

Assignment: Now turn to the glossary at the end of the book and compare your definitions.

Q3. Briefly discuss some of the ways in which bureaucracies may be said to be efficient, or inefficient. Try to provide some examples from your own life experiences.

Assignment: Apply the readings to some real life situations.

Q4. Briefly define each of the following terms and say how they relate to the debate on bureaucracy:

goal-displacement
rigidity
uniformity
routinization
division of labour

Assignment: Now turn to the glossary at the end of the book and compare your definitions

EXERCISE 2.1

This exercise is designed to make you think about the significance of bureaucracies in your own life. Do the tasks individually and then discuss your findings in small groups.

A. On a sheet of paper:

1. Itemize the contents of your wallet, purse, or pocketbook.

2. List the number of documentary items (e.g., ID cards, credit cards, etc) which link you to bureaucratic organizations.

3. Distinguish between those items which are voluntary, and those which are compulsory.

B. On the same sheet of paper:

1. Make a list of all the compulsory links that you have with bureaucracies.

2. Now, make a list of the ways in which the voluntary links you have with bureaucracies also have some compulsory aspects to them.

3. Briefly discuss how the bureaucratic items in your wallet, purse, or pocketbook would differ if you were of a different gender. How would they differ if you were an aboriginal rather than a non-aboriginal Canadian?

For the first part of the exercise, it is only necessary to examine the contents of your wallet, purse, or pocketbook. You will find that there are a surprising number of documentary links to large bureaucratic organizations contained in your immediate personal belongings. In trying to establish how important these items are for you in different situations – i.e., when opening a bank account, when joining a public library, when writing a cheque – you are also showing how much control some of these bureaucracies exercise over your life.

C. For the second part of the exercise, you should try to think of as many compulsory documentary links that you have with bureaucracies. These can include anything from birth to death certificates: bureaucracies are interested in documenting you from the cradle to the grave. Then try to think of the compulsory aspects which are often involved even in your voluntary links to bureaucracies. This may include the obligation to return library books, to pay your charge account bills, and so on. By putting together your compulsory and voluntary links with bureaucracies, you will begin to see just how much of your life is organized around these giant institutions.[21]

FURTHER READING

On the impact of bureaucracy upon our ways of thinking:
Gareth Morgan (1986) IMAGES OF ORGANI-ZATION, Chapter 1.

On the impact of corporate bureaucracy on moral behaviour:
Robert Jackall (1988) MORAL MAZES: THE WORLD OF CORPORATE MANAGERS.

Literary Images of the impact of bureaucracy on social life
George Orwell, 1984
Aldous Huxley, BRAVE NEW WORLD.
Margaret Atwood, THE HANDMAID'S TALE

The impact of corporate and public bureaucracy on women
Rosabeth Moss Kanter (1977) MEN AND WOMEN OF THE CORPORATION

K.E. Ferguson (1984) THE FEMINIST CASE AGAINST BUREAUCRACY
Nicole Morgan. (1988). THE EQUALITY GAME.
Judith Grant and Peta Tancred (1992) "A FEMINIST PERSPECTIVE ON THE STATE".
Clare Burton (1992) MERIT AND GENDER: ORGANIZATIONS AND THE MOBILIZATION OF MASCULINE BIAS.
Grahame Lowe (1987) WOMEN IN THE ADMINISTRATIVE REVOLUTION.

On the bureaucracy and efficiency debate:
Pugh, D.S., Hickson, D.J., & Hinings, C.R. [eds] 1983 WRITERS ON ORGANIZATIONS
D.S. Pugh (ed) (1984) ORGANIZATION THEORY

END NOTES

1. Cited in Handelman and Leyton (1978), pp.2-3. We have included this quote because it works at two levels – (i) in exposing the nature of bureaucratic life, and (ii) in revealing the gendered nature of reporting: the report refers only to male recipients and welfare officers.
2. Cf. Equality Now: the Minutes, Proceedings and Evidence of the Special Committee on the Participation of Minorities in Canadian Society (1984).

3. In case these concerns seem unduly alarmist, it is worth noting that similar sentiments have been expressed by the Federal Privacy Commissioner in Canada. The following was reported in the Edmonton Journal of July 14, 1993:
   "Invasions of privacy that once seemed plausible only on the pages of George Orwell's novels may soon be realities in Canada, the Federal Privacy Commissioner warned Tuesday (July 13, 1993)...
   It's not a question of paranoia (Bruce) Phillips said in his annual report.

People are being denied employment, people are being denied credit, people losing their jobs, people are losing reputations because of information being collected and used about them without their knowledge and consent".

4. See Bahro (1978), Sik (1972), Hegedus (1976), Blackburn (1991), Feffer (1992), Hartman and Vilanova (1992).

5. For a more detailed explanation of the Marxian perspective on bureaucracy, see Mouzelis (1967)

6. McDonalds is a prime example of bureaucratization. This organization has taken standardization and formalization to a fine art - detailing through a series of rules and regulations every aspect of the production process, from the exact way that burgers are to be cooked down to the requirement that employees smile.

7. See Clark (1985:48) who claims that, "The language of bureaucracy has several nested layers. It is militaristic, mechanistic, sexist, capitalist, Western, and rationalistic".

8. For recent examples of this tendency see Newson and Buchbinder (1988).

9. For a vivid account of the impersonal and intrusive character of government agencies when dealing with unemployed people, see Burnman (1988)

10. For a shocking account of one native woman's experience with the welfare bureaucracy in Western Canada see Campbell (1973).

11. The beginnings of the NATO strategy to deal with the post Cold War world are discussed in NATO review, 1991.

12. See also Bendix (1949).

13. A former minister during the 1970s, Montreal M.P., Warren Allmand, recalls friction between himself and the Department's bureaucrats because he initiated an open-door policy with native leaders. "There was a whisper campaign going on behind my back by bureaucrats. They said I was listening more to the Indians than my officials and I wasn't doing my job".

'Indian Affairs' $2.5 billion buys a lot of red tape'. Jack Aubry, Ottawa Citizen, quoted in Edmonton Journal, Nov.4, 1990.

14. For a useful review of secrecy in government see Galnoor, (1977).

15. Professor Henry Minzberg of McGill University has characterized bureaucracies into three types - the 'machine bureaucracy', the 'professional bureaucracy', and the 'divisional form' of organization, which combines 'machine bureaucracy' with semi-autonomous divisions. cf. Minzberg (1973).

16. cf. Burrell and Morgan (1979); Clegg & Dunkerley (1980); Clegg (1981; 1989), Ferguson (1984); Morgan (1986); Bell (1989); Bell, Denton & Nkomo (1992).

17. For a revealing account of the racist practices and policies traditionally employed in the British civil service to exclude Black candidates see Harris, (1991).

18. For a recent feminist critical reading of the concept of "rationality" in organization theory see Mumby and Putnam (1992).

19. Cf. Burke and McKeen (1988), Agocs (1989), Bradshaw-Campball (1991), Mills and Chiaramonte (1991), Mills and Tancred (1992), Cullen (1992).

20. The work of Wallis (1989) and Mighty (1991a, b) are rare examples.

21. We are indebted to Derek Sayer, Department of Sociology, University of Alberta, for the idea for this assignment.

CHAPTER 3

Calling the Shots:
How Organization Theory
Relates to Managers

This chapter examines some of the ways in which the topic of management has been conceptualized in Organization Theory and how these conceptualizations have been deeply
coloured by the managerialist perspective of the discipline. The chapter begins with an
exploration of management as "the fourth factor of production", and goes on to trace the
relationship between the development of big business and the growth of management
theory. Attention is paid to the impact of management and organization theory on the
character of class struggle – in particular the development of scientific management and
the "deskilling" debate. The chapter ends with an examination of management as practice.

The verb to manage, from manus, the Latin for hand, originally meant to train a
horse in his paces, to cause him to do the exercises of the manege [...] Like a rider
who uses reins, bridle, spurs, carrot, whip, and training from birth to impose his will,
the capitalist strives, through management, to control. And control is indeed the cen-
tral concept of all management systems, as has been recognized implicitly or explicitly
by all theoreticians of management (Harry Braverman , 1974, pp. 67-68).

INTRODUCTION

It is not possible to get very far in a course on Organization Theory without
encountering the topic of management. Management occupies a special place
in the hearts and minds of organization theorists and, if they are to be believed,
its importance to the operation of the modern organization can hardly be over-
estimated. Indeed, for most writers, management is not only the single, most

important factor involved in the running of an organization, it is the all-encompassing factor which influences all other aspects of organizational life. This has led many contemporary theorists to refer to management as "the fourth factor of production", in a way which rivals in importance the three other traditional factors of land, labour and capital.[1] Such an emphasis on the importance of management in OT should come as no surprise in a discipline which has evolved from a largely managerial viewpoint.

In this chapter, we shall examine some of the ways in which the topic of management has been conceptualized in OT and how these conceptualizations have been deeply coloured by the managerial perspective of the discipline. There is, in effect, something of a self-justificatory character to much of the writing on management which has come out of the mainstream traditions of Organization Theory. In spite of attempts by management theorists to establish their field as an objective, or even as a "scientific" branch of knowledge, much of the contemporary writing on management theory has never really lost its ideological character, i.e., its tendency to legitimize and to routinize the perspectives of management within the organization. This has resulted in a typically one-sided and incomplete understanding of management in much of what passes for organization theory, including management theory today. Part of the task of this chapter is to show how this narrow definition of the field of management studies has obscured our understanding of some of the broader historical, and more critical issues related to management in modern society. There is more to the study of management than managers, themselves, would have us believe. And if OT is to become more than simply an apologia for managers, the time has come for some of the broader theoretical issues of modern management to be raised in a critical and historical perspective.

In its essentials, as the opening quotation of this chapter makes clear, the most basic problem facing all managers is the problem of control, i.e., how to ensure the compliance and/or the cooperation of subordinate individuals within an organization. If managers are to run their organizations effectively, they need to be able to control the behaviour of those over whom they exercise authority and responsibility. The problem of control, therefore, defines more than anything else the central challenge faced by managers everywhere, irrespective of organizations they manage.

Very few of the definitions of management offered in the literature of OT, however, reduce the matter to such stark and simple terms. The task of management is more commonly seen as that of bringing together different resources for the purpose of accomplishing definite organizational goals. In this type of definition, the image of a manager as a controller of (potentially) recalcitrant subordinates is replaced by that of a manager as a broker for obtaining and coordinating the different institutional resources necessary for the effective operation of the enterprise or organization (cf. Edwards, 1979). The strong implication of this image, of course, is that the real job of manager is to bring together, or to assemble, a set of complementary – or non-antagonistic – elements which can be combined in order to realize the goals of the organization. There is no hint in this type of definition that the interests of any of the elements may actually be in opposition to each other, or that the relationship between them may be defined primarily by differences of power. Instead, it is usually implied that the role of management is to combine these elements into an effective functional unity which is based upon a common set of underlying interests. According to this view, an important function of management is to ensure that all elements of the organization become aware of their underlying common interests and act in accordance with these interests. This is what we may call the "functional", or "consensus" view of management, and it is this view which is typically represented in most introductory definitions of the field:

> Management is the performance of certain functions in order to obtain the effective acquisition, allocation and utilization of human efforts and physical resources in order to accomplish some goal. The activity of management is found in all organizations, profit and not-for-profit, and is made necessary when people seek to cooperate to accomplish some task (Wren and Voich, 1984: vi).

In this and similar definitions, the view of the manager as an agent of social control is largely supplanted by one in which the manager is seen more as a juggler of different human and material resources. As has been the case for many other subjects in OT, the issues of power, conflict and inequality are generally down played in management studies, and the interests of management are largely identified with the interests of the organization as a functional whole.

> We believe that the primary function of management is the coordination of human effort in a world characterized by tensions between formality and informality, between technology and humanity (Frost, Mitchell and Nord, 1990: xiii).

In this image of the manager as juggler, the practice of management (as well as the theory) implies:

[...] a myriad of balancing acts which are needed to facilitate and secure coordination and cooperation between and among individuals and groups of individuals in organizations. We draw upon the balancing image because it captures the type of actions managers must take to coordinate people with different values, self-interests and intentions and departments with different agendas [...] The balancing image captures the dilemmas managers must face and attempt to resolve in coordinating different perceptions and beliefs about what is right or wrong strategically and morally in the affairs and direction of the organizations they administer (Ibid: xiv).

The important thing to recognize about this image of management, besides the fact that it largely eschews any reference to the issues of power, conflict and inequality, is that management is seen as the only agency which is capable of bringing together the different elements of the organization. It alone can rise above the particular interests of each constituency in order to serve the operational needs of the total organization. Thus, it is only the interests of management which are fully identified with the interests of the organization as a whole. And it is for this reason that the factor of management is viewed by many organization theorists as the essential fourth factor of production which, because of its uniquely universal view of the total organization, has become the most vital and important component in the running of the modern organization.

> No job is more vital to our society than that of the manager. It is the manager who determines whether our social institutions serve us well or whether they squander our talents and resources (Mintzberg, 1975:61).

The belief in the supreme importance of management has been extended from business enterprises to government departments and non-profit organizations. Management is usually seen as that vital and creative spark which alone can bring together and coordinate the resources needed for the effective running of these organizations. As long as there are organizations, there will always be a need for their specialized management, for without management – it is implied – these resources will remain unorganized and unproductive. This sense of the universal and eternal need for professional management is well captured by Dale (1978), in a quote from – of all people – the Fabian Socialist, Sidney Webb, which appears at the beginning of a textbook on Management Theory:

> Under any social order from now to Utopia a management elite is indispensa-

ble and all-enduring [...] The question is not: "Will there be a management elite?" but "What sort of elite will it be?".

The point of examining these traditional definitions of management from a critical perspective is not to suggest that they are entirely without merit, or that they paint a totally false picture of what managers do. There is no reason why the practice of management should not be seen as the task of juggling various resources in an effort to combine and coordinate them for the realization of organizational goals. From a managerial perspective, it makes good sense to define the functions of management in these, or similar, terms. The point is, however, that such definitions offer a very partial, one-sided, and incomplete understanding of the practice of management, an understanding which remains thoroughly wedded to a managerial perspective and agenda.

As we shall see in the next section of this chapter, part of the problem with the consensus view of management is its tendency to overlook the lessons of history and to focus, almost exclusively, on the search for practical techniques of 'successful' management. This has resulted in the degradation of theory in much of what passes for mainstream OT. The absence of any critical or historical perspective has blinded much of OT to the significance of the issues of power, conflict and inequality, and has reduced it at times to the level of a managerial ideology where its only remaining function is to serve as a practical guide for managerial action. But, as we shall see, this consensus view tells us very little about the historical rise of professional management, or about the class origins of managers as a social group. In order to throw more light on these and other questions, we need a theory of management which is more than simply a guide to practical action; we need a theory which is both comparative and historical and which is free from the narrow administrative focus which underlies the practical interests of managers as a social group. What we need is a critical-theoretical perspective on Organization and Management Theory.

THE VISIBLE HAND: BIG BUSINESS AND THE MANAGERIAL REVOLUTION

There are very few mainstream OT textbooks which question the need for some kind of top-down management structure with its resultant hierarchical division of authority. For the vast majority of writers in the managerial tradition, the social functions of management and the social status of managers are largely self-evident, and require no special explanation or justification. Indeed, as one writer suggests, it isn't only management theorists who feel this way:

> If you asked most social scientists why work is run by bosses and managers and not by workers, they would likely tell you that such organization is "necessary" or "inevitable" or perhaps "efficient". Some proclaim, for example, that the hierarchical organization of work is a necessary corollary of modern production technology. Others assert that while hierarchy may not be necessary, it is efficient, making possible more profits for the employer, higher wages for the workers, and greater production for society than alternative arrangements can provide (Edwards, 1979: vii).

For writers who have remained locked in a managerial perspective, and especially for those without any understanding of the lessons of history, such assumptions are accepted as entirely natural and unproblematic. In order to examine these assumptions from a more critical perspective, however, it is important to see how the practices of management have changed over the course of recent history and how they can be understood, not so much as universal imperatives of all organizations, but as strategies used by powerful social groups to maintain direction and control over changing organizations.

While there is general agreement that management, in one form or another, has been practised in all civilized states, including those of ancient civilizations (cf. Wren, 1987), most theorists today identify the rise of, what has sometimes been called, "systematic management" with the modern age of industrialization (ibid). The roots of modern management practices can be traced back to early development of industrial capitalism, and to the greatly increased need for a disciplined work force which was associated with the origins of factory production. Many writers today, however, believe that the real turning point in management practices came with the growth of big business at the turn of the end of the nineteenth century, and the beginning of the twentieth century. With the growth of ever larger and more complex organizations – especially business enterprises – the age of the individual entrepreneur slowly gave way, in the early twentieth century, to the age of the professional manager. By the end of the second decade of the twentieth century, it had become clear to so many observers that the days of 'the rugged individualist' tycoons of industry and commerce – the Fords, Mellons, Duponts, Carnegies, Rockefellers – were numbered, and that in their places a new breed of corporate owners and directors was emerging. The age of the individual entrepreneur was passing and a new age of corporate ownership and control had already begun to replace it.

The transformation of competitive capitalism into the later stage of monopoly capitalism brought with it important changes in the management and control of large scale businesses and industrial enterprises. During the early part of the twentieth century, individual entrepreneurs still played an active role in the management and supervision of their companies. It was not uncommon, for example, for Henry Ford to visit the shop-floor of his factories in order to assess the efficiency of his machines, and the performance of his workforce. But by the end of the 1920s, this kind of personal, or paternalistic, intervention by owners of large companies had become increasingly uncommon, and increasingly improbable.[2] The transformation of ownership from individual into corporate hands was accompanied by the rise of a new class of professional managers whose businesses they managed. The rise of this new class of professional managers during the opening decades of the twentieth century is often referred to as "the managerial revolution".[3]

Some writers have suggested that the managerial revolution also resulted in a transfer of power from the traditional class of owners to that of the professional salaried managers, leading in the words of one interpreter to a "decomposition of capital" (Dahrendorf, 1959:41-48), i.e., a shift of power from a narrow elite of owners to a broader constituency of managers, owners, shareholders and other 'stakeholders'. This interpretation has been challenged by other writers who have argued that boards of directors, rather than managers, have retained their ultimate power to direct and control the companies they own.

One of the more important interpretations of the managerial revolution is provided in the work of the economic historian, Alfred Chandler.[4] In his book, *The Visible Hand*, which won him the Pulitzer Prize for History, Chandler describes the formative years of modern capitalism. He suggests that between the years 1850-1920, a new type of economic institution emerged in the United States, the multi-unit firm, which was controlled by a new class of managers operating under new conditions of capitalist production. Chandler shows how the causes of this expansion in the size and complexity of industrial and commercial firms during the years of his study were to be found in changes in demand which brought about the growth of mass markets, technological change, and high volume production.[5]

Chandler's analysis of the growth of economic organizations in the early part of the twentieth century has far-reaching implications for an understanding of the managerial revolution,[6] and of the systems of managerial hierarchy which have become established in all types of productive enterprises, and by extension, into all formal organizations in the modern world. Chandler records that when organizations began to move away from small owner-controlled enterprises towards modern multi-unit business corporations, a new class of managers appeared. These new salaried managers, who gradually displaced many of the earlier entrepreneurial owner/managers, began to transform the structural arrangements of the industrial and commercial businesses in which they worked. According to Chandler, the role of management was central to the development of the new organizational structure which came to dominate the multi-unit firms in the opening decades of the twentieth century. He suggests that, "the visible hand of management has replaced Adam Smith's invisible hand of market forces" (Chandler, 1984).

The most significant of these structural changes was the introduction of a more decentralized corporate structure which allowed for a much greater specialization of management functions. This was typically represented in the key distinctions between the general offices, divisions, departments and field units. These changes laid the foundations for the modern system of hierarchical management which, in its essentials, remains with us today.[7]

The importance of Chandler's historical analysis of the rise of the multi-unit firm, and of the corporate management structures which corresponded to it, lies in the fact that we are able to see more clearly how modern forms of management have actually evolved. There is nothing "inevitable" or "natural" about the way in which these structures came into existence; they emerged in response to a particular set of historical conditions which marked the transition from a family, or finance based capitalism, to a maturing managerial capitalism. If history teaches us anything, it is that no structures are fixed or permanent, and that everything is subject to flux, change and transformation. The managerial structures which today appear so unalterable, so stable could tomorrow be brought down by historical events as surely as the fall of the Berlin Wall. This historical understanding of the roots of modern management is a useful and necessary corrective to many mainstream OT texts which often seem to assume that present structures of management are the only rationally conceivable ones in the modern world.

Further insight into the evolution of modern systems of management, and of the changing forms of workplace supervision and control which grew out of these systems, is to be found in the recent work of labour process theorists (cf. Edwards, 1979; Burawoy, 1979 1985). In his pioneering text on the changing structures of workplace relations Richard Edwards (1979) describes three different systems of workplace control which have evolved since the Industrial Revolution. The appearance of each of these systems at different times in the course of the last hundred years illustrates the continuous attempts by managers to adapt to the ever-changing conditions of work, and to the problems of its supervision and control. What is of particular value in this approach, (and in the work of other labour process theorists), is the development of a genuinely historical perspective with which to study the evolving forms of labour man agement relations. An historical approach can often serve to move us beyond the orthodox assumptions of contemporary management principles to a point where they can be more easily questioned and critiqued.[8]

In his own work, Edwards identifies three systems of workplace control which, he suggests, can be distinguished from each other in terms of how work is directed, evaluated, and disciplined. What he calls "simple control", (and which still survives in many workplaces today), was characteristic of small owner-manager firms with tight and often highly personalized systems of workplace supervision. These systems flourished throughout most of the nineteenth century, but were progressively displaced by the growth of big business in the early twentieth century, and by the increasing size and complexity of the workplace. Under the system of simple control, work-forces were normally small and bosses were usually close and powerful. In these situations, the treatment of workers was often arbitrary, and reflected the personal styles and temperaments of individual foremen and supervisors. Because many of these early businesses were family enterprises, workers were often subject to the petty tyranny, and paternalistic authority of bosses who were, themselves, part of the family business.[9]

With the growth of big business, systems of simple control were soon overtaken by systems of technical control. In place of the highly paternalistic forms of supervision which had characterized the small family firm, big businesses were now able to control workers through the introduction of new technology. Nowhere was this more apparent than in the Ford Motor Company when, in 1914, Henry Ford installed the first form of assembly-line production: the chain-driven "endless conveyor" to assemble magnetos. The advent of assembly line production meant that workers could now be directly controlled by the technology. The machinery, itself, directed the labour process and set the pace and rates of work. Under these conditions, the supervision of workers underwent some changes. Foremen no longer initiated the work tasks as this was now done by the machinery. Instead of directing the labour process, foremen were now responsible for monitoring and evaluating the flow of work.

> The actual power to control work is thus vested in the line itself, rather than in the person of the foreman. Instead of control appearing to flow from boss to workers, control emerges from much more impersonal "technology" (Edwards, op cit:120).

In some cases, throughout much of the early period of industrialization, corporal punishment was used to discipline – especially child labourers. Fining was also a common practice against workers who had violated the rules of the company. It is of interest to note, however, that in these early paternalistic family enterprises, punishment could just as easily be exacted for supposedly moral transgressions as for breaches of industrial discipline. This is made clear from the following set of sanctions which were posted in the factories of Samuel Oldknow, considered one of the more progressive employers of the late eighteenth century:

"That when any person, either Man, Woman or Child, is heard to CURSE or SWEAR, the same shall forfeit One Shilling -And when a Hand is absent from Work, (unless unavoidably detained by sickness, or Leave being first obtained), the same shall forfeit as many Hours of Work as have been lost; and if by the Job or Piece, after a Rate of 2 [shillings] 6 [pence] per Day – Such Forfeitures to be put in a Box, and distributed to the Sick and Necessitous, at the discretion of their Employer".

This rule was posted December 1, 1797 and is reprinted in B.W.Clapp (ed), Documents in English Economic History, Vol. 1. London: G.Bell and Sons, 1976:387. Capitals from the original.

The growth of automation, and of the systems of technical control which corresponded to it, created the conditions for the managerial revolution. This first generation of professional managers increased their control over the workplace by controlling the ways in which the jobs of workers were designed. Many of these early managers came from highly technical backgrounds: some were industrial design experts, others, systems engineers or industry economists. Their most lasting achievement, as we shall see in the next section, was the creation of the classical schools of management theory, including the school of Scientific Management. But as Edwards shows, systems of technical control were unable to solve all the labour problems of production and, in fact, began to generate some new ones. More than any previous system, the technical system of control carried with it the danger that workplace conflicts could erupt into broader and more general plant-wide struggles between labour and management. When all workers were locked into an assembly-line, labour conflicts could easily escalate to include the whole plant. Work stoppages, plant sit-downs and accelerated drives for unionization throughout the 1930s, all increasingly defined the limits of technical control in modern industry.

These experiences led several major companies to move beyond purely technical systems of control, and during the post-War period, the first examples were seen of new bureaucratic systems of control. Unlike technical control, which is embedded in the physical and technological aspects of production, and is built into the design of the machines, bureaucratic control is embedded in the social and organizational structures of the firm and is built into job categories, work rules, promotion procedures, discipline, wage-scales, definitions of responsibility, and so on. As Edwards (Ibid:131) suggests, "Bureaucratic control establishes the impersonal force of 'company rules' or 'company policy' as the basis for control".

Originally, in companies like Polaroid and IBM, bureaucratic control of the workplace was introduced as a way of avoiding unionization, and the whole adversarial collective bargaining model which became established in the 1950s. With the advance of unionism in many industrial sectors, however, bureaucratic systems of control began to incorporate unions into the structures of workplace control through the rules and regulations laid out in many collective agreements. Unions were obliged to honour the terms of these agreements and to discipline any of their members who were found to be in violation of these terms.

The real success of the system of bureaucratic control, however, resided in the power it gave to management to comprehensively determine all aspects of the corporate occupational structure. Managers became responsible for how jobs were classified, how job descriptions were defined, how wage and salary rates established, how hiring and promotion procedures were adopted, and virtually every other aspect of the organization of the labour force. This form of control was extended to all sections of the labour force including blue collar and white collar workers, as well as to managers themselves. Unlike previous forms of workplace control, bureaucratic control was comprehensive in its coverage of all members of the workforce, and regulated every aspect of their lives on the job.

Today, in most work organizations, managers normally use some combination of each of these three systems of control to exact cooperation and/or compliance from their subordinates. Like everything else, management systems have undergone major changes over the past one hundred years or more in order to maintain and extend control over their work-forces. Nothing stands still, however, and with the introduction of new technology, and the development of new forms of workplace struggle, management practices which today seem so advanced and so enlightened will tomorrow give way to very different forms of industrial relations.

NOW TURN TO EXERCISE 3.1 AT THE END OF THE CHAPTER

READING BETWEEN THE LINES: MANAGEMENT THEORY AND CLASS STRUGGLE

One of the fundamental paradoxes of OT is the idea that a science of organization can be built up from the particular perspective of managers. Organizations, of course, especially work organizations, are composed of workers as well as managers. Why is it, then, that the "applied sciences" of organization have all been developed for the benefit of managers rather than workers? Why is it that managers rather than workers are seen to represent and embody the interests of the organization as a whole? Most OT textbooks take it for granted that management has a rightful monopoly over the production and application of systematic knowledge about organizations. Apparently, it comes with the territory. The job of being a manager involves learning about organizations, and how to increase their efficiency, productivity and profitability. The job of being a worker involves doing what you are told.

Today, the "science" of management is no longer paralleled by any comparable "science" of "workmanship".[10] The truth is, that many of the practical sciences of "workmanship" are passing into extinction, as traditional trades fall into disuse, and more apprenticeships are terminated – and as the accumulated knowledge of (usually male) generations is gradually lost and forgotten: interestingly, while a sizeable number of women have been recruited into the ranks of management, there has been much less progress (despite government promotions of access by women to non-traditional trades and professions) in the spread of designated skills and skilled employment among women workers. This is the real story behind the rise of organization theory and management science. It is a story in which the struggle for greater knowledge and control of work by management has always been at the expense of workers – a reduction in the skills of (mainly male) workers while supporting the continued exclusion of women from the skilled ranks.[11] Braverman (1974) refers to this process as "deskilling". When reading between the lines of OT, therefore, it is useful to bear in mind that the different theories of management, so neatly presented in the major textbooks, usually emerged from a background of struggle and confrontation between labour and management. For managers, the search for knowledge of the general principles of work organizations has always been motivated by the desire for greater control over the workforce.[12] In other words, the search for knowledge in OT has remained inseparable from the struggle for power.

The history of OT over this century has seen the rise and fall of a number of different theories of management. During the earlier part of this century, many of these ideas were developed by individual men and women,[13] who were themselves, either business people, or who had strong interests in business affairs – especially in the state of management-labour relations. Most of these early contributors to what is now known as OT came from business backgrounds and included men like the French industrialist Henri Fayol, the GM executive James Mooney, the Johns-Manville vice-president Alvin Brown, the British chocolate executive Oliver Sheldon, the New Jersey Bell Telephone Company president Chester Barnard, the British management consultant Lyndall Urwick and, of course, Frederick Winslow Taylor of the Bethlehem and of the Midvale steel companies. In fact, it has only been over the past forty years, or so, that academics have overtaken businessmen in their contributions to OT.

No one who has ever opened a standard textbook in OT can fail to have been impressed by the variety of different theoretical perspectives currently represented in this field. The historical development of OT has left behind a legacy of theoretical pluralism which continues to define the discipline up to the present day. The story behind the emergence of these different "schools" of management theory is inextricably linked to the continuing struggle of managers to expand their scope of control over the workplace, and to increase the productivity and profitability of business enterprises under the changing historical conditions of production. Each of the different schools of management theory, therefore, may be thought of as a separate landmark in the continuing struggle for power between labour and management, a struggle that – with temporary reversals – has seen labour in constant retreat.

This is not the way that management theory is normally depicted in most of the standard textbooks. To read many of these accounts, it almost seems as though management theorists have only been motivated by the disinterested search for knowledge and/or efficiency for its own sake, than by the pursuit of larger profits. But as we shall see throughout this chapter, the development of management theory has rarely been undertaken simply as an academic exercise. At stake has always been the issue of power: how to invest managers with more power – in the interests of greater efficiency, productivity, profitability, or general organizational effectiveness and how to strip power from the workers – in the interests of exacting their cooperation and/or compliance in the process of production. Nowhere is this more clearly expressed than in a recent issue of the American business magazine, FORTUNE. Under the title "New Ways to Exercise Power", the article examines the recent trend among large U.S. corporations to develop an "empowering" style of management, i.e., to share responsibility among a greater number of employees. It notes that this is a response to changed conditions:

> You can't manage today's workforce like yesterday's [...] The military command-and-control model went out with red meat. Your job is to set a strategic direction, get your people to agree, give them money and authority, and leave them alone. (Stewart, 1989:52)

However, the article is careful to point out that this new management approach is fundamentally linked to conditions of profitability or "the bottom line" as they call it. Thus, the article concludes,

> Share power, and if profits go up everyone will praise the brilliant way you unleashed the latent energy of your people. But if profits go down, everyone will condemn the sloppy way you lost control of the company. (Ibid:64)

THE PERIODIZATION OF THEORY AND THE ILLUSION OF PROGRESS: THE CASE OF SCIENTIFIC MANAGEMENT

Most OT textbooks reserve at least one early chapter for a review of past theories of management. The amount of detail covered in this historical section will vary with the organization and content of the text: from the relatively cursory treatment of past theories offered in such practical management texts as Wren and Voitch (1984), Dale (1978), Donnelly, Gibson and Ivancevich (1990), to the considerably more extensive discussions which appear in texts focusing on the evolution of management thought, such as Wren (1987). In all of these cases, however, the growth of management thought is illustrated in historical terms, beginning with the earliest known examples of management practices, (often from the ancient civilizations), and ending with the latest examples of modern management theory − exemplified in systems theory, contingency theory, or even in management science.

This almost ritualistic invocation of the founding figures and early pioneers of management theory serves a number of important functions in the teaching of modern management studies. Like any other branch of organized knowledge, it is designed to show students how the contemporary principles and practices of management owe something to the insights of earlier writers who were precursors of the modern study of organizations and management. More than this, however, the historical developmental approach to the study of management theory, (especially when introduced near the beginning of a text), creates the impression − one might even say the illusion − that the evolution of management thought may be understood as a linear progression from relatively underdeveloped to more fully developed ideas. In other words, that theories of management, much like the popular conception of physical theories of the natural sciences,[14] have progressed through different stages of growth and maturation on their way to becoming a fully-fledged "science" of management.

This linear conception of the growth of management theory acquires a special importance when comparing the "less enlightened" theories of management which flourished during earlier parts of the century with the supposedly more enlightened and more rational systems of analysis and decision-making which prevail today. Thus, in the case of Scientific Management, for example, which is commonly acknowledged to be one of the earliest traditions of systematic management, many standard textbooks will describe both its theoretical contributions and its limitations, before showing how these limitations were later addressed by other theoretical perspectives, such as the Human Relations school.[15] Similarly, the partial truths of the Human Relations school are then typically shown to be later superseded by more fully developed schools, such as the Contingency school, for example.

What is often overlooked in the "rational reconstruction"[16] of the history of management theory is the disproportionate influence which some of these early theoretical schools have exercised upon the subsequent development of management thought, and the important role that they have continued to play in shaping modern management practices. This is particularly true of Scientific Management which, in spite of its discredited reputation in some academic quarters, continues to be a powerful influence in the management of many organizations. Contrary to the illusion created by the rational reconstruction of management theory, the theory and practice of Scientific Management have not been universally consigned to the scrap-heap of history, in favour of more enlightened and more humanistic forms of management. Scientific Management, in many ways, has established the domain for all later systems of management, and its principles and practices are still embedded in the management systems of many modern business enterprises.

Although the historical periodization of management theory may seem to imply that earlier theories have been progressively superseded by later theories in the general march towards a "science of management", many management theorists still acknowledge the seminal and continuing influence of Scientific Management ideas upon the entire field of management studies. This is made particularly clear in a strong statement by the doyen of modern management theory, Peter Drucker (1986:280), which cuts straight to the heart of the matter.

> Personnel Administration and Human Relations are the things talked about and written whenever the management of worker and work is being discussed. They are the things the Personnel Department concerns itself with. But they are not the concepts of the actual management of worker and work in American industry. This concept is Scientific Management. Scientific Management focuses on the work. Its core is the organized study of work, the analysis of work into its simplest elements and the systematic improvement of the worker's performance of each of these elements. Scientific Management has both basic concepts and easily applicable tools and techniques. And it has no difficulty proving the contribution it makes its results in the form of higher output are visible and readily measurable. Indeed, Scientific Management is all but a systematic philosophy of worker and work. Altogether it may well be the most powerful as well as the most lasting contribution America has made to Western thought since the Federalist Papers.

Drucker is not alone in emphasizing the powerful influence that Scientific Management has exerted on subsequent generations of management theorists. Other writers have also defended Scientific Management against its academic critics, and have tried to rehabilitate it among contemporary students of management theory. Thus, after dismissing such charges against Scientific Management as economism, authoritarianism, exploitation, anti-unionism and dishonesty, Locke (1982:22–23) concludes his assessment of Taylor, the "founding father" of Scientific Management, by claiming not only that Taylor's ideas were "right in the context of his time" but also that "most of his insights are still valid today".

In some ways it almost seems as though the ideas of Scientific Management have come full circle. They were certainly received with enthusiasm by business groups during the early decades of the twentieth century, and were even introduced into such giant companies as Dupont and General Motors (Wren, 1987). Later, however, these ideas came under critical attack from labour groups, academics and finally from government, culminating in the notoriety surrounding the Congressional Inquiry into Scientific Management which was held in 1911.[17] Today, to judge from its coverage in contemporary textbooks, Scientific Management has been rehabilitated, and many writers now openly acknowledge its seminal influence on the development of the theory and practice of professional management. The ideas of Scientific Management have never really gone out of style, at least for businessmen and managers, for Taylor always asserted the primacy of their interests in the control of work: to him, this was the bottom line of all systems of management.

However, although most OT texts discuss the origins of Scientific Management, and show its significance for the further development of management theory, virtually none of these mainstream interpretations demonstrate any real understanding of what the practice of Scientific Management has done to the traditional skills and crafts of the (largely male, skilled) labour force, and how, in many cases, women have been crudely used as agents of deskilling.[18] The implications of Scientific Management have, like those of all other theories of management, only been understood from a managerial perspective. It is important, however, to be able to view the consequences of Scientific Management – both in theory and in practice – from the perspective of those at the bottom of the organization, as well as those from the top. In other words, we are entitled to ask: What has Scientific Management, (or any other school of management, for that matter), meant, not only for managers, themselves, but for the workers who have been subjected to its system of control?

Scientific Management, along with the "Universalist" tradition of the French industrialist, Henri Fayol, is normally classified within the Classical school of management theory which emerged at the turn of the century. These theories of the Classical School had several things in common:

1. They viewed organizations as machines, which is to say, that they focused on the formal structure and the design of organizations – the formal, or official status of managers and workers, and the technical design of jobs in the workplace.[19] Their emphasis reflected the engineering interests of men like Taylor and Fayol, who pioneered these early theories of management.

2. They tried to develop a universal set of principles of management which could be applied to any organization. Both Taylor and Fayol were committed to the goal of developing a general set of principles of management which would form the basis for a "science" of management. Later theorists would reject this Universalist approach in favour of "contingency" approaches to the study of organizations.

From the beginning, it is clear that Taylor was preoccupied with how to increase the efficiency of the workplace. He believed that the tendency of workers to engage in what was known as, "systematic soldiering", that is, in the restriction of their output on the job, constituted the greatest single obstacle to efficiency.[20] In order to eliminate the problem of soldiering, Taylor saw that it was necessary for managers to greatly increase their control over workers, and over the labour process, and to redesign jobs in ways that stripped workers of any remaining independence they may have had on the job. As is well known, Taylor accomplished these goals through analyzing different jobs in order to determine the most efficient way to perform them, and through redesigning these jobs by breaking each of them into simple tasks, and assigning workers to perform each of these fragmented tasks. By increasing the division of labour, and by transforming work from a complex set of skilled operations into a simple set of repetitive tasks, Taylor hoped to increase the efficiency and productivity of the workplace, and the general effectiveness of the total organization.

In order to achieve these goals, Taylor recommended that the reorganization and redesign of work should be done according to the basic principles of Scientific Management:

1. Managers should control the conception of work, while workers should be responsible only for its execution. In other words, that managers should make all the decisions regarding the planning and design of work, while workers should only be responsible for the implementation of these decisions. For the first time, Taylor introduced a radical distinction between mental and manual labour which was to transform the face of the modern workplace.

2. "Scientific" methods should be used to analyze, and to design all jobs.

Taylor was one of the earlier, (though not the first), to use "time and motion" studies of workplace efficiency.

3. Detailed instructions should be given to each worker of how to perform his or her job. Workers should follow these instructions to the letter, as they represented the one, "best", "scientific" way of performing the task.

4. The "best" workers should be selected to perform each type of job. In practice, this often meant replacing skilled craftsmen (sic) with unskilled workers, who would be more dependent upon management for instructions.

5. Workers should be fully trained by management to perform their jobs with management monopolizing technical knowledge and having responsibility for training workers to perform their jobs competently and efficiently.

6. Finally, work performance should be regularly monitored by management to ensure that standard procedures of work were being followed.

These, in a nutshell, are some of the basic principles which underlay Taylor's system of Scientific Management, and their contribution to the history of management thought is commonly discussed in OT texts. What has received far less attention is the impact that Taylorism has had on the occupational and educational status of workers in the modern period. Contrary to the popular textbook view, Taylorism was much more than simply an early theory of management, to be later superseded by more enlightened theories of management. In its own way, Taylorism set its seal upon all later theories of management by showing how important it was for managers to increase their control over the labour process. It was only by securing control over the way in which work was done that management could effect the transformation of the modern workplace.

For Taylor and his colleagues, the transformation of work meant, above all else, the destruction of independent 'workmanship' with its accumulated tradition of craft skills, and the corresponding monopolization and control of work by management. The advent of Taylorism, therefore, heralded the dawn of modern management. And while later theories of management drew attention to the neglected social aspects of the workplace, it was Taylorism which encouraged the drive that is now prevalent in many workplaces to turn managers into absolute controllers of work, and workers into the passive servants of the new production processes.[21] The consequences of this "deskilling", or "degradation" of work has been well documented (Braverman, 1974 Leonard, 1984).

Although the ideas of many personnel administrators today have usually been influenced by supposedly more humanistic theories of management, the principles of Scientific Management still underlie the organization and design of the workplace in many modern enterprises. This is particularly true for those industries where there is a straightforward task to perform, where the goal is to mass produce the same product again and again, where precision and standardization are deemed important and where there is a management demand for a workforce that is compliant and easily disciplined. These conditions may be found in a number of enterprises, but nowhere are they so evident as in the fast-food industry. If you really want to see the principles of Scientific Management in action today, go down to your nearest McDonalds, A&W, Burger King, Kentucky Fried Chicken, or similar fast-food outlet. In all of these establishments, the principles of F.W. Taylor are as alive today, as on the day he first introduced them. All this is apparent from the way in which managers plan and direct every detail of the work process. Workers are told what to do, managers tell them exactly how to do it. Every aspect of the work of preparing and serving hamburgers is outlined in a detailed manual of instructions.[22] Workers are expected to follow these instructions to the letter, in the interests of standardization and efficiency. Only the "best" candidates for this type of work are hired: usually young men and women of high-school age, with minimum qualifications and skills, or recent immigrants who, employers hope, will be most prepared to work under constant pressure for minimum wages because of their desperate need for any kind of employment.

Far from being a discredited and long forgotten blip in the early history of OT, the principles of Scientific Management have become embedded in the modern workplace. Indeed, the separation of the planning and direction of work from its actual performance, and the corresponding rise of professional managers as a distinct social group, (some would even define them as a distinct social class)[23] owe much to those principles, first articulated by Taylor. And while later theoretical schools emerged to focus on other aspects of management theory which had been neglected by Scientific Management theorists – the "human dimension" of work organizations, the rational decision-making processes of managers, the Contingency approach to organizational change – none of these schools seriously questioned the fundamental division of labour presupposed in all applications of Scientific Management, namely the separation of the conception of work from its execution. It was not until very recently that some management theorists have begun to look beyond this traditional way of organizing work.

The question of what managers really do, and whether it is adequately represented in the traditions of OT has preoccupied a number of writers over the past decades. Some writers have argued that management theory has played a useful role in helping us to classify, analyze, and even to explain the complex set of activities which are typically performed by all managers. Other writers have suggested, however, that these theoretical descriptions of management bear little resemblance to what managers actually do during the course of their working days. What are needed in the opinion of the latter, are more empirical studies of managers at work, and less theoretical studies.

One of the earliest attempts to classify the work of managers was made by the French writer, Henri Fayol, pioneer of the early school of Universalist management theory. Fayol suggested that the actual work of management could be broken down into five distinct activities:

- Planning
- Organizing
- Commanding (or directing)
- Coordinating
- Controlling

This attempt to reduce the practice of management to a set of all-inclusive categories was typical of many of the early classical theorists who, as we have already seen, were primarily interested in developing general principles of management. Fayol's classification of managerial work was later revised by another of the classical theorists, Luther Gullick (1937), who proposed an amended typology:

- Planning – deciding on what things to have done, and how to do them in order to accomplish the goals of the organization.
- Organizing – establishing the formal structure of the organization and implementing an efficient division of labour in the workforce.
- Staffing – recruiting and training staff members to perform the different functions of the organization.
- Directing – providing leadership to the organization by setting goals, making decisions and implementing them through instructions and orders to subordinates.

- Coordinating – making sure that the different parts of the organization work harmoniously together to fulfil a common set of goals.
- Reporting – keeping informed about all aspects of the organization through records, research and inspection.
- Budgeting – engaging in the financial planning, accounting and control of the fiscal life of the organization.

Today, most standard texts in OT further reduce these earlier classifications of management work to a set of four or five, which generally include some combination of the following elements:

- Planning
- Organizing
- Motivating
- Controlling

Thus, Frost, Mitchell and Nord (1990) distinguish between the functions of planning, organizing, leading, controlling, and the management of human resources. Similarly, Wren and Voich (1984) organize the major part of their book around the functions of planning, organizing, staffing, leading and controlling. And in his standard introduction to this area, Dale (1978) defines the primary functions of management as planning, organizing, staffing, direction, control, innovation and representation. In these respects, we can see that the earlier attempts of the classical theorists to formulate a systematic and universal classification of the work of management have continued to influence many modern writers in organizing their ideas for contemporary students of management.

Ironically, Gullick's reference to "budgeting" has disappeared almost totally from later classifications. Arguably budgeting is a key element of the practice of management.[24] Without budgeting responsibility, it could be argued, a manager is manager in name only, and is actually an administrator, or senior clerk.[25] Certainly we can note a trend in many large corporations for functions previously undertaken by middle management to be taken on by, on the one hand, senior management (tasks demanding less drudgery, faster response time), and on the other hand low paid clerical staff (more routine work, not as prioritized).[26] This can be seen in the current trend of large corporations (e.g., British Airways) to create "flatter organizations", i.e., to cut out several layers of middle management.

Other writers have rejected the classical approach, and have argued that the abstract formal categories which have been used to classify the functions of management have very little relevance to what managers really do. In place of broad theoretical generalizations, these critics suggest, what are needed are more empirical studies of how managers actually spend their working days. Most managers, unlike the theorists who write about them, do not divide up their working day into different times for planning, organizing, budgeting, etc.:

> If we ask a managing director when he is coordinating, or how much coordination he has been doing during the day, he would not know, and even the most highly skilled observer would not know either. The same holds true of the concepts of planning, command, organization and control (Carlsson, 1951).

In an influential article published several years ago, Henry Mintzberg (1975) dismissed as "folklore", the classical view of management. According to Mintzberg, Henri Fayol's categories have about as much relationship to what managers really do, as a Renaissance painting has to a Cubist abstract. Based on his own study of five chief executives over a five week period, and on the evidence of other similar studies, Mintzberg concluded that the practice of management could not usefully be reduced to the broad Universalist categories favoured by classical theorists. Contrary to the "folklore" of classical theory, Mintzberg found that the daily activities of the managers he studied were characterized by brevity, variety and discontinuity.

During the course of their workday, managers had a large number of brief, informal, two-person contacts, either over the telephone, or through unscheduled meetings. Most of their time, however, was taken up with a relatively small number of scheduled meetings which tended to last for lengthy periods of time. Mintzberg also discovered that his managers much preferred "soft" information – especially by word of mouth – to the "hard" information of written documents and computerized information systems. The reason for this was that this kind of information, obtained through gossip or hearsay, was likely to be more up-to-date than information obtained through more formal channels. "Today's gossip may be tomorrow's facts".

Mintzberg (1975:60) concluded that the spontaneous, intuitive and generally informal methods of work adopted by most managers during their workday bore little resemblance to the highly rationalized and deliberate functions of management outlined by the classical theorists:

> If there is a single theme that runs through this article, it is that the pressures of

his job drive the manager to be superficial in his actions – to overload himself with work, encourage interruption, respond quickly to every stimulus, seek the tangible and avoid the abstract, make decisions in small increments, and do everything abruptly.

In place of the classical functions of management, therefore, Mintzberg suggested that it is more useful to view the work of management as involving the performance of a number of different roles:

- Interpersonal roles, which include,
  a. Managers as figureheads
  b. Managers as leaders
  c. Managers as liaison officers.

- Informational roles, which include
  a. Managers as monitors
  b. Managers as disseminators
  c. Managers as spokes-people.

- Decisional roles, which include
  a. Managers as entrepreneurs
  b. Managers as disturbance handlers
  c. Managers as resource allocators
  d. Managers as negotiators.

Several other researchers have also concluded that the classical view of management bears little relationship to what managers actually do at work. Most of these studies have shown that managers do not methodically plan their days around the classical functions of management – at least, not in any systematic sense. These functions are normally performed in jumbled and fragmented ways, as the typical manager struggles to pack a multitude of different activities into the limited time-span of a single day. The evidence from Sweden (cf. Carlsson, 1951), the United States and Canada (cf. Sayles, 1964 Mintzberg, 1964, 1975), Great Britain (cf. Stewart, 1967 Lawrence 1984) and Germany (cf. Lawrence, 1984), is all fairly consistent on most of these points. The greater part of the typical manager's day is spent on informal discussions which are usually unplanned, and are often only between two people. With the exception of scheduled meetings, most managers are unable to spend more than thirty minutes on any project without interruption or diversion. The vast majority of contacts that the manager has with other personnel in the organization last less than five minutes. Most of these contacts are initiated by subordinates in some cases, less than five percent were initiated by superiors.[27]

The results of these empirical studies have convinced some critics of OT, that if students are to learn anything useful about the management of organizations, they should begin with an understanding of how managers actually spend their time,[28] rather than by learning about how classical theorists think that managers should spend their time. Management, for these writers, is not simply a science, but also an art, which cannot easily be reduced to a set of broad abstract principles.

There are, of course, still some defenders of the classical view of management. In a recent review of 21 management textbooks published between 1983-86, for example, Carroll and Gillen (1987), found that 17 of these texts still used at least four of the classical functions (proposed by Fayol) to organize their ideas. These authors also report that several attempts to replicate the results of Mintzberg's study of managers have failed to produce similar results, while other studies have shown the utility of retaining classical definitions of the functions of management. Although the work of managers often appears to be diverse and fragmented, it becomes more comprehensible when analyzed through the categories of classical management theory.

> [...] there appears to be sufficient evidence to say that managers do perform a wide variety of specific activities which can be classified under the functional typology developed by Fayol and others in the classical management school; also, greater managerial success (organization and unit performance and management mobility) is related to skill and time in the functional responsibilities (Carroll and Gillen, 1987:43).

These authors conclude by upholding the classical view of management as the best way of teaching students in a clear and logical manner about the different functions of management, and of providing an intellectually coherent framework for the organization of basic textbooks in the field.

> The classical functions still represent the most useful way of conceptualizing the manager's job, especially for management education, and perhaps this is why it is still the most favoured description of managerial work in current management textbooks (Ibid:48).

In closing this chapter on management and its relationship to OT, we should not lose sight of the fact that managers are real individuals who run organizations in our society. Beyond its importance as an historical phenomenon, therefore, or as a series of theoretical schools, or set of administrative practices, the institution of management remains a way of life for those whose job it is to plan, direct and supervise the work of others. In this sense, we can even regard the institution of management as part of a culture, in much the same way as recent theorists have begun to study organizations as cultural systems (cf. Deal and Kennedy, 1982; Gerloff, 1985; Leavitt, 1986; Mills, 1988b). Like all cultures, the management or corporate culture of any organization contains its own values and philosophies, its rituals and symbols, its myths, and its legendary or heroic figures. Every major organization seems to have a celebrated cultural hero: Wardair had its Max Ward, Chrysler its Iacocca, McDonalds its Ray Kroc, Amway its Devos, Mary Kay Cosmetics its Mary Kay Ash, and so on.

Today, some of the more traditional features of management culture in our society have fallen into disrepute. This is especially true of the tendency for managers to be drawn from a relatively narrow cross-section of society from which women and minority groups have been largely excluded. The traditional management culture has remained resolutely androcentric and ethnocentric, as well as middle class in nature; the overwhelming majority of individuals working in top management positions have – until very recently – been white males. This patriarchal dominance, with its corresponding exclusion of women and minorities, has left a very strong imprint on the management culture of organizations in our society, although it is an imprint which has been largely overlooked in mainstream texts of OT (Mills, 1988a: Due Billing and Alvesson, 1994).

Until recently, many of the least desirable aspects of the managerial culture were assumed to be inevitable features of the corporate world. Many writers on OT have taken for granted the need for managers to be aggressive and competitive in their attempts to successfully scale the corporate ladder. Everyone knows, so it would seem, that the corporate world is often a ruthless jungle, and in order to survive in it, successful managers must demonstrate the necessary qualities of aggression, competition, and ruthless ambition. Life at the top of many organizations – and not just business organizations – is invariably stressful and often characterized by loneliness, fear, anxiety, and insecurity.[29] But according to the received wisdom, this is the way the world is, and only those who can demonstrate these gladiatorial qualities can hope to prevail in the corporate culture of management.

More recently, however, some feminist critics of mainstream (and malestream) OT have questioned the inevitability of these predatory aspects of the corporate culture. In their view, the climate of competition, aggression, lone-liness and fear which often typifies the corporate culture owes more to the resolutely "male ethos" of life at the top of the organization than to any other institutional imperative. According to this view, the dominance hierarchies as-sociated with so many organizations in our contemporary corporate structure derive from the patriarchal structures of male power and authority. It is these gendered structures, rather than any more general organizational imperative, which breed the gladiatorial qualities so often associated with managers – both male and female – within our organizations. The real force of this feminist cri-tique of traditional OT lies in its implication that, with a radical redirection of organizational values – away from competition, aggression, hierarchy, and in-dividualism towards cooperation, empathy, equality and reciprocity – our or-ganizational cultures could be transformed into more humane and fulfilling sets of social relationships. This is the great challenge of thinking our way beyond present structures and values in order to actively reshape our institutions. We shall return to some of these issues when looking ahead to the future of OT in the final chapter of this book.

KEY TERMS

budgeting	deskilling	scientific management
bureaucratic systems of control	directing	time & motion studies
classical approach	informational roles	simple control
commanding	interpersonal roles	staffing
consensus view of management	managerial revolution	reporting
controlling	managerial viewpoint	systematic soldiering
coordinating	organizing	planning
corporate culture	technical control	universalist tradition
decisional roles		

Q1. What is management? And how do we know?

Assignment: In answering this question, read one account from the Universalist, from the feminist, from the people of colour, and from the Mintzberg approaches. (see the text and Further reading for guidance to the literature) compare the approaches of each – what do each say about what managers actually do? what do each say about how management should be studied? what difference does gender and colour play in 'what managers do'?

Q2. Briefly define each of the following terms, and discuss their contribution to our understanding of management.

consensus view of management

classical approach

universalist tradition

managerial viewpoint

Assignment: Now turn to the glossary at the end of the book and compare your definitions.

Q3. What is meant by the term "the managerial revolution" and what does it tell us about the practice of management?

Assignment: In answering this question, you should review the appropriate sections of the chapter

Q4. Briefly define each of the following terms and try to provide examples of each from your own work experience(s).

bureaucratic systems of control

simple control

technical control

Assignment: Review the appropriate chapter sections, and apply to your own work experiences.

Q5. What is meant by the terms "deskilling", and "degradation of work", and how may these terms be related to gender and skill in the workplace? Give some examples from your own experience(s) or observations to show how these terms may be applied to different work situations.

Assignment: Review the appropriate chapter sections, and check your definitions with the glossary at the end of the chapter.

Q6. Briefly define each of the following terms and say how classical theorists relate each to the "practice" of management:

> Budgeting
> Commanding
> Controlling
> Coordinating
> Directing
> Organizing
> Staffing
> Reporting
> Planning

Assignment: Now turn to the glossary at the end of the book and compare your definitions.

FS: What is the corporate culture of an organization and how does it relate to management?

Assignment: Read any mainstream OT account on management and the role of corporate culture. Now, compare that account with any feminist accounts of management. How do the two approaches compare? What do feminist accounts tell us about corporate culture and how it might be changed?

EXERCISE 3.1

This exercise is designed to make you think about the significance of management as a set of practices – its impact upon the lives of people generally and your life in particular. Do the tasks individually and then discuss your findings in small groups.

A. From the list that begins on the following page indicate which of the activities you are involved in on an ongoing, or regular, basis, whether you manage the activity alone or whether someone else manages for you. On a separate sheet of paper indicate the type of actions involved in managing the activity. [An example is given of a 'checking account at the Bank']. Try to be as detailed as possible when describing the kind of managing activities involved.

EXAMPLE

ACTIVITY	YES/NO	SELF MANAGED	OTHER MANAGED
Bank checking account.	yes	Keeping track of the day to day trans-actions, making payments, ensuring that monies received are paid in; record keeping.	Bank manager – offical recording of accounts; ensuring that account is 'in balance'.

ACTIVITY	YES/NO	SELF MANAGED	OTHER MANAGED
Bank Checking Account			
Bank savings Account			
Owning a car			
Driving a car			
Enrollment in a course of higher education			
Preparing for an examination			
Membership of a social club			
Committee membership or organizer of a social club			
Being part of a group of friends			
Being a father or mother to young children			
Being a father or mother to grown children			
Being a member of a family			
Being part of a Community organization			

ACTIVITY	YES/NO	SELF MANAGED	OTHER MANAGED
Being a member of a choir			
Being a member of a native band organization			
Being a member of a church			
Being a member of a music band or group			
Being a member of a sports group			
Being an organizer of a community organization			
Being the leader of a music group/band			
Being a native band leader			
Being an employer			
Being an employee			
Buying household groceries and other items			
Responsibility for child care.			
Dating			
Going to the movies, the theatre, or some other activity			
Being a brother or sister			
Eating out in a cafe or restaurant			
Going to the doctor for medical advice or treatment			
Going to the hospital for medical treatment			
Going to confession			

ACTIVITY	YES/NO	SELF MANAGED	OTHER MANAGED
Going on strike or engaging in other forms of organizational disputes			
Editing a student newspaper			
Writing for a student newspaper			
Being disciplined by school, university or employer			
Reading a book			
Writing an essay or assignment			
Other activities not listed above.			

B. Now, in small groups discuss your lists, and attempt to summarize the following questions:

1. As a group, how much of your regular activity is self managed and how much of it is managed? (You might indicate which activity is wholly self managed, wholly other managed, or involves a combination of self and other management).

2. Now examine the forms of control used in managing different types of activity and attempt to classify activities according to the dominant form of control. What is the range of control experienced by group members? (Give examples). What is the form of control that is most experienced by group members? (Give examples).

3. Is the range and/or form of control most experienced different depending upon a person's gender, ethnic/race, or class background? What does your answer — albeit yes or no — tell us about managerial control?

4. What is the central difference between forms of self control and other control?

5. Are any specific forms of control associated with some activities but not others?

6. Which activities, if any, could be managed differently and under what circumstances?

FURTHER READING

On the history of management thought and development
Stewart Clegg and David Dunkerly (1980) ORGANIZATION, CLASS AND CONTROL.
Gareth Morgan,(1986) IMAGES OF ORGANIZATION.
Albert J. Mills and Stephen Murgatroyd (1991), Chapter 1. ORGANIZATIONAL RULES.
Michael Rose (1975) INDUSTRIAL BEHAVIOUR.

Literary Images of Management Control:
A.J. Cronin. THE STARS LOOK DOWN

The non-managerial alternative:
Ivan Illich (1981) DESCHOOLING SOCIETY.
Michel Foucault (1977) DISCIPLINE AND PUNISHMENT.

On the impact of management theory on the conceptualization of women workers.
R.L. Feldberg and E.N. Glenn (1979) MALE AND FEMALE: JOB VERSUS GENDER MODELS IN THE SOCIOLOGY OF WORK.
Marta Calas (1992) AN/OTHER SILENT VOICE? REPRESENTING "HISPANIC WOMEN" IN ORGANIZATIONAL TEXTS.

On the neglect of gender in labour process theories
Scott Davies (1990) INSERTING GENDER INTO BURAWOY'S THEORY OF THE LABOUR PROCESS.
Peta Tancred-Sheriff (1989) GENDER, SEXUALITY, AND THE LABOUR PROCESS

On the problem of 'women in management'
Marta Calas and Linda Smircich (1992) USING THE "F" WORD: FEMINIST THEORIES AND THE SOCIAL CONSEQUENCES OF ORGANIZATIONAL RESEARCH.

On the resistance of female employees to management control
Anna Pollert (1981) GIRLS, WIVES, FACTORY, LIVES.
Susan Porter Benson (1992) THE CLERKING SISTERHOOD.

On management and people of colour
Ella Bell and Stella Nkomo (1992) REVISIONING WOMEN MANAGER'S LIVES
Toni Denton (1990) BONDING AND SUPPORTIVE RELATIONSHIPS AMONG BLACK PROFESSIONAL WOMEN: RITUALS OF RESTORATION.

END NOTES

1. See Wren (1987: 36). The economist, Alfred Marshall also subscribed to the view that management – or, what he called, "organization" – should be treated separately from the other factors of production. In this regard, he suggested that:

   "The agents of production are commonly classed as land, labour and capital [...] it seems best sometimes to recognize organization apart as a distinct agent of production" (cited in Dale, 1973: 157).

2. In this regard Max Ward was something of a modern anachronism. Ward used to run his Canadian airline, Wardair, like his personal fiefdom. Intervening in everything from general management decisions to the degree of starch that went into his aeroplane table cloths. In the end, partially as a result of Ward's entrepreneurial style, Wardair succumbed to corporate takeover and is now under PWA ownership.

3. Cf. Berle and Means (1933), Dahrendorf (1959), Burnham (1960), Galbraith (1967) and Chandler (1977; 1984). James Burnham, a disillusioned Trotskyist, became impressed by the fact that alongside the growth of professional management in the West, in Soviet Russia – with its bureaucratic state control – a new class of professional managers had developed to run state enterprises 'on behalf of' the state.

4. See Rinehart (1987:100-107) and Krahn and Lowe (1988:28-30) for the Canadian terms of this debate.

5. This explication of Chandler's ideas is indebted to Pugh et al (1983: 50-54).

6. Chandler makes a distinction between horizontal and vertical growth – see Wren (1987:82-83).

7. Another writer whose work has paralleled that of Chandler in some respects is that of Oliver Williamson (1975). The thesis of the managerial revolution was also anticipated in the writings of Karl Marx, who was quite prescient in his analysis of the growth of professional management, as the following quotation reveals:

"Just as the first capitalist is relieved from actual labour as soon as his capital has reached that minimum amount with which capitalist production, properly speaking, first begins, so he now hands over the work of direct and constant supervision of the individual workers and groups of workers to a special kind of wage-labourer. An industrial army of workers under the command of a capitalist requires, like a real army, officers (managers) and NCO's (foremen, overseers), who command during the labour process in the name of capital. The work of supervision becomes their established and exclusive functions (Marx, Capital I. Cited in Nichols and Beynon, 1977:30).

8. Burawoy (1979:12), arguing for the significance of the historical perspective, states that,

"Industrial sociology and organization theory proceed from the facts of consensus or social control. They do not explain them. It is necessary, therefore, to break with the transhistorical generalities of industrial sociology and organization theory and to dispense with metaphysical assumptions about underlying conflict or harmony [...]. To do this we must restore historical context to the discussion"

9. Wren (1987:43), provides some graphic examples of the kinds of dictatorial management practices which prevailed at this time.

10. To date the struggle between management and labour has traditionally been represented as a struggle between groups of males – the male manager and the skilled male worker. This debate misses the fact that women have traditionally been excluded from management and from positions and definitions of skilled work. cf. Cockburn (1985). Labour process and management theorists alike have been guilty of ignoring gender from their analyses, cf. Tancred-Sheriff (1989); Davies (1990).

11. Not only have women been excluded from many skilled jobs but very few female-dominated jobs have – regardless of skill requirement – been classified as "skilled". Cf. Cockburn, op cit.

12. Tancred-Sheriff (1989) argues that in the labour process women have been used as a form of "adjunct control" in which their sexuality has been used by organi-

zations as a form of mediation between the business and its clients.

13. Several women have made important contributions to Organization and Management Theory but, as part of the general gendered nature of the field, have been somewhat neglected until recently. Dr. Lillian Moller Gilbreth who, with her husband Frank, pioneered the system of Scientific Management during the early decades of this century. Similarly, Mary Parker Follet, who was another proponent of Scientific Management , later played an important part in presaging the development of the Human Relations school. In later years Joan Woodward played a central role in the development of the contingency approach to management. See Wren (1987) for biographical sketches of these and other historical contributors to O&MT; Tancred-Sheriff and Campbell (1992) specifically discuss the contribution of women management theorists.

14. For a critique of this popular view of science, see Kuhn (1962); Feyerabend (1975).

15. For example, in his review of Scientific Management, Robbins (1990:35) concludes with a qualification which is typical of many historical interpretations:

"In retrospect, we recognize that Taylor offered a limited focus on organizations. He was looking only at organizing work at the lowest level of the organization – appropriate to the management job of a supervisor [...]"

16. This term was originally used by Imre Lakatos (1972) to describe the inductivist, or incremental view of modern science in which the history of science is portrayed as the gradual and inevitable progress towards the truth. Lakatos has criticized this received view as inconsistent with the way in which the history of science has actually developed. For further critical discussion of the inductivist historiography and epistemology of science see Kuhn (1962) and Feyerabend (1975).

17. See, Hearings before Special Committee of the House of Representatives to Investigate the Taylor and other systems of Shop Management under authority of House Resolution 90, Washington, D.C., U.S. Government Printing Office, 1912.

18. See footnote 10 above. While Braverman (1974) revealed how female workers were used by managers as cheap labour to perform the newly deskilled tasks of previously skilled male workers, it was left to Cockburn (1985) to remind us that the notion of "skill" is itself a gendered concept and that Scientific Management helped to strengthen the tendency to exclude women from categories of skilled work.

19. See Morgan (1986: Chapter 2) for an excellent discussion of how the Classical school of management drew its inspiration from the image of the organization as a machine. Morgan shows how the machine metaphor is far from dead in the modern world, but continues to inform ideas about management in many modern business enterprises.

20. Taylor's obsession with the problem of soldiering in the workplace has been observed by many writers. Krahn and Low (1988:105), for example, quote Taylor as saying that, "There could be no greater crime against humanity than this restriction of output". Even given the seriousness (and self-righteousness)

with which Taylor looked upon industrial efficiency, this statement seems quite obsessive in the degree of its exaggeration..

Braverman (1974: 98) also shows the importance that the problem of soldiering had for Taylor in a quotation which reveals just how central this issue was to him:

"The greater part of systematic soldiering [...] is done by the men with the deliberate object of keeping their employers ignorant of how fast work can be done. So universal is soldiering for this purpose, that hardly a competent workman can be found in a large establishment, or under any of the ordinary systems of compensating labour, who does not devote a considerable part of his time to studying just how slowly he can work and still convince his employer that he is going at a good pace. The causes of this are, briefly, that practically all employers determine upon a maximum sum which they feel it is right for each of their classes to earn per day, whether their men work by the day or piece".

21. Although some O&MT textbooks suggest that the principles of Scientific Management presupposed the full cooperation of workers in the "scientific" reorganization and redesign of their jobs, Taylor (1967: 83), himself, was never in any doubt about how such cooperation should be secured:

"It is only through enforced standardization of methods, enforced adoption of the best implements and working conditions, and enforced cooperation that this faster work can be assured. And the duty of enforcing the adoption of standards and of enforcing this coopera-tion rests with management alone [...] All those who, are proper teaching, either will not or cannot work in accordance with the new methods and at the higher speed must be discharged by the management"

22. Some indication of how precisely McDonald's workers are trained in the details of fast food preparation and service can be seen from the following description of the operating manual used in all McDonald's franchises:

"It told operators exactly how to draw mill shakes, grill hamburgers, and fry potatoes. It specified precise cooking times for all products and temperature settings for all equipment. It fixed standard portions on every food item, down to the quarter ounce of onions placed on each hamburger patty and the thirty-two slices per pound of cheese. It specified that french fries be cut at nine-thirty seconds of an inch thick. And it defined quality controls that were unique to food service, including the disposal of meat and potato products that were held more than ten minutes in a serving bin."

The manual also defined those specialized production techniques that made the operation of McDonald's like an assembly line [...]". Cited in Love (1986:141-2).

A similar account is offered by Ester Reiter (1986; 1990), based on her own experiences as a fast-food worker for Burger King. But perhaps the quintessential example of Taylorist principles come from the slogan which was popularized by the management of Kentucky Fried Chicken in the form of the acronym, KISS: Keep It Simple Stupid. Surely, there has never been a more parsimonious expression of the basic principles of Scientific Management!

23. See Burham (1960); Dahrendorf (1959); Berle and Means (1933); and in the context of the East European managers, Djilas (1982).

24. Mills and Murgatroyd (1991:122-124), for example, argue that "accounting rules" are an essential element of the functioning of organizational management.

25. Kanter (1977; 1979) has noted that many managers in large corporations have little discretion over resourcing and, as such, are powerless – managers in name only.

26. We are grateful to Peter Saunders for these observations about the centrality of budgeting.

27. To date, in true gendered fashion, studies of what managers do have only focused on males. In-depth, empirical studies of women managers have yet to be done.

28. Feminist organization theorists rightly argue that this should be learned of women as well as men managers.

29. Many examples of the predatory aspects of the corporate culture of management exist. The following comments taken from the reminiscences of one former CEO provide a vivid illustration of life at the top for many managers.

"Fear is always prevalent in the corporate structure. Even if you're a top man, even if you're hard, even if you do your job – by the slight flick of a finger, your boss can fire you. There's always the insecurity. You bungle a job. You're fearful of losing a big customer. You're fearful so many things will appear on your record, stand against you. You're always fearful of the big mistake[...] The executive is a lonely animal in the jungle who doesn't have a friend. Business is related to life. I think in our everyday living we're lonely." (Terkel, 1974:406)

CHAPTER 4

Creating the Psychic Prison

The central objective of this chapter is to challenge the reader to think about the impacts of organizational arrangements on the way persons come to relate to each other and come to view themselves and other persons. To this end the chapter explores the relationship between the construction of human subjectivity and social factors that contribute to the construction of organization life. The chapter then examines six important critical approaches to the understanding of the psychic life of organizations – critical theory, humanist, Marxist, postmodernist, psychoanalytic, and feminist. The chapter ends by suggesting a synthesis of critical approaches

Work and Identity – An Interview With Sharon Webb[1]

Sharon Webb was born on her parents' tobacco farm in Ontario in the late 1950s. It was a very traditional environment in which the men worked the land and the women cooked and cleaned. From an early age, Sharon's father impressed on her the importance of the relationship between work and sense of self, constantly warning his children that if they didn't grow up like him they "were going to be nothing but ditchdiggers." It was a message which he directed more at his sons than at Sharon. He had a different message for her: "You're going to get pregnant, you're going to get married and you're going to be stupid." This might have molded her into his image of her but he was a harsh man who had little time for his children and that fuelled in her a determination to resist.

She left home at fourteen and entered the world of work where she faced many challenges to her sense of self and identity. As a parts' truck driver, for example, Sharon faced many problems. The company that she came to work for had never hired a female driver before and was in the process of contesting accusations of discrimination when Sharon applied for the position. She was hired but it was made clear to her that she wasn't wanted. To impress on her that it was a "man's job" they made her pick up sixty pound cylinder heads as part of the job. She later found out that the men were expected to use forklifts to pick up the cylinder heads. Next her driving skills were questioned. If she didn't complete her deliveries in a certain time she was told, "We'll find someone more capable." Then her supervisor prohibited her from talking with anyone else in the workplace: "I got so mad and I used to cry. And I thought, No, I'm not giving in, I'm not giving in to this bullhead. Oh, and I'd be so mad – I'd get in my truck, I'd bawl my eyes out half way across the city and then calm down again."

Any attempts that she made to learn more about the job was met with hostility: one time she was in the office attempting to learn something about computing and was "literally torn out of the office" by the supervisor and told, "That's not your job and you're not to learn anything that I don't teach you. If you're caught in here again you're fired." On other occasions she was demeaned when the supervisor attempted to show her "how to hold a pencil correctly" to improve her efficiency and when she was expected to "wash toilets, empty ashtrays, do the garbage" – jobs not connected with the employment of a parts' driver. Sharon was also sexually harassed but "warned off" her male colleagues. She had more problems with the male customers: "They'd say, here's a hot little number working in here – she must service everyone. They'd try it because there's people out there who think that all the time." Eventually Sharon was forced to quit this job. She moved on to other work and other sets of organizational experiences.

INTRODUCTION

Organizations are human creations. They are established by persons for given and changeable ends and they employ or recruit other persons to help achieve those ends. The activities of the people involved become linked and regularized through various processes of coordination and control, and in time these activities create a sense of something objective, something standing above the members of the organization – a sense of structure, of organization, is created. In turn, the "objective" sense of organization helps to create the illusion that organizations are places devoid of human subjectivity and emotion: worries, concerns, dreams, desires, family, and sexuality are expected to be submerged in the day-to-day activities of the organization and its goals.

This feel of the organization is a familiar one but it is not the only impression. People do not leave their selves behind when they come to work. The workplace is charged with emotionality, family concerns, sexuality, worries, hopes and dreams: try as they may, persons cannot divorce their selves from the workplace. Organizations are composed of persons with diverse psychological needs and behaviours which inevitably come to influence, and are shaped by, working relationships.

In describing her work experiences Sharon Webb was to say that "most of the jobs that I found unpleasant had to do with the people I've had to work with, not the work itself." In her job as a parts truck driver she confronted questions about her womanhood, her physical capabilities, her intelligence, her skills, her ability to learn, and her moral values. She had to survive an organizational context in which "real women" were those who appeared weak, got pregnant, and were primarily committed to home and family. It was an organizational context in which overt displays of heterosexuality were an expected sign of masculinity and femininity.

The specifics of such non-task related experiences are peculiar to Sharon Webb, but the experiences themselves are a general part of everyday work life. The experiences were not incidental to Sharon's job: her ability to complete her work tasks and earn a wage was framed by non-task experiences. That Sharon was able to survive tells us something about her psychological strength and the ability of persons to resist organizational pressures, but not everyone is capable of resisting pressures. In part this may have something to do with the fact that not all organizational pressures are experienced as negative, in part it has to do with the individual strengths of the people involved, in part it has to do with the fact that most organizational experiences confront us as "normal", but largely it has to do with the fact that, at an individual level, most people have little or no organizational power.

Organizations have come to exert a powerful influence over people's lives. Power, social status, income, and wealth are often gained in and through organizations. Those whose relationship to the modern organization is tenuous ("housewives"), disrupted ("unemployed"), undeveloped ("preschooler"), or terminal ("retirees") find themselves labelled as somehow less than whole persons. For those inside the organizational world hierarchical relationships determine various material, social, and psychological outcomes.

That organizations can have a powerful influence on the way persons come to think about themselves and others have rarely been of interest to organizational theorists and managers. Where there has been a focus on the psychological well-being of persons in organizations it is linked with a concern to improve organizational goals. Indeed, much of organization theory and organizational behaviour (OT/OB) has served to reinforce managerialist views of the role of organizations and the persons who serve them (Clegg, 1981). That is why we examine the role of OT/OB theory in the following section of this chapter.

To uncover the links between organizational structures and personality we need to go beyond traditional OT/OB theory. Through an examination of critical theory, humanist, Marxist, postmodernist, psychoanalytic and feminist studies of organization the remainder of this chapter sets out to introduce a range of alternative theories and to identify some of the key relationships between organization and personality.

PSYCHIC PHENOMENA AND ORGANIZATIONAL BEHAVIOUR

An interest in the psychology of people at work began in the early stages of the development of OT and OB. Scientific management theory developed at a time when employers believed in the absolute right of managers to command and the clear duty of the employees to obey. This was reflected in the work of Frederick Taylor, the originator of Scientific Management theory. On the surface Taylor's theory of management has nothing to do with psychology but his implicit views of human nature play a central role. Taylor viewed the employee as a simple organism who responds to reward and to threat: this notion of human nature became an important factor in the way Scientific Management was applied and how employees were treated (Rose 1975).

It was the Hawthorne Studies which began the focus on the psychological aspects of employees. The series of studies commissioned by Western Electric at its Hawthorne Works (Chicago), beginning in the mid 1920s and ending in the mid 1930s, was motivated by management concerns with low productivity and high turnover. Unlike Taylor, the Hawthorne researchers drew on explicit theories of human personality – including the work of Durkheim, Pareto and Freud; theories which were used to legitimize the development of specific forms of workplace control. What was implicit throughout the Hawthorne research is a view of women as psychologically inferior to men (see Chapter 5).

Durkheim's theory of social solidarity was used to argue that the modern workplace fulfils a need in people for group solidarity (Roethlisberger and Dickson, 1939). Workplace control, from this viewpoint, was not some undemocratic series of dictates but an important form of social integration in an otherwise fragmented society. Pareto's elitist theory of leadership was used to legitimize a view of employees as "irrational," and thus in need of the "rational" leadership of the modern manager. From this viewpoint management was not simply a right but an important form of social leadership. Freud's work on neurosis was used to explain that negative behaviour and attitudes at work were not so much due to dissatisfactions with the work as to deep-seated, psychological problems rooted in unresolved family and childhood factors. To this end the Western Electric company, for a time, required all their Hawthorne employees to undergo psychoanalytical counselling sessions to 'help' them to see that certain of their attitudes were problematic and interpersonal rather than work related (Rose 1975).

This elitist view of human nature had a major impact on the development of theories of organizational behaviour and was no doubt aided and abetted by the fact that it struck a cord with existing management views and needs, and by the misappropriate classification of this school of thought as 'Human Relations'!

After World War II a concern with psychological aspects of the workplace developed in a number of directions – focusing on motivation, leadership style, resistance to change, organizational climate, psychological well-being and satisfaction, and, more recently, organizational culture. The sheer number of studies on the relationship between psychological factors and organizational outcomes led, in North America, to the development of Organizational Behaviour as a specific area of study distinct from Organization Theory and its focus on the relationship between structural arrangements and organizational outcomes.

The development of OB and OT has been somewhat paradoxical. At its worst, a concern with people's needs has been turned into a strategy for achieving management objectives – the focus on psychological and/or social needs has become a tool for achieving organizational ends. Here is a recent example, taken from Daft (1989, pp.511-12):

> Organizational culture is an important management tool of strategy implementation. When a shift in strategy is needed, leaders may have to change cultural values to fit and reinforce the new strategy. When strategy and culture are already in alignment, the role of leaders is to embody culture. Indeed, in some organizations the culture is so strong that leaders will attempt to choose a strategy consistent with culture rather than vice versa. When cultural values must be changed, managers can design ceremonies and slogans, devise symbols, and repeat stories to infuse the underlying values and philosophy that support company strategy.

Here, in crass form, is an invitation to management to manipulate the values, beliefs and relationships of persons at work to fit the company business strategy of the time. There is little consideration of the potential disruption and dislocation of the persons involved.

At its best, a genuine concern with the psychological needs of people has been linked with the achievement of organizational ends – a search for an appropriate balance between individual and organizational well-being. Here is an example, taken from Schermerhorn, Hunt, and Osborn (1988, pp.37-39):

> A psychological contract is the set of expectations held by the individual and specifying what the individual and the organization expect to give to and receive from one another in the course of their working relationship. This contract represents the expected exchange of values that causes the individual to work for the organization and causes the organization to employ that person […] When the individual and the organization both feel the exchange is fair, a state of inducements-contributions balance exist.

Here the authors are concerned to find an arrangement which benefits the individual employee while being of value to "the organization." Such an approach fails to see the paradox of seeking psychological growth and development in the context of unequal arrangements of power. Rarely do OT and OB studies question existing arrangements of power and control. By referring to "the organization" Schermerhorn and his colleagues manage to convey the impression of an equal arrangement between two parties – the individual and the organization but organizations are not entities, they consist of powerful persons who manage and control the activities of others. At least Daft leaves us in no doubt who is in charge and what that means for employees.

The very issue of control and its impact on personality is left out of account in studies of organizational behaviour. Thus, it is not surprising that most OB and OT studies also leave out of account issues of gender, ethnicity/race, and class. Much of OT/OB research fails to take the gender of their subjects into account in their findings and to date has largely neglected non-white workers as subjects. Likewise blue-collar workers have received only a fraction of the attention given to white-collar, professional and supervisory staffs. Industrial work – with its technological means of control (for example, the conveyer belt), its payments-by-results system of motivation, and its clear lines of authority – seems a less appropriate area for studying the improvement of techniques of motivation and leadership, or of human growth! What we are left with is an area of study that focuses, at best, on the psychological well-being of the non-manual, white, male employee.

By ignoring issues of control and its dimensions of class, gender and race OT and OB have contributed to, rather than exposed, the nature of organizational power and its impact on our sense of self. In the next section we explore the relationship between organizational power and personality through a review of six critical approaches to organization.

NOW TURN TO EXERCISE 4.1 AT THE END OF THE CHAPTER

IMAGES OF THE PSYCHIC PRISON

> [The] idea of organizations as psychic prisons [is a] metaphor [which] joins the idea that organizations are psychic phenomena, in the sense that they are ultimately created and sustained by conscious and unconscious processes, with the notion that people can actually become imprisoned or confined by the images, ideas, thoughts, and actions to which these processes give rise. The metaphor encourages us to understand that while organizations may be socially constructed realities, these constructions are often attributed an existence and power of their own that allow them to exercise a measure of control over their creators (Morgan, 1986, p.199).

An interest in the relationship between the development of self and the character of modern organization can be traced back to the work of Marx, Weber, and Durkheim (see chapter 1). Durkheim's concerns have been taken up within the OT/OB literature only briefly and the most thoroughgoing development and syntheses of Marx's and Weber's ideas were undertaken outside the emergent OT/OB fields by the Institute of Social Research. Founded in Frankfurt (Germany) in 1923, the Institute was established to undertake interdisciplinary research concerned with grasping 'the ultimate causes of (the) processes of (social) transformation and the laws according to which they evolve'.[2] Marxist in orientation, the Institute attracted a number of radical scholars interested in research into the nature of capitalism and its transformation. Scholars who came to work at the Institute include Max Horkheimer, Theodore Adorno, Erich Fromm, Wilhelm Reich, and Herbert Marcuse.

Critical Theory

The broad theoretical perspective which developed at the Institute became known as the 'Frankfurt School' or 'critical theory' and was shaped by several factors – including the rise of fascism in Germany and the development of Stalinism in the Soviet Union. Those factors led many of the critical theorists to broaden their interest in the transformation of capitalism to encompass issues of personality development and the impact of bureaucratization on social life: events in Germany and the Soviet Union were revealing that, given the right conditions, large and increasing numbers of persons were able to act in a cold, heartless and brutal manner. To make sense of the impact of organizational arrangements on personality critical theorists drew primarily on the work of Weber, Marx, and Freud.

The issues and debates generated by critical theory are complicated and outside the focus of an introductory text[3] but three areas of discussion raise important questions about the relationship between personality and organization and warrant our attention. The first area of discussion – on 'consumption'- deals with the issue of economic power and dehumanization and suggests that the nature of capitalist organization reduces persons to 'things', or commodities thus making them susceptible to organizational influences. The second area of discussion – on 'bureaucracy'- deals with the issue of ideological power and organizational behaviour and suggests that bureaucratic rules and expectations encourage people to internalize bureaucratic ways of thinking and acting: people *become* bureaucrats. The third area of discussion – on 'personality' – suggests that capitalism as a system is structured in a way that stifles creativity and human growth, encouraging and rewarding repressive and authoritarian behaviour.

On Capitalism and Consumption: Critical theorists argue that capitalism reduces persons to the level of 'things' .[4] Capitalism is defined as a system in which goods are produced not for immediate consumption but as items for sale on the market; the potato, for example, is viewed by the producer not so much as a vegetable for eating as a thing to be sold, a commodity for sale. Similarly, the productive capacities of persons are viewed as commodities for sale. To live people have to sell their ability to work (their 'labour power') to an employer for wages. This has important consequences for the employee. S/he is employed not so much as for who he or she is as what he or she can do. Personality features, except where they have a direct bearing on the job, are normally irrelevant to the employer. Thus, workplace relations take on a thing-like quality, with employee contributions to the organization being valued as a commodity. This can be seen in the everyday phrases such as 'he was worth employing,' 'her productivity is too low,' 'he isn't producing enough'.

Another consequence of capitalist organization, according to critical theory, is that the employee's energies are directed at the production of things for sale. The carpenter, for example, is not engaged in creating something to sit on when she makes a chair but she is, rather, producing an item for sale. The electronic engineers who make Nintendo games are not creating a world of magic for children but a high level of profitable items for the Nintendo company.[5] The recent spate of PG-rated movies is due more to a concern with the maximization of profits than specifically in entertaining children (Corliss, 1993).

The employee is surrounded by a world of things and as a result begins to see him- or her- self as a thing. Many persons find it hard to escape the feeling that they are just a cog in the wheel, a faceless number who is ultimately replaceable. It is a process which is exacerbated by the fact that employees have little or no control over the work process, that the nature of their work is specialized and separate from the work of others, that employees are placed in a competitive relationship with other employees, and that the nature of work usually involves tasks which inhibit creative and autonomous thinking. In short, the nature of capitalist production inhibits the ability of the employee to experience his/herself as a creative and meaningful human being. This process is further compounded by the organizational character of the workplace which is increasingly bureaucratic in nature.

On Instrumental Reason and Bureaucracy: On the face of it bureaucracy is a particular form of organizational structure, defined by a combination of specialization, standardization, formalization and centralization (see chapter 2), a neutral instrument of organization. Yet critical theorists argue that bureaucracy is not simply a way of organizing but is also a way of thinking and acting that is far from neutral in its impact on employees.

Max Weber had earlier argued that bureaucracy is a form of organizing that arises out of, and depends on, a form of rational, calculative thinking. According to Weber the modern world is characterized by instrumental reasoning whereby persons act according to a series of means and ends calculations and this has contributed to the development and efficiency of the bureaucracy form of organization (see chapter 2). Building on the work of Weber, the critical theorist Herbert Marcuse argues that bureaucracy is not simply a form of organizational structure that is neutral in its functioning and outcomes: it is a form of organizational life which forces persons to think and act in narrow ways for those in charge. Bureaucracy, according to Marcuse, affects employees in three crucial ways – (i) domination, (ii) atomization, and (iii) the destruction of creative thought and reflexivity.

Domination – within a system of private ownership and control instrumental reasoning, or means-end calculability serves the ends of the powerful within the organization. The relationship between capitalist and worker, manager and managed, profit and wages are masked by a complex system of organizational rules and regulations. Bureaucratic structures, for instance, appear to the worker as a neutral organizational form – a scientifically devised mean for achieving certain ends. Bureaucratic rationality reduces everything to calculable dimensions. The worker's productive activities are reduced to a calculable performance to be "motivated, guided and measured by standards external to him, standards pertaining to predetermined tasks and functions" (Marcuse, 1941: 417). Organizational ends, far from being seen as the narrow ends of those who stand to profit, are experienced as a neutral set of activities. In the process the organizational means take on a life of their own – technical rules become things in themselves; rules, in other words, become important for their own sake rather than the end they are supposed to serve.

Atomization – specialization, a key element of bureaucracy, atomizes the workers, according to Marcuse: as tasks become increasingly mechanized they present fewer and fewer opportunities for mental and reflective labour. Work experiences become fragmented and knowledge of the whole work process becomes remote. Occupations – which have increasingly been atomized and isolated – now seem to require for their cohesion coordination and management from above (Held, 1980:68). The resulting outcome of the overall process of bureaucracy is that the experience of class diminishes and domination becomes ever more impersonal. Bureaucracy masks the underlying power relations with a sense of instrumental reason and technical rationality.

The Death of Creative Thought – the combination of impersonal domination and atomization helps to create a set of work experiences which encourage narrow, rigid thinking and which, as a consequence, help to inhibit the development of creative thought and action; this can, as other critical theorists have argued, lead to the arrest of personality development and the rise of the authoritarian personality.

On Personality Development, Sexuality, and Authoritarianism: Following Marx, many of the critical theorists argue that persons have innate capacities or potentialities for creativity; that through productive activity persons create their world and in so doing create themselves. In the processes of human development productive activity has not been freely engaged in by people but instead has been subordinated to situations of private ownership and control: as a result the individual has become a "worker" and his/her labour activity has been engaged in the production of things and a world not of his or her making. This "unfree" labour has led to the development of a world which appears alien and beyond the comprehension and powers of the individual. Instead of feeling in command of the process of creativity the modern worker experiences powerlessness and a distinct lack of creative abilities.

Concern to understand human subjectivity led several of the critical theorists to the work of Freud, and, as a result, the concepts of 'life instinct' and 'repression' became central to the analysis of organizational realities. In their various ways critical theorists argued that a striving for life – sexual and self-preservation instincts – is at the core of a person's being and the more that this instinct is suppressed the more distorted and disturbed, the less creative and less human the person is likely to become. Capitalist organization is seen as playing a more or less direct role in the process of repressing the person's life instinct. Horkheimer, for example, argues that organizations repress the life force (or libido) to ensure sufficient energy for production but that this tends to reduce persons to the status of mere functionaries of economic mechanisms and enforces suffering on a massive scale. The experience of repression causes feelings of guilt and/or inadequacy and increased aggression towards self and others (Held, 1980:44).

Focusing on sexuality – by which he meant genital sexuality[6] –Wilhelm Reich argues that capitalist organization represses sexuality and in the process blocks people's impulses for liberating experiences:

> It was not until relatively late, with the establishment of an authoritarian patriarchy and the beginning of the division of the classes, that suppression of sexuality begins to make an appearance. It is at this stage that sexual interests in general begin to enter the service of a minority's interest in material profit; in the patriarchal marriage and family this state of affairs assumes a solid organization form[....] The moral inhibition of the child's natural sexuality [through the formation of a strong super-ego], the last stage of which is the severe impairment of the child's genital sexuality, makes the child afraid, shy, fearful of authority, obedient, 'good,' and 'docile'[....] It has a crippling effect on man's

rebellious forces because every vital life-impulse is now burdened with severe fear and since sex is a forbidden subject, thought in general and man's critical faculty also become inhibited (quoted in Held, op cit., p.117).

This process results in rigid, conservative and reactionary thinking that, for Reich, is characteristic of capitalist organization but which was at its apex in Nazi Germany.

In attempting to explain the rise of fascism and the appeal of the Nazis Reich and Adorno developed Freudian analyses. Adorno's work centred on the issue of ego weakness and narcissism. Adorno believed that capitalism had progressively weakened the position of the father as an authority figure and that as a result the growing child develops a weak ego and the inability to keep in check a striving for gratification. The person become self centred and absorbed (or 'narcissistic') Such a person becomes susceptible to powerful, organized agencies. This happens through two powerful mechanisms – (i) the provision of an outlet for repressed urges, and (ii) identification with a strong leader. *Repressed urges:* Certain groups encourage the release of repressed urges and allow the transfer of energy to the service of the group. The Nazis, for example, attracted recruits by encouraging the use of violence and destruction. In today's world organized soccer hooliganism and the rise of neo-Nazism in Europe have attracted a number of young followers bent on destructive activity. *Identification and leadership:* In Freudian theory the central mechanism for transforming human energy or libido into a bond between follower and leader is identification. The self-absorbed person with a weak ego is often prey to the attractions of a strong leader. Identification involves an essential, primitive narcissistic aspect, one which makes the 'beloved object part of oneself'. The authoritarian leader becomes, according to Adorno, an enlargement of the subject's own personality. Thus, strong narcissistic impulses can be satisfied by identification and idealization of a leader (Held, 1980:135).

To date, the works of the critical theorists remain the most thoroughgoing analysis of the relationship between personality and organization. In recent years a growing number of studies have revived interest in the relationship between organizational realities and human personality – revisiting, in the process, many of the issues raised by critical theory. Humanist approaches, for example, have taken up the issue of the impact of organization on human growth while challenging the pessimism of critical theory. Humanist theory takes psychological well-being rather than neurosis as its starting point. In a similar way, Marxist analyses, while retaining a focus on the transformation of capitalist organization, have tended to turn away from Freudian explanations of psychology, turning instead to phenomenological approaches. Here the emphasis is on understanding how the human actor's view of the world is constructed and can be transformed through action rather than through psychoanalysis. In many ways psychoanalytic approaches to organization are the direct heirs of critical theory. The work of Christopher Lasch and Manfred Kets de Vries, for instance, utilizes psychoanalytic theory to explain the problems and dangers of modern organization. Lasch focuses on the relationship between capitalist organization and narcissism, and Kets de Vries focuses on the impact of neurosis on organizational management. Postmodernist analysis has revived an interest in the relationship between organizational arrangements and the self but has questioned the use of essentialist concepts of the self: while critical theorists focused on the impact of organization on the (preexisting) self postmodernists argue that the self is created in and through organizational discourses. Feminist theory, with its focus on women's liberation, is concerned with the impact of organization on the construction of discriminatory (gendered) selves. To this end, it has questioned an over-reliance on orthodox Freudian concepts and essentialist notions of the self which lay the blame for discrimination on women themselves.

Humanist

Within mainstream organizational behaviour analysis of the impact of organizational arrangements on human growth and personality has been limited to a small group of humanist psychologists. Foremost among these psychologists is Abraham Maslow and Chris Argyris.

Maslow's work, like that of Max Weber, has been bastardized by most OT texts and reduced to a parody. Successive generations of OT students have come to associate Maslow with little more than the "hierarchy of needs" theory of human motivation, a theory – they are informed – that has not been verified and is of little predictive value for managers (Robertson and Cooper, 1986).

If we look at the body of Maslow's work we find a concern with the human condition – a concern that did not end with a focus on the white male but encompassed women[7] and native people.[8] Maslow, unlike many other psychologists of his day or the earlier critical theorists, was interested not so much in "illness" (for example, neurosis) but in "wellness." He wanted to know what keeps people mentally healthy. From that starting point, he came to believe that there were a number of fundamental needs – physiological, security, social, esteem, and self-actualization – that had to be satisfied if people were to become or remain psychologically healthy. Implicit in Maslow's hierarchical ordering of human needs is a theory of maturation and human development; that as we grow from infant to adult – moving through various processes of socialization – we acquire a number of socially defined needs beyond our basic physiological needs. Maslow was acutely aware that persons do not rigidly move hierarchically through a series of need demands but that in human society some needs have become of more profound significance than others. Maslow's theory of needs could have served as a fundamental critique of the nature of organization had he used it as a measure of the contexts in which persons develop. His description of the nature of self-actualization, for example, stands in sharp contrast to what is possible in the confines of hierarchically arranged organizations: Maslow – disappointingly, utilizing the male dominant language and imagery of the time – described self-actualization thus,

> A musician must make music, an artist must paint, a poet must write, if he is to be ultimately happy. What a man can be, he must be. This need we may call self-actualization... It refers to the desire for self fulfilment, namely, to the tendency for him to become actualized in what he is potentially [...] the desire to become more and more what one is, to become everything that one is capable of becoming (Maslow, 1943, p.382).

Certainly, three decades earlier, research in Alberta on the Blackfoot Indians had led Maslow to conclude that competitiveness within American culture was harmful.[9] Yet Maslow chose to work within the system, advising management how to alter some of their systems of work to allow employees greater degrees of freedom.

In the application of Maslow's work to OT two important areas of research have been left out of account – his work on knowledge and inquiry, and on dominance and sexuality. Besides the five needs noted in the hierarchy of needs' model, Maslow's research suggests two further needs – (a) freedom of inquiry and expression needs, and (b) a need to know – a need for curiosity, learning, philosophizing, experimenting, and exploring (Hoffman, 1988). It is not clear why those needs did not come to form part of Maslow's final model but had they been included they could – with their emphasis on control and domination – have contributed to a more critical examination of the existing character of modern organizations.

Maslow's work on domination was not made much of by Maslow himself, and, for reasons which are not entirely clear, he appears to have suppressed much of his thoughts on sexuality and female psychology.[10] From initial work with primates extended to studies of people, Maslow became convinced that "dominance" was an extremely important force in social relations, arguing that a dominance drive was a key determinant of social behaviour and organization (Hoffman, 1988:69-70). If indeed, as Maslow contends, persons develop different dominance needs this has important implications for organizational research. For instance, to what extent are organizational arrangements a reflection of the dominance needs of those who came to found and control them? To what extent do hierarchical arrangements encourage and provide expression for dominance needs? Had Maslow developed these ideas he may have been able to further our understanding of the relationship between organizations and authoritarian behaviour.

Maslow's work on sexuality provides some clue to the potential relationship between organizations and dominance. He felt that the influence of social values in shaping male-female relations had an important impact on dominance, feeling that it affected daily life at work as well as in marriage. He observed that, "The very definite training that most women in our culture get in being 'ladylike' (non dominant) exerts its effect forever afterwards" (quoted in Hoffman, 1988:234-5).

Maslow believed that "definite inborn psychological differences exist between men and women"[11] and that "male and female basic needs must be fulfilled prior to self-actualization." But he also believed that self-actualization involves a synthesis of traits associated in North American culture with both masculinity and femininity – an aspect of the concept of self-actualization that OT accounts have been completely silent about! Despite his belief in the existence of some innate psychological differences between men and women Maslow nonetheless recognized the role of male dominated cultural forces in holding back the potential for female self-actualization, arguing that because our western culture denigrates the feminine modes, "our conceptions of the universe, of science, of intelligence [and] of emotion are lopsided and partial because they have been constructed by man." Continuing in this vein, he went on to say that, "If only women were allowed to be full human beings, thereby making it possible for men to be fully human" then western culture might finally generate a balanced, rather then male, approach "to philosophy, art, science." Unfortunately, these words were confined to a letter to a friend which concluded with the statement that, "If ever I get up courage enough to write anything on the subject I shall send you a copy" (quoted in Hoffman, 1988:234-5)!

The work of Chris Argyris also raises important questions about the relationship between personality and organizational structure. Argyris's work focuses on human maturation and growth, arguing that as people move from infancy to adulthood they move from (i) a state of passivity to a state of increasing activity (ii) dependency to relative independence (iii) limited ways to various ways of behaving (iv) limited to deep-rooted interests (v) short to long time perspectives (vi) being in a superordinate position to aspiring to occupy an equal position as an adult and (vii) a lack of awareness of self to awareness and control over self. As persons mature and grow a great deal of their time is spent in organizations but, as Argyris notes, the existing structures of those organizations do not encourage maturation; they do not permit persons to use their capacities and skills in a mature and productive way. For Argyris, far too many jobs in modern industry were so fragmented and specialized that they prevented workers from using their capacities and from seeing the relationship between what they were doing and the total organizational mission (Schein, 1980:68). Argyris's solution to this problem was to argue for "participative management," that is, to allow employees a say in the decision-making processes, without dismantling the existing systems of power and control.

The work of Maslow, Argyris and others has been influential in drawing attention to human needs and growth but the impact of their observations has been weakened by a commitment to change *within*, rather than of, the existing frameworks of power. Their analysis is also weakened to some extent by notions of "human" development premised on male-associated characteristics and processes of development (Gilligan, 1982; Cullen, 1992).

Marxist

The work of Peter Leonard occupies an interesting position within Marxism in that it straddles the humanist/structuralist (Burrell and Morgan, 1979) schism that has characterized Marxist thought since the development of critical theory: in *Personality and Ideology* Leonard combines a focus on the structural imperatives of capitalism with a focus on human agency and subjectivity. Unlike critical theory, Leonard attempts to synthesize the social psychology of George Herbert Mead with the political economy of Marx.

At its simplest, Mead argues that the self is socially constructed. We are not born with a particular self or personality but, rather, we develop a sense of self through interaction with others. Interaction includes the capacity to relate to symbols and part of that process involves the designation of the self with a symbol. Thus, the person becomes an object in his/her own world (Leonard, 1984:71). The process through which the self is developed involves a relationship of 'I' to 'me'. The 'I' refers to the process of thinking and acting, whilst the 'me' refers to the reflective process. The 'me' represents the organized attitudes of others which confronts the 'I' and in turn is worked on by the 'I'. Mead's view of the self, thus, is fairly complex and suggests a self which is never finally formed but is always to some degree in a state of flux and mediation. Mead's approach however lacks an adequate theory of the social order in which symbolic interaction takes place. Leonard sets out to correct this by utilizing Mead's psychology within the framework of historical materialism. In this way, argues Leonard, we can analyze how the self – for the large majority of working people – develops in contexts in which the 'I' is confronted by more powerful symbols and actors.

In capitalist society social relations centre on production and reproduction, and are based on class, gender and ethnic domination. Thus,

> contexts are penetrated by meanings, definitions, and 'common sense' assumptions which reflect the ideologies through which a class, gender, ethnic group or other collectivity maintains its internal coherence, makes sense of the world, and either legitimates its dominant position in the social order or validates its resistance to domination (Leonard, 1988:109).

Turning to the structure of personality and "use-time" in the process of production, Leonard argues that an important factor in the development of personality is how the person uses the time available to him or her for various kinds of activities. Under capitalism the necessity to labour predetermines the general distribution of use-time and the time utilized in labour is usually "abstract and does not, for most, allow the expanded development of capacities" (Leonard, 1988:91).

> On the other side, the opportunity to develop capacities within personal, concrete activities are for many also restricted, except in so far as they further the interests of capital in maintaining labour power or increasing the consumption of commodities (Ibid.).

The structure of capitalist organization is such as to have the effect of, "reducing the motivation to continue one's capacities, and so the personality will become stagnant and ossified "(Leonard, 1988:98).

Despite his observations about the impact of work on personality Leonard is far from pessimistic about the potential for liberation, and argues that involvement in groups and activities that resist capitalism can help to stimulate creative contexts in which the self can develop – leading to a process of self and social emancipation.

The work of Leonard – along with that of Illich (1981), Clegg (1975, 1983), Burrell and Morgan (1979), and Benson (1977) – signalled an important and promising development in Marxist theory. This work was important not only in applying Marxist theory to an understanding of the relationship between organizational realities and personality but in attempting to do so through a synthesis of Marxist and phenomenological theories. But the promise ended with the series of events that rocked the communist world – beginning with the appearance of glasnost in 1985 and continuing through the fall of the Berlin Wall, and, the subsequent break up of the Eastern bloc into several, often warring, states. Those changes, among other things, have led some to characterize the era as a crisis of Marxism, or "the end of history" (Fukuyama, 1989), that is, the irrevocable triumph of liberal capitalism. It has led numerous Marxists to search for alternative ways of thinking, with many being attracted to postmodernist analysis (Morgan, 1986; Burrell, 1989; Clegg, 1990). But the changes of the last decade – an era of change unprecedented since the French and American Revolutions – have not heralded a triumph of capitalism as much as a collapse of modernity, as peoples and what were once nations struggle to rebuild a sense of self and identity. It is a time when now more than ever persons are questioning the old ways of

> A 1992 issue of Maclean's describes how Canadians are a characteristic part of the trend towards questioning old ways of viewing the world:
>
> "Across the nation, Canadians share that troubling erosion of faith in their economic future.... There is a sense across the nation that the economic rules are profoundly and permanently changing.... For many Canadians, that loss of economic faith represents a profound spiritual crisis. The recession has eroded their fundamental belief in the inevitability of economic progress, but there is no satisfying replacement for that secular faith. Canadians are resentful, anxious and cynical about their way of life ... they are on the cusp of an enormous social change ... grasping for new certainties and new dreams."

viewing the world and, as a result, postmodernist analysis has become attractive to a range of scholars.

Post-Modernist

Over the last decade or so postmodernist analysis has replaced Marxism and critical theory as the predominate school of radical thought.[12] In terms of organizational analysis the work of Michel Foucault has been of particular interest to radical theorists,[13] and has much to say about the relationship between subjectivity and the development of particular forms of organization.

Foucault's work fundamentally challenges the modern(ist) notion of the individual as something essential, fixed, or "deep inside" us. For Foucault, the individual comes to be through a series of "disciplinary" and "confessional" practices – practices which, in the modern world, are organizational in form. Who we are and how we see ourselves is a product of the network of (largely) organizational practices within which we work and exist.

Foucault sees the development of modern society as a series of developments in which power, knowledge, and the body are closely interrelated. A concern with knowledge of and over the body characterizes the development of modern society. In the new manufactories of the eighteenth century new forms of knowledge assisted the emerging class of entrepreneurs to regularize the extraction of time and labour from the bodies of their workforce. Increasingly entrepreneurs and government took an interest in the control and regulation of the body. The state became interested in the health, numbers and condition of the population. This generated an array of new organizations and professionals concerned with translating and regulating the developing interest in the body. In the process concepts and practices of "normalization" were produced:

> These practices are supported and exercised by the state and by new bodies of knowledge, especially medicine and the human sciences. Under the humanistic rubric of the state's interest in and obligation to the creation and protection of the "well-being" of its inhabitants, global surveillance of its members is increasingly instituted. The state needs experts to amass the knowledge it requires and to execute the policies said to effect and maximize this well-being and protection. Instances of such knowledge and associated practices include medicine, education, public health, prisons, and schools (Flax, 1990, p.207).

Foucault calls this "disciplinary" practices – practices that are concerned with concrete and precise knowledge of the body, and as such constitute "biopower" in their outcomes of control. A major outcome of the nature and widespread existence of disciplinary practices has been, according to Foucault, the creation of the individual self; a constant placing of individuals in situations where they are forced to think about themselves and are simultaneously provided with the answers.

Alongside these practices,

> the individual subject is also created through confessional practices. The primary exemplars of these practices are psychoanalysis and psychiatry. These discourses produce sexuality as a dangerous force within us that can be controlled only by the person exercising surveillance upon her- or himself. Such surveillance is said to lead to both "self-knowledge" and freedom from the effects of these forces. However, in order to attain such self-knowledge and self-control, the individual must consult an expert whose knowledge provides privileged access to this dangerous aspect of the person's "self" (Flax, op cit., p.208).

Thus, the modern(ist) era confronts us with powerful discourses in which notions of the "self" are primary notions that create various senses of "self" in the image of the – largely organizational – practices from which they arise. In a world of dominant, organizational relationships this raises interesting and disturbing questions about the construction of self and reality: it has led several radical organizational theorists to study the relationship between organizational practices and subjectivity (Knights and Willmott, 1985; Knights and Collinson, 1987; Collinson, Knights and Collinson, 1990; Morgan and Knights, 1990). Authors like these have been drawn to several key notions developed by Foucault. One is Foucault's 'unique emphasis on the body as the place in which the most minute and local social practices are linked up with the large scale organization of power' (Dreyfus and Rabinow 1982: xxii). Another is Foucault's theory of power, with it's notion that power is everywhere and no-where, 'ubiquitous, but ultimately uncentred power relations' (Boyne and Rattansi, 1990:18), not possessed by individuals, groups or functions but always a relationship that involves positive as well as negative outcomes. Still another is Foucault's argument that meta-narratives (that is, general or universalizing theories of how societies function) are but competing truth claims that threaten to replace one set of power relations with another. For the postmodernist these three elements "provide a valuable means for comprehending the complexities of social control" (Ferguson, 1984: xii). They help to explain why it is that individuals comply with processes of power that may ultimately work against them – i.e., they are not simple victims of an all-powerful system but are contributors to a series of relationships through which power is created and maintained, and they help to explain how, through seeking radical change, individuals come to substitute one set of power relationships (e.g., capitalism) with another (e.g., communism) – i.e., though acceptance of a particular theory of society individuals buy into a set of truth claims which serve as a new power influence over the way they come to view themselves.

Postmodernist ideas are currently proving attractive to a growing number of radicals[14] but several critical questions about this viewpoint remain unanswered. The ultimate triumph of postmodernist thought may well depend on the responses provided to these questions. *Power* – it has been argued that post modernism underestimates the role of power holders in organizations:

> While it would be extremely foolish not to recognize diverse forms and locations of power ...(it) remains legitimate to talk of power 'holders'. That is, power is both a relationship and held by individuals or groups (Thompson, 1991)

Self – the post modernist concept of the self as fragmentary has been challenged for failing to come to terms with:

> The fact [...] that we live one life not several, our ability to chose which other "worlds" we wish to inhabit is very much dependent on our position in this world [Marx Memorial Library Bulletin, #117, 1992]

Radical change – finally post modernism has been criticized for an inability to encourage radical change:

> Postmodernism [...] is recognized as having abandoned any attempt to make any sense of (change). David Harvey notes postmodernism's: – 'total acceptance of the ephemerality, fragmentation, discontinuity, and the chaotic. It does not transcend it or counteract it. Postmodernism swims, even wallows, in the fragmentary and the chaotic currents of change as if that is all there is' (Ibid.).

Psychoanalysis

In the last decade or so a number of psychoanalytical studies of organization have drawn attention to the links between self and organizational reality, and in ways that are reminiscent of the early work of the critical theorists. Christopher Lasch's (1983) study of narcissism in American life raises a number of interesting questions for organizational analysis. Lasch suggests that there is a strong relationship between the way we come to conceive of ourselves and of organization:

Every age develops its own peculiar forms of pathology, which expresses in exaggerated form its underlying character structure. In Freud's time, hysteria and obsessional neurosis carried to extremes the personality traits associated with the capitalist order at an earlier stage in its development – acquisitiveness, fanatical devotion to work, and a fierce repression of sexuality. (Lasch, 1983: 87–88).

According to Lasch, our own time is characterized by a "culture of narcissism," signified by the widespread evidence of "borderline" personality disorders. In terms of clinical observations, patients who symptomize the malaise suffer from pervasive feelings of emptiness and a deep disturbance of self-esteem (Lasch, 1983, p.89). Lasch's description of the general malaise of narcissism complements Foucault's notion of the construction of the self in suggesting that the end product of discourses concerned with self-knowledge is the creation of individual self obsession:

Medicine and psychiatry – more generally the therapeutic outlook and sensibility that pervade modern society – reinforce the pattern created by other cultural influences, in which the individual endlessly examines himself for signs of aging and ill health, for telltale symptoms of psychic stress, for blemishes and flaws that might diminish his attractiveness, or on the other hand for reassuring indications that his life is proceeding according to schedule. (Lasch, 1983:99)

Drawing upon the work of Heinz Kohut, Lasch contends that narcissism arises out of the "unavoidable shortcomings of maternal care" (Kohut, 1971) which results in the child coming to realize that s/he is not the centre of the universe, that the mother is ultimately separate from the child and not there solely for his/her total gratification. The resulting disappointment and frustration lead the child to strive to reverse the situation and "involves either creating a tyrannical idealized self-image or the incorporation of tyrannical idealized parent image for the self" (Walter, 1983:262).

Far from containing narcissistic disorders the structure of modern society both reflect and encourages them. As Joel Kovel expresses it,

(The) stimulation of infantile cravings by advertising, the usurpation of parental authority by the media and the school, and the rationalization of inner life accompanied by the false promise of personal fulfilment, have created a new type of "social individual." The result is not the classical neurosis where an infantile impulse is suppression by patriarchal authority, but a modern version in which impulse is stimulated, perverted and given neither an adequate object upon which to satisfy itself nor coherent forms of control.... The entire complex, played out in a setting of alienation rather than direct control, loses the classical form of symptom – and the classical opportunity of simply restoring an impulse to consciousness." (Quoted in Lasch, 1983: 90).

Narcissism finds its expression in the modern organization in a number of ways:

> For all his inner suffering, the narcissist has many traits that make for success in bureaucratic institutions, which put a premium on the manipulation of interpersonal relations, discourage the formation of deep personal attachments, and at the same time provide the narcissist with the approval he needs in order to validate his self esteem.... The management of personal impressions come naturally to him, and his mastery of its intricacies serves him well in political and business organizations where performance now counts for less than "visibility," "momentum," and a winning record. As the "organization man" gives way to the bureaucratic "gamesman" – the "loyalty era" of American business to the age of the "executive success game" – the narcissist comes into his own. (Lasch, 1983: 91-92)

In the organizational world the exteriors of offices, the interiors of offices, and the presentation of self within offices have come to symbolize narcissism – symbols that not only reward but require narcissistic behaviour (Walter, 1983).

The narcissistic organizational culture gives rise to a type of leader who "sees the world as a mirror of himself and has no interest in external events except as they throw back a reflection of his own image" (Lasch, 1983:96). Such leaders are often more concerned with image than substance – advancing "through the corporate ranks not by serving the organization but by convincing his associates that he possesses the attributes of a "winner," in getting to the top he manipulates persons and symbols and, in an organizational culture created out of intersecting male values (Mills and Murgatroyd, 1991), many of those symbols utilize females and images of femininity:

> A graciously and perhaps even sumptuously decorated office reception of a company communicates opulence and self-assurance.... So too does the presence of a comely lady receptionist. These individuals are clearly not of goddess stature but are reminiscent of the nymphs who served as handmaidens to mythological gods in a variety of ways. (Walter, 1983: 259).

The organizational "gamesman":

avoids intimacy as a trap, preferring the "exciting, sexy atmosphere" with which the modern executive surrounds himself at work, "where adoring, miniskirted secretaries constantly flirt with him. In all his personal relations, the gamesman depends on the admiration or fear he inspires in others to certify his credentials as a "winner." (Lasch, 1983: 93-94)

This type of leadership contributes to an organizational culture in which certain images of leadership and of masculinity is expected to be "mirrored" (Kets de Vries, 1989a). For males the narcissistic organizational culture holds up images of certain types of male-associated behaviour that they are expected to mirror if they are to be deemed simultaneously successful and male. Mirroring is facilitated by excessive dependency between executives and subordinates: in these situations subordinates may come to identify excessively with the leader (Kets de Vries, 1989a, 1989b, 1990). In its extreme form this may involve over-identification "to the point of madness," as in the case of the relationship between Henry Ford and his lieutenants – Liebold, Sorensen, and Bennett, and the FBI under J. Edgar Hoover (Kets de Vries, 1990). On the other hand, failure to mirror the appropriate behaviour can result in organizational/sexual innuendo and rejection, as in the firing of an executive by Henry Ford II who deemed that the man's tight trousers signified a lack of manliness and, ergo, managerial competence (Iacocca, 1984).

What is striking about the psychoanalysis of organizations is its male reference points – reference points which are inherent in the way psychoanalysis is conceived (Mitchell, 1975; Squire, 1989) right down to the gendered way that maternal care is seen as the root of narcissistic development (Flax, 1990). It is far from clear to what extent narcissism can be said to be a characteristic of both males and females: indeed there is some evidence that gender constrained differences of experience between males and females (and between working and middle-class females) is associated with different forms of psychological distress and neurosis (Nahem, 1981), and "doing" is more likely to be encouraged in/associated with males than females, i.e., aggression and a striving for dominance will be characterized as male rather than female traits (Gemmill and Schaible, 1990). Nonetheless, psychoanalytic studies of organization indicate the type of dominant discourses within which male and female selves are constructed.

Feminist

For women organizational cultures hold out a whole different set of problems about identity formation. Women are confronted with organizational discourses which not only shape notions of femininity (and of masculinity) but whose rules and practices are male dominated. From a feminist psycho-analytical perspective Jane Flax (1990:120) argues that psychoanalytic theories "lack a critical, sustained account of gender formation and its costs to self and culture as a whole." Contending that children have acquired a "core identity" by the age of three, Flax urges a reconsideration of the mother-child dyad and the mother's power in the unconscious lives of men and women:

> This is an important step in the process of doing justice to the subjectivity of women and undoing the repression of experiences of ourselves as mothers and as persons who have been mothered (Flax, 1990: 123).

The significance for the mother-child dyad however should not be viewed separately from all the other social relations of which it is a part:

> Although part of the child's self is constituted through her or his internaliza-tion of the caretakers, in the process the child incorporates more than his or her experience of specific persons.... To some extent the parents' entire social histories become part of the child's self. An adequate theory of human devel-opment from an object relations perspective would have to include an account of all these different levels and types of social relations and their interactions, mutual determinations, and possible antagonisms. It would have to include an expanded concept of families – families not merely as a set of immediate rela-tions among individuals but also as permeable structures located within and partially determined by her social structures, including those of production, culture, and race, class, and gender systems. (Flax, 1990:124)

This perspective seems to suggest that the influence of organizational dis-course on the shaping of gender identity is significant but more so in the early stages of core identity formation. Nonetheless she goes on to argue that disci-plinary and confessional practices influence the way we categorize one another by gender and the way we come to view ourselves.

What is not clear from Flax's analysis is the extent to which involvement in any number of disciplinary and confessional practices influences, shapes, or modifies the core self and its gendered character. She does, however, offer the advice that a feminist deconstruction of the self would point to locating self and its experiences in concrete social relations:

> A social self would come to be partially in and through powerful, affective re-lationships with other persons. These relations with others and our feelings and fantasies about them, along with experiences of embodiedness also mediated

by such relations, can come to constitute an "inner" self that is neither fictive or "natural." Such a self is simultaneously embodied, gendered, social, and unique. It is capable of telling stories and of conceiving and experiencing itself in all these ways. (Flax, 1990:232)

Recent feminist studies have indicated ways in which people's sense of gendered self becomes shaped by organizational discourse. Blustein, Devenis and Kidney, (1989:200), for example, found a relationship between "the exploration and commitment processes that characterize one's identity formation … and an analogous set of career development tasks." Marshall and Wetherall interviewed a group of male and female law students about their perceptions of the characteristics required to be a lawyer. What they found was that there tended to be a shared view about the masculine nature of the traits required to be a successful lawyer, and that this had different implications for male and female students:

> Effectively, the relation between women and occupational identity became problematized, whereas the relation between men and occupational identity became normalized.... Women and lawyers were portrayed as dissonant, the identity relationship became a site of struggle but, in contrast, the masculine and the law became synonymous, with the masculine personality portrayed as identical with the legal personality. (Marshall and Wetherall, 1989, p.121)

For some of the female respondents this meant that becoming a lawyer involves learning to overcome feminine traits. Some of the other female respondents saw women as positive agents of change – improving the law through feminine characteristics. In either case women were faced with gender and occupational identity as "conflict and a site of struggle" (Marshall and Wetherall, 1989:123).

Gendered images of occupations and organizational realities are not simply reflected in the ideas of actors, reproduced by rote. It is through discourse that particular versions of reality and of self are produced/reproduced, modified and changed. As Marshall and Wetherall (1987:125) argue:

> there is no one 'true' representation of self and identity. At any given moment there will be varying possibilities for self-construction [...] identities are actively negotiated and transformed in discourse and [...] language is the area where strategic construction and reconstruction of self occurs.

Continuing the theme of gender and identity, Wetherall, Stiven, and Potter (1987:61-62) argue that notions of career are imbued with intersecting and contradictory discourses concerning gender and employment opportunities. Studying a group of final year university students, Wetherall found that,

> Two particular kinds of talk tended to dominate participants' discourse about women in the workplace, careers and children. These could be called the 'equal opportunities' and 'practical considerations' themes.

The equal opportunities theme was a form of talk which endorsed liberal values of egalitarianism, freedom of choice for the individual, equally shared responsibilities, and so on. The practical considerations theme, on the other hand, combined notions of the reproductive role and maternal urges of females with supposed understandable employer reluctance to risk hiring females over men. This quotation from a male respondent illustrates the latter theme:

> I suppose you can always see how an employer's mind will work, if he has a choice between two identically qualified and identically, identical personalities, and one is male and one is female, you can sympathize with him for wondering if the female is not going to get married and have children (Wetherall et al, 1987: 62).

These themes did not clearly represent differences of opinion between re spondents but were often made by the same person. Wetherall et al argue that "these contradictions may be responsible for the force and continuity of the ideology" that continues to maintain discriminatory differences between men and women, contradictions which help people – men and women – to "make sense" of a changing world in which gender notions remain strongly unchanged in the face of equity struggles and laws. Through the contradictions respondents were able to support the growing discourse of employment equity and yet, in a way that distanced themselves, explain why equity wouldn't work.

From a different perspective Ella Bell (1989) has shown how contrasting mythological images of black and white women in literature – respectively "the mammy and the snow queen" – is negatively reflected in management expectations of women of colour. Race and ethnicity, of course, add a whole different set of features to given organizational discourses and raise questions about the relationship between organization and sense of racial self. In recent works Bell and Nkomo (1992) discuss Black women's experience of racism and how it influences their ability to seek and attain managerial positions. Mighty (1991) has analysed the triple jeopardy of being female, black and an immigrant in today's Canada. The overwhelming neglect of race and ethnicity in theories of organization is discussed at length in chapter six.

Radical theories of organization indicate several links between the structure of organization and the development of human personality and identity. The schools of thought that we have reviewed disagree – often fundamentally – on the specific influences of organization on human life but they share a basic concern with the potentially distorting and destructive outcomes of those influences. Each school of thought encourages us to analyze the relationship between how organizations are structured and our experiences of self – how we become women and men, black and white, middle class and working class; how we come to feel about ourselves and others; how we come to express ourselves; how we shape our sexual preferences and those of others around us.

Despite the varying differences between each radical school, we can still draw some conclusions about organizational theory from considering various contributions. We need a theory of organizations that focuses on structure and personality, and on societal realities. This theory must incorporate issues of class, race, ethnicity, and gender, be concerned with issues of micro and macro power structures, and be continually aware of and questioning towards competing meta-narratives, including those from radical as well as non-radical perspectives. Finally, the goal of such an organizational theory must be nothing less than human liberation. Developing this perspective will not be easy, particularly in the face of postmodernist critique. But in the current debates among Marxists, feminists and postmodernists we can see the promise of such a new perspective which will combine the radical intent of feminism and Marxism with the scepticism of postmodernism.[15]

KEY TERMS

identity	*self*	*subjectivity*
repression	*rationality*	*instrumental reason*
post-modernism	*critical theory*	*biopower*
authoritarian personality	*dominance*	*disciplinary practices*
self-actualization	*psychic prison*	*confessional practices*
narcissism	*mirroring*	*discourse*
life instincts/Eros		

Q1. Briefly define "narcissism" and explain how a "culture of narcissism" can influence organizational personality.

Assignment: Compare your answer with the definition in the glossary of terms and the discussion in the chapter section on psychoanalysis.

[FS: For a broader understanding read C. Lasch *The Culture of Narcissism*, chapters 2 and 3]

Q2. In what ways can organizational arrangements have an influence on gender?

Assignment: List and discuss three (3) organizational factors (for example, sexual discrimination) associated with gender. Explain how each organizational factor influences the way people view men and women.

[FS: For a broader understanding of the factors involved read Wetherall, Stiven and Potter (1987) Marshall and Wetherall (1989) and Ferguson (1984: chapter 1).

Q3. Write short notes on each of the following terms and say how critical theory relates them to organizations
    Authoritarian personality
    repression
    Eros/life instinct

Assignment: Compare your answer with the definitions in the glossary of terms and the discussion in the section of the chapter on critical theory.

[FS: To gain a more in-depth understanding of the terms read Held (1980: chapter 4) or any other work that summarizes critical theory and psychoanalysis].

Q4. List and discuss three ways that critical theory sees bureaucracy as affecting employees.

Assignment: Read chapter 2 and the section on Instrumental Reason in this chapter and compare your answer.

[FS: For a more advanced understanding read Held (1980) and the Introduction and chapter 1 of Marcuse (1970)]

Q5. What did Maslow mean by the term "self-actualization" and to what extent is it attainable within the confines of the present structure of work?

Assignment: Compare your answer with the discussion in the chapter section on Humanism.

[FS: For a fuller understanding of self-actualization read chapters 9, 13 and 15 of Hoffman (1988)]

Q6. What is the relationship between identity and use-time?

Assignment: Compare your answer with the chapter section on Marxism

[FS: For a fuller understanding of the relationship between identity and use-time read Leonard (1984: chapter 4)]

Q7. Briefly define the following terms and discuss how they help us to make sense of organizations:
    bio–power
    disciplinary practices
    confessional practices
    subjectivity
    dominance
    discourse

Assignment: Compare your answer with the discussion in the postmodernism section of the chapter.

[FS: For an in-depth understanding of these terms read Burrell (1988)]

Q8. What is "mirroring" and what can it tell us about the problems of organizational leadership?

Assignment: Compare you answer with the discussion of psychoanalysis section of the chapter.

[FS: For a greater understanding of mirroring read Kets de Vries (1989)]

EXERCISE 4.1

This exercise is designed to make you think about the relationship between organizations and how we see and feel about ourselves.

For this exercise you will need a notebook to use as a diary. Keep a diary of your organizational experiences during the next seven days. In terms of your self focus on the following factors:

    self esteem- sexuality-identity
In terms of organizational experiences focus on the following factors:

hierarchy-rules-structure-space

time-status-interpersonal relationships-task

Hierarchy – refers to levels of authority in an organization.

Rules – refer to written and unwritten, formal and informal, rules which guide and control behaviour in an organization.

Structure – refers to the way an organization organizes its affairs, for example, the extent to which it is formal, standardized, centralized, highly controlled.

Space – refers to the physical layout of a place and the ways that the space is used. For example, there is a difference between the way McDonalds and The Keg structure their organizational space. There is also a difference in the use of space - for example, some organizations – such as colleges - allow their employees free access to most aspects of the organization and other organizations - such as prisons and nuclear power stations – restrict employees to a limited area.

Time – refers to the time span within which an organization operates, (for example, 9.00–5.00) and to the way time is used, (for example, the way an organization controls the use of time by requiring a certain level of speed, or expecting assignments and exams to be completed at certain times only)

Status – refers to the importance of one group over another.

Interpersonal-relationships – refers to the way persons relate to each other, for example, sharply, friendly, rude.

Task – refers to the actual duties or actions that a person carries out within an organization, for example, digging, reading, calculating.

Task #1: At the beginning of the notebook write some short notes on yourself.

A (I) Self-esteem: under this heading say something about how you feel about yourself and how you would ultimately like to feel about yourself. Using the following seven point scale, rate where you feel that you are usually:

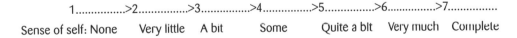

1...............>2...............>3...............>4...............>5...............>6...............>7...............
Sense of self: None   Very little A bit   Some   Quite a bit Very much Complete

A (ii) Now say something about how you usually feel. Write down ten adjectives that best describe you, for example, lonely, happy, restless, defensive, etc.

B (I) Sexuality: Under this heading write some short notes on your experience of your self as a man, or a woman. Write down ten adjectives that best describe the kind of woman or man that you are, for example, macho, gentle, strong, intellectual. Now write a brief note on the kind of man or woman that you would like to be.

B (ii) Write a brief note on how you see your sexual orientation, for example, heterosexual, bisexual, lesbian, gay. What makes you feel good about your sexuality, what makes you feel bad?

C (i) Identity: Under this heading write short notes on who you are. Write down ten adjectives that best sum up the kind of person that you are, for example, intelligent, athletic, driven, deep, etc. Note down the type of job that you would like to be doing if you had a free choice.

Task #2: Over the next week you will experience a variety of organizational situations at college, at work, in the stores, at a library, at an organized sporting event, at a political meeting, etc. Using the list of organizational factors above, note down each time an event or situation has a noticeable effect (e.g., makes you laugh, depresses you) and try to identify which factors were involved.

EXAMPLE:-

DAY 1

Organization: Political Party Meeting

Incident: Turned up at meeting a few minutes late, made to feel inadequate and unorganized. Asked to make coffee during the meeting. Ignored when trying to put forward suggestions.

Feelings = depression, anger, weakened self-esteem, made to feel that I'm "only a woman," feel that I'm not seen as a real person with any direction.

Organizational factors: 1. Time - the meetings are always inconvenient as far as childcare arrangements are concerned. 2. Space - the men seen to dominate the meeting room. 3. Location - meeting above a bar reinforces my feelings of vulnerability as I have to negotiate drunks. 4. Status - as one of the few women involved I am made to feel somehow different and less than adequate.

Task #3: At the end of the seven days reflect upon your diary and write notes on your overall experiences. Compare notes with other students and in small groups discuss the following questions:

a) To what extent do organizations influence the way we feel about ourselves?

b) To what extent do organizations contribute to the construction of our sense of self?

c) To what extent do we enter organizations with a developed sense of self?

d) What features of an organization are more likely to influence how we feel about ourselves?

e) What features are least likely to influence how we feel about ourselves?

f) How can we address some of the more psychologically damaging aspects of organizations?

FURTHER READING

Critical theory:
David Held (1980) INTRODUCTION TO CRITICAL THEORY

Humanist Psychology:
Edward Hoffman. (1988) THE RIGHT TO BE HUMAN: A BIOGRAPHY OF ABRAHAM MASLOW

Marxism:
Peter Leonard (1984) PERSONALITY AND IDEOLOGY

Post-Modernism:
Martin Parker and John Hassard [eds] (1993) POSTMODERNITY AND ORGANIZATIONS

Psychoanalytical Theory:
Manfred Kets de Vries and Denny Miller (1984) THE NEUROTIC ORGANIZATION

Feminist Theory:
Kathy Ferguson (1984) THE FEMINIST CASE AGAINST BUREAUCRACY

END NOTES

1. Interview with Albert Mills for a study on "Women at Work". The name is a pseudonym.
2. Carl Grunberg, the Institute's first director, quoted in Held (1980), p.30.
3. For a fuller discussion read Held (1980).
4. Here critical theory draws heavily upon Marx's theories of alienation (1967) and commodity production (1959) and Lukacs' theory of reification (1971).
5. David Sheff's (1993) excellent book on the Nintendo company exposes the "bottom line" focus of the company.
6. This is a much narrower interpretation of Freud's concept than the notion of life instinct which encompasses numerous aspects of human strivings.
7. Betty Friedan's ground breaking feminist work, *The Feminine Mystique*, drew attention to the significance of Maslow's little known but "seminal" 1930s studies on female sexuality and dominance.
8. In the mid-1930s Maslow undertook a study of the Blackfoot Indians of Southern Alberta.
9. Maslow associated the Blackfoot emphasis on generosity with the high levels of "emotional security" that he found among members of the tribe (Hoffman, 1988).
10. A recent analysis of Maslow's work on sexuality and dominance reveals a number of methodological and, not least, sexist problems with the research. Cullen (1992) argues that Maslow's research methods involved elements of coercion

in regard to the recruitment of "low esteem" female respondents, and that his notion of "self-actualization" was premised on a male notion of self fulfilment.

11. This world view no doubt underlay his understanding of "self-actualization", see footnote 10 above.

12. It should be made clear that not all postmodernist theory is radical in intent.

13. Cf. Burrell (1988); Clegg (1990). Other postmodernist writers that have been of particular interest to radical organizational theorists include Derrida (cf. Cooper, 1989; Calas, 1992), Deleuze, Lyotard, and Baudrillard (cf. Thompson, 1991).

14. A recent article has argued that, postmodernism is "a cultural climate as well as an intellectual position, a political reality as well as an academic fashion". "Post Modernism", Bulletin of the Marx Memorial Library, #117, 1992.

15. We are currently in the beginning stages of the development of new syntheses which include 'post feminism' (cf. Calas and Smircich, 1992) and 'post–Marxism' (cf. Jameson, 1989).

CHAPTER 5

Sex and Organizational Analysis

This chapter focuses on the significance of gender as a feature of organizational life. Issues of masculinity, sexual harassment, heterosexuality, sexuality, and power are explored. The main objective is to reveal the deep-seated nature of the gendered character of organizations, encouraging the reader to think more deeply about the relationship between organizational construction and sexual discrimination in its broadest sense (from employment equity to the gendering of self).

In/digestion at a Quebec Hospital

In September 1988 Line DesRosiers broke off her relationship with Henri Proud'homme, an event that in itself is quite unremarkable. Yet she happened to be employed as a pharmacy clerk at a hospital at which he was the assistant director, and that led to unexpected consequences. Immediately after the breakup Proud'homme took a week's sick leave, and DesRosiers was told by Jack Jackson, the hospital's executive director, not to return to work. It was strongly suggested to her that she find a job at another hospital. Line DesRosiers refused to leave. As far as she was concerned she had done nothing wrong, and certainly her personal life had nothing to do with the hospital. Nonetheless, DesRosiers felt compelled to hire a lawyer to safeguard her position.

At this stage the hospital insisted that DesRosiers stay home on full pay until they could arrive at a satisfactory conclusion. In November of 1988 DesRosiers' lawyer negotiated an arrangement with Jackson and the hospital's personnel director that she would remain home of full pay until January 15 of the following year, and that her position would be reassessed on January 8. In January the stay-at-home arrangement was extended for a farther two months – until March 19. When the new date was reached the hospital again signed an agreement to keep DesRosiers at home on full pay. This time, however, DesRosiers insisted that the agreement include a return

SEX AND ORGANIZATIONAL ANALYSIS 131

to work date. The hospital conceded and the date of May 29 was fixed as DesRosiers' return to work date.

By the end of May 1989 Line DesRosiers was back at work after eight months enforced paid leave, at $391 a week. During the eight months the hospital hired a replacement worker at the same rate of pay as DesRosiers — a cost of around $20,000. This at a time when the centre — which serves as both an hospital for chronically ill elderly patients and a nursing home for senior citizens — was running a budget deficit of $280,000, and when they were proposing to cut the patient's food (by $10,617) and leisure activity (by $5,390) budgets, reduce building maintenance (by $51,177), and cut back on nursing supplies.

When the story became known in June 1989[1] DesRosiers was unwilling to say much for fear that she would lose her job. Proud'homme, on the other hand, seemed unmoved: "I'm not obliged to go over all this stuff. As far as the hospital is concerned it has done nothing wrong or illegal or immoral." He finished by commenting that Jackson was attending the International Conference on AIDS and was not available for comment.

INTRODUCTION

The story of Line DesRosiers illustrates the theme of this chapter — the relationship between sex and power within organizations. Here is a case where the actions of two mature adults (DesRosiers was 41 and Proud'homme 44 at the time) were made the subject of organizational inquiry and decision making. It was an inquiry and a set of decisions that were not, however, equal in their deliberation. Only her action (in breaking up with Proud'homme) was seen as disruptive to the organization, and she was suspended. He, on the other hand, was seen as 'wronged' and in need of time to 'recover'. The story is a typical one of sex-power disparities in the workplace, that is, a male-dominated setting in which females have little or no power. In this instance the key administrators all were male, including DesRosiers' former lover Proud'homme: DesRosiers herself occupied a fairly lowly position within the organization. The administrators interfered in the situation and took his side and that is due to the shared experience of maleness and of organizational power. The story of Line DesRosiers is unusual only in that it made the newspapers. The dismissal of female subordinates by male supervisors following a breakup in their emotional relationship is a fairly common occurrence throughout organizations

(Quinn, 1977; Hearn, 1985; Harrison and Lee, 1986; Collinson and Collinson, 1989).

Sex is usually regarded as something quite separate from organizational life. Indeed, it is often considered illegitimate to bring such matters into the affairs of the organization. Yet, as we shall see throughout this chapter, sex is a central feature of organizational life.

To make sense of sex at work we need to begin by making a distinction between sex, gender, and sexuality. At its most basic level 'sex' refers to the biological differences between men and women.[2] However, our notions of the nature of men and women are not restricted to biological differences – through culture we come to associate women and men with varying sets of characteristics, for example, soft/rough, weak/strong. We refer to culturally acquired characteristics as 'gender'.

'Sexuality' is an important aspect of gender and refers to a "person's sexual self; those aspects of a person that make them sexually attractive to another." (Mills, 1994). Thus, a person is born with certain biological features (sex) and, using those features as a basis, people attribute particular characteristics (gender) to the person so that they are viewed as male or female. An important part of the process of becoming a man or a woman involves assumptions about the physical attractiveness (sexuality) of that person.

SEX AND ORGANIZATIONAL LIFE

The process of becoming a man or a woman involves many stages and contexts in a person's life. Each stage and each context involves a number of power relations in which people are rarely equal. Definitions of womanhood and of manhood are often influenced and shaped by powerful forces in society. The current U.S. debate on gays in the military is a good example. The debate shows how powerful people in the armed forces and government managed, for many years, to shape an approved image of masculinity; one that was 'rough,' 'tough' and decidedly heterosexual.

Organizations are powerful contexts in which people spend much of their lives. As such they are important cultural sites which contribute to our understandings of what constitute men and women. This is achieved in any number of ways, ranging from decisions about what men and women are capable of through to the use of sexuality for organizational ends:

The association of types of work with "masculinity" and with "femininity": In

1981 the great majority of Canadian women were concentrated in clerical, sales and service occupations, and in jobs that were generally low paying. This situation did not improve much throughout the 1980s (Peitchinis, 1989). Each time an organization classifies a job as for 'men only' or 'women only' they are not only discriminating but they are helping to create narrow images of men and women. Steel work, for example, is so closely associated with men that steel work is seen in some communities as part of what it means to be masculine.[3]

The underrepresentation of women in the top echelons of organizational office-holding: when an organization fails to promote women to positions of management it is not only discriminating but, at the very least, is insinuating that leadership qualities are a masculine trait. In Canada fewer than twenty-five percent of all "management, administrative, and related occupations" are held by women, and few of them are in the management end of that category (Abella, 1984). In 1983 women constituted fewer than four percent of upper-level management in the country's largest Crown corporations and less than five-and-a-half percent of all management positions in the federal public service (Abella, 1984). There were no women chief executive officers of the top 500 companies in Canada. A more recent study indicates that there have been only slight improvements in the overall picture. Looking at "selected departments" in the federal government, Peitchinis (1989) found that just over nine percent of executive and senior management positions were held by women. The private sector, however, has changed little. As late as 1990, for example, women constituted less than six percent of company Board membership in Canada (Bradshaw-Campball, 1991).

Pay inequities: when an organization pays a woman less than it does a man who is engaged on roughly similar work it is not only discriminating but it is contributing to the notion that womanhood is worth less than manhood. In Canada the average female wage is 65.8% of that received by men (Statistics Canada, 1990):

> One of the most graphic illustrations of the wage gap was provided by the Ontario Coalition for Better Daycare when it pointed out that zoo keepers and farm hands, predominantly male, were making $21,200 to $22,400 per year in 1983, compared with day-care workers, predominantly female, who were making only $13,000. Do employers value animals more than children? Do employers value zoo keepers more than child-care workers?" (Cuneo, 1990).

The use of sexuality to sell products and services: an organization helps to shape public images of sexuality each time it uses sexuality to sell its products (Task Force on Sex-Role Stereotyping, 1982 MediaWatch, 1982, Crean, 1985). On the whole, companies use young, white women and men to sell their products. By featuring certain kinds of women and men in their advertising companies are not only selling their products but they are selling the idea that a person is not sexually attractive unless they conform to a certain look.[4]

Sexual harassment: acts of sexual harassment are among the clearest examples of sexual behaviour at work. Sexual harassment, in its most explicit form, involves unwanted attention of a sexual nature, whether through acts of a physical, verbal or otherwise suggestive nature: the overwhelming majority of cases involve the sexual harassment of a woman by a man. Studies of sexual harassment at work indicate that there is a relationship between the incidence and type of harassment and the character of the workplace itself (Gutek, 1985; DiTomaso, 1989; Gutek and Cohen, 1992). Some workplace environments, for example, encourage or fail to discourage sexual harassment.

Power is a central issue in sexual harassment. Organizational arrangements create countless contexts of power inequity in which men occupy the majority or the only positions of power and authority. In many cases of sexual harassment organizational power is a factor where the woman is bothered by an organizationally more powerful male and/or has to rely on a male power structure to intervene to prevent harassment.[5]

Prohibitions and norms against homosexuality: a central and recurring theme of organizational sexuality is heterosexuality. Signs of sexual preference other than heterosexuality are rarely tolerated within or-

In 1987 Wardair attempted to prevent one of its male flight attendants from wearing an earring. The company argued that it was bad for business because passengers would associate the earring with homosexuality and, by association, AIDS. Around the same time the United Church of Canada became deeply divided over the issue of the ordainment of homosexual ministers. It took until the end of the 1980s to resolve the question at the level of policy making – in favour of ordaining ministers regardless of their sexual preference (although not regardless of their sex; women were still excluded from the ministry). Nonetheless controversy still continues to rage at the local level. In March of 1991, for example, the congregation in Athabasca, Alberta, split over the issue – with eighty of the one-hundred parishioners, along with the minister, breaking away because of deep objections to the new policy. Female sexual preference is no less sensitive an issue.

ganizations.[6] Very little research has yet been done on homosexuality at work but what evidence there is indicates that gay women and men are usually expected to conceal their sexual preferences from organizational view (Schneider, 1982, 1984) and this places severe strains on the gay person (Hall, 1990). When an organization discriminates against a person on the basis of their sexual preference they contribute to the suppression of sexual difference.

It should be clear from these various examples that sex is not only a constant feature of organizational life but has numerous implications for organizational and personal outcomes. Yet, OT has remained silent on the subject. As we saw in chapter one, organizational texts make little or no mention of sex, gender, or sexuality. In this chapter our central objective will be to challenge you to think about the relationship between sex, organization, and power, and about the implications of those relationships for organizational and personal outcomes.

NOW TURN TO EXERCISE 5.1 AT THE END OF THIS CHAPTER

SEX AND ACADEMIA

> In 1986, the Association of Universities and Colleges of Canada passed a "Statement on the Status of Women in Canadian Universities," which pointed out the need for ... institutions of higher learning to assume a leadership role in ensuring equality for women in the workplace. Unfortunately, there is little evidence to suggest that Canadian universities have taken this responsibility seriously.... In general, universities appear to be no farther ahead than other organizations in ensuring equity for women[...] Little attention has been paid to the gender inequities in university management... However, it is not difficult to see that, just as in other organizations, women very seldom make it to upper management levels in Canadian universities. The number who have become university presidents is few indeed. (Brindley and Frick, 1990, p.1).

The pursuit of "knowledge," as with other pursuits, takes place in the context of power relationships (Burrell and Morgan, 1989; Clegg, 1980). Universities are no less prone to the utilization of power to achieve decisions than many other organizations. Where universities differ from many other organizations is in masking the use of power behind claims of "scientific method" and "objectivity."

That the Universities — no less than other organizations — are male dominated means that a key aspect of the exercise of power involves a gendered dimension, that is, it reflects unequal power relationships between men and

Table 5.1

Proportion of Tenured and Leading to Tenure Appointments held by Women by Province and Rank, 1989-90.[7]

	Full	Assoc.	Asst.	Lect.	Total
Newfoundland	7.2%	20.1%	32.4%	55.6%	19.6%
Prince Edward I.	5.3	13.0	24.2	0.0	13.5
Nova Scotia	7.8	18.2	43.6	56.3	20.8
New Brunswick	8.6	21.0	30.7	50.0	17.4
Ontario	6.5	18.0	34.2	52.0	17.3
Manitoba	6.7	19.1	29.5	25.0	15.6
Saskatchewan	4.6	19.5	27.3	57.1	13.5
Alberta	8.6	19.7	36.8	64.3	17.4
British Columbia	5.4	17.6	29.3	40.0	16.3
Canada (excluding Quebec	6.8	18.5	33.6	52.4	17.2

Note: Data for Quebec are not available for 1989-90.
These percentages were calculated for each rank by dividing the number of women holding tenured positions or positions leading to tenure by the total number of faculty in such positions.

women (Bannerji et al, 1991). Only a minority of senior university administrators are women (Dagg and Thompson, 1988; Brindley and Frick, 1990), and this reflects that very few tenured or tenure-track faculty positions are held by women (see table 5.1). In terms of pay equity for university faculty, a recent study concluded that, "At all ranks women earn less than men (a pattern which has changed very little over time . . .)" (Dagg and Thompson, 1988).

Sadly this appears to be just the tip of the iceberg. A 1988 study of Canadian universities found widespread evidence of sexual discrimination to the degree that it could be described as an "incredible anti-woman ambiance" (Dagg and Thompson, 1988). The authors found a climate of sexism which included posters of scantily clad or naked women on university walls; orientation rituals that degraded women;[8] the use of course materials which made little or no reference to women, or which marginalized them; male professors who use derogatory terms for women, tell sexist jokes, and use images of women as sex objects to make a point in class;[9] a relative lack of funding for

Dagg and Thompson, (1988) cite two surveys which make horrific reading: (i) a 1986 survey of five hundred women at Simon Fraser University in which sixty-one percent of female graduates stated that they had been sexually harassed at university – mainly by male faculty members, and (ii) a study of ten Ontario campuses which reported two hundred and thirty-five incidents of physical and sexual violence against women in one year (1985-86) alone. And there are many other cases not picked up by the authors. In 1986 a male professor in the educational psychology department of the University of Alberta was suspended for six months and fined $2,000 for sexually harassing female students, but the action was only taken after some reluctance on the part of the University. More recently the University of Western Ontario's business school was the subject of media attention when a female member of faculty resigned, charging that she was sexually harassed.

feminist research; the under-funding and downgrading of women's studies programs[10] and widespread sexual harassment and sexual assault.[11] For women of colour the Universities present a double bind of racism and sexism (Carty, 1991).

SEX AND ORGANIZATIONAL RESEARCH

An 'anti-woman ambiance' (or, institutional sexism) is the context in which academic research is conceptualized, developed, funded, carried out, and disseminated; it is a context not dissimilar from other organizational contexts that the academic researcher encounters. The impact of institutional sexism can be seen in the bulk of organizational research, which reflect sexist attitudes.

Reading through OT research one is struck by the fact that women are either ignored or marginalized. It is as if the researchers were not so much occupants of an 'ivory tower' as cloistered away in a monastic order! From the classic studies to current texts gender has been neglected and ignored in studies of organization. This neglect has contributed to sexual discrimination by helping to normalize the idea that women are somehow peripheral to the public sphere. As Clegg (1981) argues, mainstream theories of organization help to reproduce the status quo of class, gender and race inequities.

The Hawthorne Studies provides a classic example of the way OT ignores gender even where it is a major, and obvious, element in the workplace. The Hawthorne Studies played an important part in the development of OT – particularly in suggesting that people need social solidarity and leadership – but gender was a central variable that was left out of account (Acker and Van Houten (1974). Gender was a key factor in the research design itself. The two main groups studied were an all male ('Bank Wiring Room') and an all-female ('Relay Assembly Test Room') group. The groups were studied in different ways. Study of the Bank Wiring Room involved observation of the existing work group: the men were free to continue their usual work practices, including autonomy to develop and maintain their own work norms. The 'Relay Assembly Test Room,' on the other hand, involved an artificially created work group; a small group of women was selected to take part in the experimental group situation. Unlike the men, the women were carefully recruited, closely supervised, and in numerous ways, told that they should improve their productivity:

> Group norms relating to productivity did develop in both work groups, but they developed in relationship to the external environment of each group and the external demands in regard to increasing production were different for the groups. Furthermore, the immediate external environment was controlled by males in both experiments. But maleness constitutes a different kind of external environment for a female group than for a male group because the effect of sex-based hierarchy of the larger society is added to the structuring of control in the organization. For the women's group, the relationship was between powerful males and weak females, that is, the females being weak, had to please the supervisors if they wished to stay in the test room, so they adopted the norm of increased production (Acker and Van Houten, 1974, p.156).

Sex-based power differentials are evident throughout the research. The women selected for the experiment were young (around 20), unmarried, and, with one exception, living at home with their parents in traditional, first-generation immigrant families. All those in positions of authority and power – from supervisors to researchers – were men. When the young women were asked separately if they wished to participate in the experimental group, "it is not surprising that they all agreed" (Acker and Van Houten, 1974:153). In the published reports of the research there is more than a suggestion of paternalistic attitudes and manipulation by the researchers as evidenced, for example, in the repeated use of the term "girls" throughout the texts.

Acker and Van Houten's (1974) analysis of the Hawthorne Studies indicates that sexuality is not only a feature of the workplace but of the study of the workplace itself. The disparities between the men's and the women's group were ignored in the research findings. For instance, the researchers failed to notice that it was the female group which increased output and the male group which restricted output. The findings of these studies went on, instead, to suggest that the results were applicable to all (genderless) employees.

> Since the research treatment was very different for the males and for the females, there still remains the question of whether the group of males would have responded similarly to the same combination of rewards and punishments. Of course we do not know (Acker and Van Houten, 1974, p.156).

A similar error of this kind was made by French and his colleagues in their now-classic participation studies. Lester Coch and John French carried out a study of a pyjama factory to study the effects of employee participation in decision-making on resistance to change. Their results – which indicated a positive relationship between participation and change – played an important role in influencing research into participation and 'democratic work climates' (Coch and French, 1948). Twelve years later French attempted, without success, to replicate the earlier findings (French et al, 1960). Various reasons were offered to explain the difference in results but not that the original study involved female employees and the replication study involved male employees: the male subjects were less willing to accept the legitimacy of participation schemes, were more attached to norms of restricted output and, as a result, working practices were not 'improved'.

Where organizational studies have taken gender into account they have done so in a way that has trivialized it. The work of Blauner (1967) provides a prime example. Studying workplace alienation, Blauner analyzed the statements of male and female workers in different ways. When dealing with men Blauner interprets their activities and responses as being primarily job related, that is, he uses a 'job's model' of analysis (Feldberg and Glenn, 1984). Thus, when men expressed discontent Blauner recorded this as valid expression of work-related dissatisfaction. When dealing with women Blauner interprets their activities and responses as being primarily related to their gender (but in the crudest biological sense), that is, he uses a 'gender model'. Thus, when women expressed discontent Blauner recorded this as being due to their "weaker physical stamina" and "family commitments."

In recent years a number of feminist studies have exposed the extent to which gender has been ignored in many of the leading studies of organization. Weber's theory of bureaucracy has been questioned for assuming that the underlying character of "rationality" is a universal, rather than a male-associated, characteristic (Martin, 1990). It has been argued that the male character of rationality explains why bureaucratic environments have served to inhibit female entry and opportunity (Ferguson, 1984: Morgan, 1988). Likewise, Crozier's (1964) study of bureaucracy has been challenged for ignoring gender in explaining organizational conflict (Acker and Van Houten, 1974): although the machine operators were women and the maintenance workers, on whom the operators depended, were men Crozier explained antagonisms between the groups in terms of bureaucratic structure. Herbert Simon's "bounded rationality" model of decision-making has been taken to task for ignoring the role of emotionality in organizational decisions (Mumby and Putnam, 1990), and Beynon and Blackburn's (1972) work has been criticized for using a gender model of explanation in determining female perceptions of work (Feldberg and Glenn, 1984). And doubt has been cast on the generalizability of the pioneering leadership studies of Lewin, Lippitt, and White (1978): the studies, which indicated that employee productivity could be improved by a "democratic style of leadership", were based on experiments with ten years old boys (Mills, 1988a).

Radical theories of organization have not been exempt from the problem of gender neglect. Allen's (1975) Marxist analysis of organizations, and Burrell and Morgan's (1979) radical critique of organization theory provides no references to 'men,' 'women,' 'sex,' or 'gender' in their indexes. Burawoy's (1979) contention that structure rather than gender determines workplace consent and resistance has been contested on the grounds that "gender matters not only for the structuring of the labour process, but also in interpersonal relations within the structure" (Davies, 1990). And Silverman's (1970) action frame of reference, which challenged functionalist theories of organization by stressing the importance of the actor's perceptions has been critiqued for its use of male reference points. Silverman, for example, argues that in understanding the worker we must see "his actions [...] as the outcome of his perceptions of the various options open to him and of which alternative best meets his priorities at the time". But, as Clegg and Dunkerley (1980:405) point out, this can also be applied to "her definitions, her actions, her perceptions of the various options open to her, and her priorities."

Finally, not only have women been ignored or marginalized within the various foci of research they have been ignored as researchers. Sheriff and Campbell (1992) point out that the work of Mary Parker Follett presaged the transition from the Scientific Management School to the Human Relations

School but there has been very little recognition of her pioneering role until very recently.

In summary, the neglect of gender by the great majority of organizational analysts has served to ignore some of the most crucial features of organizational life, led to an overlooking of organizational dynamics, contributed to the development of flawed methodologies and, by far the most damning aspect, has contributed to sexual discrimination in the workplace.

ISSUES IN SEX AND ORGANIZATIONAL RESEARCH

Despite the widespread and deep-rooted relationship between sex and organizations, research into that relationship has only begun to develop during the last decade. In this last section of the chapter we want to raise some issues for further research, indicate examples of the type of research that is underway, signal some of the conflicts involved in the research strategies involved, and to help you to understand better some of the problems involved in this area of research.

Throughout the chapter we have indicated the various issues involved in research into sex and organizations. These can be summed up under four broad headings – Equity Issues (including sexual discrimination, employment equity), Sexuality, Power and Authority Issues (including women in management, resistance, sexual harassment and abuse, sexual preference, workplace romance), Identity Issues (including notions of self, self worth, and self esteem) and Research Issues (including implications for research and for the researcher).

Equity Issues

The issue of employment equity is a political one. Sex discrimination legislation has been, since the mid-1970s, a growing reality throughout the western industrial nations[12] and yet things have moved slowly. This has prompted some researchers to examine the workplace for clues to the bases of sexual discrimination so that we might better understand how to bring about change. This research has gone in various directions. At one level there is a wealth of descriptive analysis detailing the extent of sexual discrimination in the workplace (Peitchinis, 1989). This is valuable in indicating the levels of inequities that exist and any trends or patterns of change. Research, at another level, is aimed at uncovering barriers to change.

Barriers to change

The direction of a research project depends on how the researcher views organization. To take four examples, organization is viewed as networks of communication, organizational cultures, systems of production or labour processes, and pathways to organizational careers.

Communication networks: some research focuses on the role of communication in inhibiting employment equity. Cava (1988), for example, focuses on effective male forms of communication to identify communicative strategies that will help women to be more effective in existing networks of communication. Cox (1986), on the other hand, is more interested in altering existing communication practices to ensure a successful "integration of women" into the organization. Cox identifies the problems for women of existing communicative strategies to encourage top management to alter their practices. Borisoff and Merrill (1985) develop this latter aspect by encouraging men and women at work to examine the nature of communicative strategies and their potential for effective organizational practice. In the process, they argue, people will find that some male-associated practices (e.g., interrupting) will be seen as ineffective and some (e.g., assertiveness) will be seen as effective; some female-associated practices (e.g., attentive listening) will be seen as effective and some (e.g., passivity) will be seen as ineffective. The aim is a fine mixture of effective male and female communication styles. Pearson's (1985) concern goes beyond the organization and is aimed at exposing the roots of gendered communication. Pearson argues that sexism in communications needs to be dealt with not only by weakening the hold of gendered practices in the workplace but also through fundamental changes in the way we socialize children.

In a different vein Meissner (1986), Putnam (1982, 1983, 1985), and Mills and Chiaramonte (1991) set out to reveal the role that communication plays in the construction of gender. Meissner argues that "communication reproduces dominance relations," indicating that inequities might be more effectively addressed through resistance to certain communicative practices. Putnam's research focuses on the socially constructed nature of organization and the centrality of communication to that process. Putnam (1982:7) argues that we can free ourselves from the taken for granted assumptions that inhibit equity by understanding, "The specific grammars, codes, and recipes that determine appropriate human behaviour in specific contexts." Mills and Chiaramonte takes this one step farther. They argue that we need to understand the concept and practice of organization that precede organizational communication. They contend that strategies aimed at inner-organizational communication alone will not get to the heart of inequities because the very concept of organization *per se* is deeply gendered. Thus, a more effective long-term strategy should be aimed at altering the way we think and do organizing.

Organizational culture: The organization as a culture is another way of viewing organizations. Ironically, given that gender is a culturally devised phenomenon, there is little research on the relationship between organizational culture and sexual discrimination. Hofstede's (1984) international study of workplace values was among the first to link the notion of gender with organizational culture. Hofstede argues that countries differ in the dominance of masculine values and that this can be correlated with equity factors in the workplace. Hofstede classifies countries into high or low "masculinity" (or MAS) according to the extent to which respondents (of both sexes) "tend to endorse goals usually more popular among men (high MAS) or among women (low MAS)". Hofstede found that countries with high MAS scores have lower numbers of women in professional and technical jobs. It is not clear, however, whether lowered masculinity factors lead to enhanced opportunities for women at work or vice versa.

Hostede's work draws on traditional notions of masculinity but the work of Smircich (1985) shifted attention towards feminist analysis of organizational culture, arguing that, "A feminist perspective on culture calls for analysis and critique of the underlying gender basis of the production of knowledge and the prevailing social order." Two Canadian studies that were conducted in a feminist vein were the Abella Commission Report (1984) and Nicole Morgan's (1988) study of the Canadian Federal Public Service; both focused attention on the significance of culture for employment opportunities. The Abella Commission pointed the way in their description of the problem as "systemic discrimination":

> Rather than approaching discrimination from the perspective of the single perpetrator and the single victim, the systemic approach acknowledges that by and large the systems and practices we customarily and often unwittingly adopt may have an unjustifiably negative effect on certain groups in society[...]

The Report goes on to argue that systemic patterns of discrimination have "two basic antecedents":

> a) a disparately negative impact that flows from the structure of systems designed for a homogeneous constituency and

b) a disparately negative impact that flows from practices based on stereotypical characteristics ascribed to an individual because of the characteristics ascribed to the group of which he or she is a member. The former usually results in a system designed for white, able-bodied males, the latter usually results in practices based on white able-bodied males' perceptions of everyone else (pp.9-19).

Morgan shows how prevailing social and political attitudes combine with organizational arrangements to create organizational cultures. Taking a broad view of the interrelationships between organizational and wider cultural factors, Morgan reveals how:

> some settings create possibilities for women to advance from entry-level to managerial positions while other settings have attempted to inhibit their advancement, or have relegated them to low-status, unskilled, part-time, and poorly paid jobs.

In a similar vein, Mills (1988a, 1988b) studies the combination of social and organizational features to examine the ways in which different rules of behaviour combine in the creation of an organizational culture and what the implications of different configurations are for sexual discrimination. Recent feminist accounts of organizational culture include Martin's (1990b) attempt to reveal the way in which male dominant culture suppresses evidence of gender conflicts, and Hood and Koberg's (1990) typology of female adaptation to the business organization and the associated psychological consequences of being "acculturated without being assimilated." Outside the OT literature excellent studies of women's resistance to male culture have been carried out by Pollert (1981), Lamphere (1985), and Benson (1988).

Labour processes: Cockburn (1985), Lowe (1987), and Tancred-Sheriff (1989) focus on the organization as a system of production or labour process. Cockburn's historical analysis of the development of techniques of production indicates that the process is deeply gendered – with men controlling technology. Techniques of production – passed on from male to male in a series of training situations – create knowledge, power and status in the workplace and make the possibility of employment equity impossible unless 'an autonomous women's movement inside and outside the trade unions can be created to develop women-only training and to transform the nature of technology and the relations of work'. Lowe's work shows how the different relation of women and men to production techniques facilitates processes of "deskilling" which have transformed types of work from male to female dominated and, in the process, created low-paid and unskilled jobs. Tancred-Sheriff focuses on issues of control and explores how different managements have used female sexuality to facilitate control over clients and consumers.

Organizational pathways: Focusing on individual 'pathways' to organizational careers Gutek and Larwood (1987) and Brindley and Frick (1990) study successful women (and men). They collect information on the ways that women have become successful to understand how existing barriers can be breached by the next wave of female aspirants. Kanter (1977) takes a totally different approach by focusing on the organization as a structure and concluding that structural factors rather than gender differences account for much of the perceived difference between men and women at work. Kanter urges management to restructure in ways that can allow fuller opportunities to men and women.

Sex, Power, and Authority issues

Within OT research much of the focus on gender has been on the problem of (an absence of) women in management. This has generated an extensive literature of its own. The work of Gutek and Larwood (1987), and Brindley and Frick (1990) are examples of this kind of focus. Much of the women in management (WIM) research mirrors the broader inequities literature in attempting to describe and analyze barriers to women's entry into management. This literature has focused on the improvement of women within current hierarchical arrangements. For example, Morrison et al (1987) in the U.S., and Agócs (1989) in Canada identify ways that women might "break the glass ceiling" into top managerial positions. Within this frame research evaluates the role of mentors (Burke and McKeen, 1988), sex role stereotyping (Schein, 1989), leadership style (Rowney and Cahoon, 1988), stress (Beatty, 1991), and the impact of family (Lee, 1991).

Much of the WIM literature is rooted in a 'sex differences' approach which focuses on the difference between men and women (as essential categories of person). Radical challenges to the WIM framework have come from Sheppard (1989) and Hearn and Parkin (1987) who take a 'gender focused' approach. From this perspective the focus is on the ways that persons become seen as men and women and it is argued that the very issues of management and leadership themselves need to be questioned because they are as 'gendered as they are problematic'.

The WIM literature focuses on **positions** of power and authority but few studies take up the issue of the **exercise** of power and authority. From outside the WIM literature, Pollert (1981), Collinson (1988), Sheppard (1989) and Davies (1990) draw attention to the ways in which sexuality is used as a form of control, and Mills and Murgatroyd (1991) take up the issue of resistance to gendered organizational control – showing that women are not passive recipients of male notions of their value and worth.

The biggest area of research into sexuality and power in organizations is focused on sexual harassment but a growing body of work is concerned with the relationship between sexuality and organizational outcomes. The literature of sexual harassment is far ranging and includes descriptive accounts (Cooper, 1985); analysis of 'sex-role spillover' that is, the extent to which people's non-work sex roles (husband/wife father/mother) influence work roles (Gutek and Cohen, 1992), and the relationship between sexuality and power (DiTomaso, 1989).

Other areas of sexuality research have looked at the relationship between work practices and masculinity, for example, the ways that men are expected to act at work if they are to be accepted as "real men" (Collinson and Collinson, 1989), the contribution of organizational factors to the construction of particular types of sexuality (Hearn and Parkin, 1987), for example, the way women are expected to be caring as nurses but 'sexy' as flight attendants; the impact of notions of sexuality on the way certain organizations have come to be constructed (Burrell, 1984; Ranke-Heinemann, 1991), for example, the introduction of celibacy into the Catholic Church in the twelfth century; the contribution of organizations to acceptable images of sexual preference (Schneider, 1982, 1984; Hall, 1989), for example, the exclusion of homosexuality from organizational life; the use of sexuality as a means of organizational control (Pollert, 1981), for example, the use of paternalist language by managers to control female employees; and the impact of masculinity on organizational development (Maier, 1991), for example, the dominance of aggressiveness or competitiveness as expected forms of organizational behaviour.

Race/Ethnicity and Sexuality: the relationship between sexuality, race/ethnicity, and organizational life has been greatly under-researched. The work of Bell (1989) in the U.S., and Mighty (1991) in Canada are rare attempts to study these relationships through a focus on black women. Little or nothing has been done on Hispanic (Zavella, 1985, and Calas, 1992 are rare examples), Chinese, south Asian (Wallis, 1988) or native women.

Identity Issues

A relatively new area of research deals with the impact of organizational arrangements on gender and sense of identity. As opposed to earlier research which focused primarily on the impact of sexist work practices on women's sense of self worth (Cooper and Davidson, 1982), this newer research is concerned with the impact of organization on the construction of a person's sexual identity, attempting to uncover the extent to which notions of "male/female," "masculine/feminine" are created by the organizational context (Leonard, 1984; Hearn and Parkin, 1987; Livingstone and Luxton, 1989; Mills, 1991).

Research Issues

Gender focused research has helped to reveal some of the problems of the research act itself; as Acker and Van Houten's (1974) work indicates, sex is a research issue as well as a focus. The situation of male researcher and female subject is problematic. The male researcher all too often represents one more male authority figure and as such is in a powerful position vis-à-vis the female subject. Hearn and Parkin (1983) have responded to this question in part by combining the research efforts of a male and a female researcher. Hearn (1985) urges, "men concerned about sexism" to study male environments with the aim of unearthing the ways in which men "control and fix'" those environments to the detriment of women. Similarly Maier (1991) advocates work with males to help men see that they too have a "self-interest in promoting gender equity."

The relationship of male researcher to female subjects is also problematic in terms of methodology. A number of female researchers have argued that a feminist approach to women in organizations needs to be rooted in the experiences of being a woman, and thus it is problematic if not impossible for a man to get at understandings born of a particular set of gendered experiences. This viewpoint is not uncontested and it has raised several questions. For example, if it is not possible for a man to understand a woman is it possible for female researchers to understand male experiences except through the impact of those experiences on women? If gender is a phenomenon of males and females then cannot men and women equally be involved in gender research? If gender is a cultural phenomenon, and men and women social constructs, then isn't it contrary logic to exclude some persons from gender research because they are men? If, however, men are able to talk to the experiences of women doesn't that add to the furtherance of a male dominance in which women's sense of self is always being defined for them? These are difficult questions which are far from resolved.

The relationship of female researcher to female subject is also problematic if the research supports the existing male dominant character of organizations. Tancred-Sheriff and Campbell (1992) take issue with leading female researchers whose work, they argue, has lent itself to managerialism.

From feminist research outside OT two bits of fundamental advice are worth noting. Kirby and McKenna (1989) argue that the self – the gendered self – cannot and should not be divorced from the research act. Examination of self will help to keep in front of the researcher her or his own gendered nature and biases. Stanley and Wise (1983) argue that to reduce the power relationship between researcher and subject the researcher needs to work fully with groups of persons to develop a research strategy, that the research strategy should arise out of the needs, concerns, and perceptions of the group itself.

KEY TERMS

authority	**employment equity**	*femininity*
gender focused research	*masculinity*	*power*
sex based power	**sex differences research**	**sexual harassment**
sexual preference	**sexuality**	**systemic discrimination**

REVIEW QUESTIONS

Q1. Define sexuality.

Assignment: Check the definition of sexuality in the introduction of this chapter.

[FS: To improve your understanding of the term read and compare the definitions from the following articles and book chapters – Burrell (1984), p.98 Hearn and Parkin (1987), pp.53-58 Mills (1989), pp.30-33].

Q2. What is the relationship between sex, organization, and power?

Assignment: Read through your diary notes for exercise 5.1., and write brief notes on the following: a) compared with when you first completed the exercise, how would you now assess the role and extent of sexuality in your organization? b) what general conclusions do you draw about the relationship between sexuality, organizations, and power? and c) if you had to re-peat the exercise what, if anything, would you do differently, and why?

Q3. What are some of the main research issues involved in studying sex at work?

Assignment: Write short notes on each of the following problem areas: (i) methodology, (ii) definition, and (iii) understanding barriers to change. Compare your answer with the discus-sion in this chapter.

[FS: Read Hearn and Parkin (1987), Chapter 1, and (i) note down the main points identified as problem areas, and (ii) comment on each point, stating how it might be dealt with].

Q4. What is the difference between a "sex differences" and a "gender fo-cused" approach to research?

Assignment: Compare your answer with the definitions in the 'Sex, Power and Authority Issues' section of this chapter.

[FS: Read and contrast the following two studies of gender and leadership – Hearn and Parkin (1988) and Harriman (1985, Chapter 9). Write short notes on five major differences between each approach].

Q5. What part do masculinity and femininity play in organizational life?

Assignment: Compare your answer with the discussion throughout this chapter.

[FS: For a deeper analysis of the question read Mills and Murgatroyd (1991: Chapter 4)].

Q6. How can the study of sexuality and organizations help us to understand (a) sexual preference and (b) race/ethnicity at work?

Assignment: Compare your answer with the discussion throughout this chapter.

[FS: (i) Read Quinn (1977) and Hall (1989): what are the main similarities and differ-ences between the two approaches?

(ii) Read Cox (1986): how do you think this study would differ if the focus had been on women of colour?].

Q7. Briefly define each of the following terms, and say how each might in-fluence the way organizations operate:
employment equity

systemic discrimination

sexual discrimination

sexual harassment

Assignment: Now turn back to the chapter and compare your definitions.

EXERCISE 5.1

This exercise is designed to help you to arrive at your own conclusions about the nature of the relationship between sexuality, organization, and power.

For this exercise you will need a notebook to serve as a diary:

A. Power, Authority and Gender Divisions.

Find out the sex composition (i.e., relative numbers of men and women) of (i) your university/college administration, (ii) the faculty as a whole, (iii) the faculty in which you are studying. Note down the results in your diary, and leave space for comments. Over the next week note down – one way or another – any events, actions, or policies that suggest to you that the sex composition of the authority structure has/has not a significant influence on the life of the organization.

B. Observations.

Over the period of a week keep a diary of your observations within the university or college. Try to observe as many aspects of college life that you can:

• Note down the graffiti from the toilet walls – does it tell you anything about some people's concern with sexuality?

• Look at notice boards – can you learn anything from the types of events and activities that are advertised? For example, how many of the activities encourage direct participation by men and women equally? How many activities are sex-typed, i.e., for men or for women only?

• Read the student newspaper, and sum up the extent to which it reflects sexual concerns.

• Look through the university or college calendar – count the photographs and note down the respective percentages that include males and which include females; compare the number of photographs of men and women in which the person in depicted in a passive role, e.g., sitting, observing, and those which depict an authoritative role e.g., lecturing, administrating, directing, etc.

• At the various break, arrival and departure times spend time reflecting upon the conversations around you. Note down your thoughts. How much of the discussion revolves around things sexual? To what extent do you think they have a bearing on any of the other activities of the college?

• Observe relationships – both inside and out of the classroom. How are people relating to each other? Is there a sexual dimension and, if so, what role do you think it plays in the way things are organized or done?

• Pay attention to issues of sexual preference. To what extent to any or all of the things you note down reflect a concern with heterosexuality?

At the end of the week's observing write down some general conclusions about the role and extent of sexuality in your institution.

FURTHER READING

An overview of issues of sexuality:
Jeff Hearn & Wendy Parkin (1987) 'SEX' AT 'WORK'
J. Hearn et al (1989) THE SEXUALITY OF ORGANIZATION

Barbara A. Gutek (1985) SEX AND THE WORK-PLACE

An overview of issues of gender and organization theory:
A.J. Mills & P. Tancred [eds] (1992) GENDERING ORGANIZATIONAL ANALYSIS

END NOTES

1. "Hospital in red paid ex-lover to stay home", William Marsden, The Gazette, June 8th, 1989 edition. Despite the fact that the story is public we have used pseudonyms throughout to spare the victim further unease.

2. Oakley (1972) makes this distinction but Rakow (1986) argues that 'sex', itself, is a socially constructed concept and should be considered part of the concept of gender.

3. In 1980 a successful complaint to the Ontario Human Rights Commission forced the Stelco steelworks in Hamilton to recruit females. A major study of the changes in the industry found that a number of male steelworkers felt their 'manhood' as well as their jobs to be under threat due to the entry of women

into the industry (Livington & Luxton, 1989).

4. The Canadian airline Wardair is a prime example of this form of advertising that reached deep into its recruitment practices. In the late 1980s the airline was the subject of a Canadian Human Rights Commission case. The company was accused of recruiting only attractive, slim, and young women, who were then required to follow a set of company rules which dictated how they were to look – from their make-up right down to their underwear.

5. In recent years it has become evident that sexual abuse is also a feature of some organizations. In the late 1980s Canada was rocked by a series of revelations about the sexual abuse of children in orphanages, churches, and reform schools. For example, in Ontario

six members of a Roman Catholic order were charged with physical and sexual assaults against former students at Ontario reform schools, and in New-foundland eight priests were tried for the sexual abuse of children at the Mount Cashel orphanage in St. John's.

6. See Hall (1989).

7. From the Bulletin of the Canadian Association of University Teachers, April, 1991, Vol.38, No.4., p.13 of the "Status of Women Supplement".

8. The authors cite a ceremony by the University of Toronto engineering students which involved an assault on a life-size inflated female doll. In 1990 there were similar incidents at the University of Alberta which led to the setting up of an enquiry. In one incident engineering students put on a "skit-night" at which some of the males were said to have shouted at a female student, "shoot the bitch", a remark which – following the shooting deaths of the fourteen female students at the Montreal Polytechnique in December 1989 – was in unusually poor taste. Another incident involved a student newspaper – *The Bridge* – which made crude remarks about the city's female Mayor.

9. More recently, in 1990, the University of Calgary reprimanded a group of male medical faculty members after several female students had make similar complaints about the use of jokes and anti-women examples in the classroom.

10. In 1991 the women's studies programme at the University of Lethbridge came under attack from a male physical education professor who publicly called on the University to re-evaluate its support for the programme. Describing the development of women's studies programmes in Canadian universities as a "cancerous growth", the professor argued that 'such programmes are for the promulgation of radical feminist ideas rather than objective scientific research'. The professor failed to take issue with such "objective" programmes as management, theology, history, or physical education!

11. See Dagg and Thompson, (1988).

12. In the UK there are the Equal Pay (1970) and Sex Discrimination (1975, 1986) Acts; in the U.S. the Equal Pay Act (1963) and provisions against sex discrimination in the 1964 Civil Rights Act; and in Canada a 1984 Royal Commission on Equity in Employment led to the Employment Equity Act (1986).

CHAPTER 6

Out of Sight, Out of Mind: Race, Ethnicity and Organization Theory

This chapter examines the increasing significance of race and ethnicity in modern organizations. It begins by looking at some of the barriers which have excluded minorities from a full participation and representation in the dominant institutions of Canadian society, and shows how these barriers have a long historical legacy in this country.

The chapter then proceeds to trace developments in public policy and academic theory as these relate to ethnic and race relations in Canada. This is followed by an analysis of the treatment of race and ethnicity in studies of organizations, with an examination of the influence of assimilationism, and the predominance of the ethnicity paradigm in the literature of organizational theory and research.

The chapter concludes with an assessment of the contemporary backlash against minority rights, including current political and ideological attacks on multiculturalism and other programs for equality rights.

October 20th, 1983. Proceedings of the Special Committee on the Participation of Visible Minorities in Canadian Society.

> *Mr. Aziz Khaki, President, Committee for Racial Justice of British Columbia, gives testimony. He states that there is widespread employment discrimination against non-White Canadians:*
>
> *"Let me give you an example", he states. "At Simon Fraser University every year we get a number of banks and chartered accountant firms who come to recruit graduates from commerce, from economics, from business administration. Unfortunately, the acceptance rates of the non-Whites, the visible minority, has been almost*

An ethnic group is one defined primarily on the basis of cultural criteria: a human group whose members share common ties of nationality, language, or religion. Sometimes the term "ethnic" may be used to distinguish those groups in society which differ from the dominant majority group, only in language, religion or nationality, but not in physical appearance. Thus, White, non-Anglophone immigrant groups in Canada (Italians, Poles, Germans, etc.) are defined as "ethnic", but not as "racial", groups.

A racial group is one that distinguishes itself, or is distinguished by other groups, in terms of its physical appearance such as skin colour, hair texture, or some other arbitrary physical characteristic which may be used as a basis of social distinction. In common usage, "racial" groups are "non-White" groups, or what are often referred to as "visible minorities" or as "people of colour".

A minority group is a group which occupies a subordinate, or relatively powerless position in society, and is often subject to the control or domination of other, more powerful groups. Minority groups are defined primarily in terms of their lack of power in relation to other groups, and may include visible minorities (i.e., racial groups) or gender minorities (women, gays) among others.

zero in many areas. They are told the average grade point cutoff […] you must have a minimum of 3.5 and even if they have 3.7 they are told: 'Oh, we are looking for someone who has a personality'. By personality you really do not know whether they are looking at the colour of your skin or your height or your breadth or they are looking at whether you speak English without an accent or you use symbols to which those people are accustomed, and this is where we feel that some sort of a definite affirmative action is required.

Let me quote another example, and I hope you will bear with me. Last year we had an advertisement by the CBC, the B.C. region […] and we had billboards all over the province: beautiful, good-looking, seven to eight faces on the billboard. We see eyes and ears. Not one of those faces shown there was the face of a non-White. This makes you feel that there is reinforcement to say: This is a white man's country." (From the minutes of the Proceedings and Evidence, Issue #16).

How important are the topics of race and ethnicity to the study of organizations?[1] If you look over the table of contents of any of the major OT textbooks, you may be forgiven for concluding that these topics are of no great importance at all to organizational studies. Most of these texts make little or no reference to non-White, non-Anglophone individuals, or to individuals whose national origins are different from the mainstream White Anglo-Saxon Protestant culture.

Blauner (1972) has distinguished between what he calls "immigrant minorities" of European background who came voluntarily to the U.S., and have been successfully assimilated into American society; and "colonized minorities" of non-European background – Aboriginals, Blacks, Chinese, Mexicans, etc. – who were forcibly incorporated into American society through conquest and colonization, and have remained marginalized and disadvantaged. There is, in other words, an important difference in the way that White and non-White peoples entered the New World.

Yet clearly, the topics of race and ethnicity continue to be of great importance in plural societies, such as Canada and the U.S., the populations of which have been drawn from a variety of different racial, ethnic and national backgrounds[2]. Indeed, the very history of these New World societies has been the history of different population groups who have been thrown together through the processes of immigration and colonization[3].

Unfortunately, the history of racial and ethnic relations in Canada and the U.S. has frequently been characterized by conflict and inequality, and even violence. Racial intolerance is nothing new in Canada and can be traced back to the earliest period of settlement and colonization.

Chinese immigrants, for example, were subjected to discriminatory head taxes around the turn of the twentieth century, and were later completely prohibited from entering Canada during the years 1923-1947, under the Chinese Immigration (Exclusion) Act. Another example of early racial discrimination in Canada was that practised against the Black Loyalists who emigrated from the U.S. to Nova Scotia after 1776, and who were refused land grants which had been promised them in return for their support of the Crown. There is no shortage of other examples of racial intolerance in Canada. The summary internment and confiscation of the personal property of Japanese Canadians during World War Two; the colonial administration of the aboriginal peoples under the Indian Act – including denial of their voting rights until 1960; the refusal of landing rights to Jewish political refugees from Nazi Germany and of East Indian passengers of the Komagata Maru in 1914; are only some of the more shameful cases of officially sanctioned racial intolerance in this country.

In addition to the particular history of racial discrimination against non-White groups, however, there have been numerous other examples of ethnic discrimination against "foreign" White immigrants in Canada. The historical reluctance of English Canadians to acknowledge the legitimate language and cultural rights of French Canadians, both inside and outside of Quebec, contributed to the long-term inequality of Francophones in terms of their educational rights, employment opportunities and cultural development.

Other ethnic groups have, at different times, also experienced prejudice and discrimination at the hands of the Anglophone majority, including such groups as Ukrainians, Italians, and others once classified as "non-preferred" immigrants. The history of many ethnic groups in Canada, therefore, has been marked by struggles for greater justice and equality within the institutions and organizations of the majority culture.

In Canada today, there can be little doubt that racism – prejudice and discrimination directed against an individual's physical differences from the majority culture – has become a serious national problem. And while racism is nothing new in Canadian society, its periodic re-emergence during times of economic crisis has always resulted in increased tensions in race relations.

As the opening quotation also shows, racism may be perceived in the media, especially when non-Whites appear to be excluded from any positive representation. For many visible minority people, the mass media have sometimes reinforced the impression that the dominant image of Canada remains that of a White Man's country. In the words of one observer,

> Advertising simply reflects what is true about the entire Canadian attitude towards mass communication – namely, WHITE SELLS. The President of Labatt actually said these very words, when he was asked why there were no non-Whites in his company's commercials, (quoted in *Equality Now*, 1984;91).

Since the mid 1980s, and following from some of the recommendations contained in the Report of the Special Committee on the Participation of Visible Minorities in Canadian Society entitled, Equality Now, the picture seems to have improved somewhat. Today, it is not uncommon to see news reporters on the major television networks who are members of visible minority groups.

However, notwithstanding the democratization of some forms of advertising, such as departmental store catalogues, soft drink and fast food commercials, there are still some industry hold-outs. For the brewery industry, as for the tobacco industry, it appears as though the maxim, WHITE SELLS, still continues to hold true.

Besides the issue of media representation, however, employment is another area where racism is often experienced by visible minority Canadians. Many organizations have refused to accredit the overseas qualifications and experience of Third World immigrants, (and sometimes of White immigrants, as well), thereby forcing these immigrants either to obtain Canadian qualifications, or to accept unskilled, or underskilled forms of employment. Non-Whites have also found that their access to promotion and career mobility may be blocked by subtle forms of prejudice and discrimination within the organization; although as Beattie (1975) has shown, other minorities, including Francophones, may also experience some of these barriers to occupational mobility. In some cases, non-Whites have been excluded from employment where they would be highly visible to a largely White clientele[4].

Further dramatic evidence of employment discrimination was uncovered in a Toronto study conducted several years ago (Henry and Ginzberg, 1985) in which equally matched Black and White job applicants (who were actually professional actors) were compared in terms of their success in obtaining employment. The result of this study showed that there is a considerable amount of racial discrimination in hiring practices. Discrimination typically involved a Black applicant being told that a job was filled, while half an hour later, the White applicant was invited to fill out an application. Black applicants were often treated discourteously, while White applicants were treated with warmth and encouragement. When both telephone and in-person contacts were combined, the overall ration of discrimination was three-to-one, that is, Whites had three job prospects to every one for Blacks with equal qualifications. There is no reason to believe that these discriminatory practices are peculiar to Toronto; to a greater or lesser extent, they are typical of every large Canadian city.

These, and similar studies, have tended to confirm the experiences of many visible minority people that preference is normally given to White candidates in most fields of employment in Canada today. Non-White applicants have traditionally suffered job discrimination for a number of different reasons – e.g., non-Canadian citizenship, no Canadian training and educational credentials, poor English or French language skills, etc. – which, taken together, have constituted a formidable set of obstacles to the career aspirations of many visible minority immigrants to Canada. And while some of these reasons may have also been used to discriminate against other less visible immigrants from European backgrounds, it is only non-White immigrants who have felt the full force of racial as well as cultural discrimination in Canada. The reality of this picture of systemic, or institutional discrimination against visible minorities was already acknowledged in a 1982 Federal Government Report which recommended that some remedial action be taken to end the informal colour-bar which has continued to operate in the Canadian job market:

> [T]raditionally most firms have regarded the white non-disabled man as the desired worker for most positions aside from those traditionally regarded as women's work. Employment practices have consequently evolved based on the physical and cultural attributes of this favoured typed of worker, placing other workers and job applicants at a disadvantage regardless of their abilities and qualifications. Over time, these practices have been so greatly accepted and deeply embedded in the customary processes of the organization that they are seldom questioned or altered (Canada Employment and Immigration Commission, Affirmative Action Technical Training Manual, Ottawa, 1982;34).

There can be little doubt, therefore, that the topic of ethnicity is of burning interest to the study of organizations. Without some knowledge of how different ethnic and racial groups are represented in the labour force, in the education system, in law enforcement statistics, in housing surveys, and in other strategic areas of public life, an important part of our picture of Canadian society and its institutions is missing. More specifically, by excluding the topic of ethnicity from organizational studies, and thus rendering the experiences of visible minority people invisible (and inaudible), we are all the more tempted to succumb to the myth of Canadian tolerance: that racism is something you find in the United States and Great Britain, but not here in Canada.

NOW TURN TO EXERCISE 6.1 AT THE END OF THE CHAPTER.

THE POLITICALIZATION OF RACE AND ETHNIC RELATIONS

Studies of race and ethnicity in Canada have remained closely influenced by government policy, and by the debates and controversies which have frequently surrounded major changes of policy. Over the past several decades, but especially since the 1960s, the Canadian government has focused on three broad areas of concern in the field of race and ethnic relations policy: Francophone-Anglophone relations, Immigration and Multiculturalism, and Indian Affairs. Together, these areas have encompassed the major priorities of government policy, and are representative of much of the academic research undertaken on the topics of race and ethnicity in recent years.

The Evolution of Government Policy

One of the landmark events in the study of ethnicity in Canada was the creation of the Royal Commission on Biculturalism and Bilingualism (B&B) in 1965. This Commission was set up to inquire into the continuing separation of Francophone and Anglophone communities in Canada, and to examine the implications of this split for national unity. Some of the recommendations contained in the Report of the B&B Commission were later adopted by the Liberal government of the day, and became the basis for the Official Languages Act which, for the first time in Canadian history, established both French and English as official languages of the Federal government and its agencies. Beyond these immediate ramifications for Federal policy, however, the B&B Report provided a major incentive for further research into Francophone-Anglophone relations in this country, an initiative which has resulted in a growing proliferation of such studies.

The B&B Commission report also opened the door to further studies of other ethnic groups in Canada. With the publication in 1969 of Book IV entitled *The Cultural Contribution of other Ethnic Groups*, a political climate was created to extend to non-charter ethnic groups (i.e., groups other than English and French) some public recognition of their importance in Canadian society. This recognition was further reinforced in 1971, when the then–Prime Minister Trudeau formally introduced the policy of Multiculturalism[5]. The declared intent of this policy was to provide official recognition and support to those ethnic groups who sought to preserve their distinctive cultural heritages and ethnic identities within the framework of a pluralistic society. This aspect of the B&B Commission report inspired a new wave of research into the status of non-charter ethnic groups in Canada.

If bilingualism was the Federal government's answer to demands for Quebec sovereignty, Multiculturalism was its answer to the demand of non-charter groups for greater recognition and respect. It seemed, at the time, a neat and elegant solution to the problem of how everyone fitted into Canadian society.[6]

Over the past three decades, other events have also led to a renewal of interest in the study of Canadian ethnic and race relations. In 1974, for example, the Federal government released its Green Paper on Immigration and Population, a document which was intended to serve as a discussion paper for a national review of Canadian immigration policy. While the Green Paper proved to be a controversial document, it contributed to a renewed interest in studies of non-White, (i.e., visible minority), immigrants in Canada. Although certain parts of the Green Paper presented a highly provocative (many would say, irresponsible) discussion of Third World immigration to Canada, in its own way it also motivated a new wave of Canadian ethnic studies into the status of visible minority groups. This tradition was further strengthened in 1984 with the publication of the Report of the Special Committee on the Participation of Visible Minorities in Canadian Society. The Report, entitled *Equality Now*, provided a contemporary picture of race relations in Canada focused on the problems of institutional racism, and on measures for addressing and alleviating these problems.

In addition to *Equality Now*, another report appeared in 1984 which addressed the issues of institutionalized discrimination against minority groups, including women, visible minorities, Native peoples and the physically handicapped. This was the Report of the Commission on Equality in Employment which examined the particular problems of job discrimination. A number of recommendations for programs of affirmative action, (or what in Canada are more commonly referred to as programs of employment equity), were also contained in this report.

Since the publication of these reports, several significant pieces of legislation have been passed[7].

The other major area of ethnic studies in Canada, of course, has been that of Native studies. In 1966-67, a landmark study of Native peoples was published entitled *A Survey of Contemporary Indians in Canada*. Commissioned by the then-Department of Indian Affairs, this report became known as the Hawthorn Report, after its primary author Harry Hawthorn. It has remained to this day the singular, most comprehensive report on the status of Indian people in Canada, and has drawn much attention to the problems of poverty, unemployment and general neglect which have long confronted so many Native communities across this country. Two years later, in 1969, the Federal government released a White Paper on Indian Policy entitled *Statement of the Government of Canada on Indian Policy*. This document, which advocated among other things the repeal of the Indian Act, the abolition of the Department of Indian Affairs, the termination of universal aid programs, and the ending of any special status for Indians, was met with almost universal opposition from all Native communities across the country. In the face of this opposition, the White Paper was withdrawn in the Spring of 1971, and none of its recommendations were ever implemented. The defeat of the White Paper marked the end of an era: from this point on, it would no longer be possible for any Federal government to pursue an overt policy of forcible assimilation of Native peoples.

More recently, the former Federal conservative government of Brian Mulroney established a Royal Commission on Aboriginal affairs. This is the first comprehensive survey of Indians in Canada to be commissioned since the Hawthorn Report of 1966-67[8].

These, then, are some of the landmark studies of ethnic and racial minority groups in Canada which were completed over the past three decades. Together, they help to define the big picture of race and ethnic relations in Canada, and the political context in which these studies were undertaken.

Academic Theory

In Canada, as we have seen, studies of race and ethnicity have traditionally been related to three major areas of concern for Canadian public life: Francophone-Anglophone relations, Immigration and Multiculturalism, and Native Peoples. These concerns have helped to chart the course of much of the work which has been done in the area of race and ethnic studies in Canada. However, unlike their American counterparts, most Canadian scholars have not been strongly motivated by the ideology of assimilationism and integration.[9] In matters of race and ethnicity, Canadians have traditionally distinguished themselves quite sharply from their American cousins; in place of the melting pot, Canadian society has more often been seen as an ethnic mosaic which, for over two decades now, has been influenced by the government policy of Multiculturalism.

One of the most influential studies of ethnic relations ever to be published in Canada was that undertaken by the sociologist John Porter in *The Vertical Mosaic* (1965). This study, which was developed as a critique of the dominant model of ethnic (or cultural) pluralism in Canada, established a critical framework for Canadian ethnic studies, and set the direction of subsequent research for many years to come.

In his study, Porter documents the extent of ethnic inequality in Canada through an analysis of census data covering a twenty-five year period from 1931-1951. Porter found that there were major inequalities between different ethnic groups in terms of their average levels of income, education and occupation. According to Porter's research, Canadians of British background tended to be overrepresented in the higher socioeconomic strata, while Canadians of Southern and Eastern European backgrounds fell consistently into the bottom of the social class structure. These, and other findings, led Porter to question the value of the policies of ethnic pluralism in Canada, (or what later came to be called, Multiculturalism), and to challenge the image of Canada as an "ethnic mosaic". Although the passage of more than a quarter of a century has necessarily dated the conclusions of this analysis, it remains unsurpassed as a comprehensive study of Canadian society in which the fundamental themes of ethnicity and social class are analyzed in the classical sociological tradition.

According to John Porter, therefore, Canada has always been an hierarchically-organized society in which there has been very little mobility from one socioeconomic level to another. Different ethnic groups, because of their different entrance statuses, became trapped into segregated occupations within the labour force. The highest positions in the structures of wealth and power were occupied by those of British decent, followed by those from Northern and Western Europe. Those from Eastern and Southern Europe occupied the lower levels of the stratification system, while those of French-Canadian and Native descent found themselves at the very bottom of the social pyramid. This is why Porter referred to Canadian society as a "vertical mosaic": a society made up of a mosaic of different ethnic groups, but rigidly arranged in a vertical hierarchy of wealth and power.

Since the appearance of *The Vertical Mosaic* in 1965, there have been other studies of ethnicity, class and social mobility in Canada, although none has equalled the breadth and scope of Porter's original study. The general conclusion of many of these studies has been that the structure of ethnic relations in Canada is characterized by a much greater degree of social mobility than was indicated in Porter's research (cf. Heap, 1974; Tepperman, 1975; Pineo, 1976; Darroch, 1979; Lautard and Loree, 1984). While British and American groups have remained overrepresented at the top of the socioeconomic system in comparison to groups from other ethnic backgrounds, these differences have tended to diminish over several generations. Other ethnic groups have not, for the most part, remained trapped in their original entrance statuses as Porter had concluded. Over a period of several generations, the rate of social mobility within many of these ethnic communities has begun to approach the Canadian norm. This does not invalidate Porter's evidence of an Anglo-American domination of the system of ethnic stratification in Canada, but it does suggest that the system displays a much greater degree of social mobility than he had acknowledged.

However, as other researchers have pointed out, evidence that the stratification of traditional ethnic groups has diminished does not mean that ethnicity is now no longer related to socioeconomic status in Canada. It only means that the inequalities that Porter observed have progressively declined. But it should be remembered that Porter's analysis was based largely on the comparative status of White ethnic groups – that is, those of European descent – whether from continental Europe, or from Britain or the United States. This limitation of Porter's "ethnicity model" prevented him from analyzing the social status of long-established non-White racial groups in Canada, rendering them "invisible subjects" of Canadian ethnic studies.

Since 1967, however, with the introduction of the universal points system, there has been a spectacular increase in the percentage of immigrants originating from non-European source areas. Based on the evidence of this "new immigration", more recent studies have shown that although many of these new immigrants (from the Caribbean, India, Hong Kong, the Philippines, etc.) came to Canada with higher levels of education than their previous European counterparts of the 1950s and early 1960s (those from Italy, Spain, Portugal, Greece, etc.), many often have difficulty in obtaining employment commensurate with their higher education and qualifications. This is because many visible minority immigrants face problems of prejudice and discrimination in the workplace which seriously impede their occupation mobility, and trap them into lower paying job ghettos. Indeed, the notable disparity between the earnings and the educational attainments of many non-European immigrants in Canada has led some researchers to conclude that the institutionalized ethnic discrimination faced by the earlier generation of European immigrants (which has all but disappeared as a significant social force)[10] has now been replaced by an institutionalized racial discrimination against the current generation of Third World immigrants (cf. Ramcharan, 1982; Satzewich and Li, 1987; Li, 1988).

Public Reaction and Debate

If the political climate of the 1970s and 1980s proved more responsive to the concerns of racial and ethnic minorities in Canada than in earlier decades, this momentum appears to have ground to a halt in the 1990s.

The ascendancy of a neo-conservative agenda in many parts of the country, preoccupied with the politics of the debt crisis, has already begun to threaten the Multicultural vision of Canadian society, and the public consensus upon which this vision depended.

Today, there are numerous indications of the growing unease with which many Canadians seem to view present policies of Multiculturalism [11]. In a national public opinion survey undertaken during the Winter/Spring of 1990-91, the Citizen's Forum on National Unity, chaired by Keith Spicer, reported that a significant proportion of its informants and respondents were critical of how policies of Multiculturalism had been administered. Many people believed that Multiculturalism had become an unnecessary extravagance which the nation could no longer afford at a time of economic recession.

Others had more pointed criticisms which reflected a belief that Multiculturalism increasingly favoured the rights of ethnic minority groups over those of the dominant cultural majority. During the past couple of years, several well-publicized cases may have served to reinforce some of these anxieties and frustrations. Among many Canadians, for example, the decision to permit the wearing of turbans by Sikh officers, or the wearing of braids by Aboriginal officers in the RCMP, was an unpopular one. Rather than welcoming these changes as evidence of the removal of cultural barriers to the recruitment of minority groups into the Federal law enforcement service, many Canadians appeared to see these changes as unreasonable concessions to the pressures of visible minority communities. Similarly, plans announced by some public school trustees to allow baptized Sikh students to wear kirpans, (that is, ceremonial daggers) in public schools aroused opposition and protest in some quarters[12]. For many Canadians, these and other measures which were designed to enable ethnic minorities to fully participate in the institutions of Canadian society without necessarily having to sacrifice their own traditions – particularly when the maintenance of these traditions was seen as a matter of religious conscience – have not always evoked sympathy or understanding. In fact, as the political platform of the Reform Party now demonstrates, as well as other fringe parties of the right (such as the Confederation of Regions Party), Multiculturalism and Bilingualism, have become popular political targets[13].

Even some scholars have expressed misgivings about the role of Multiculturalism in Canadian public life. In a recent book entitled *Mosaic Madness*, sociologist Reginald Bibby has lamented what he sees as some of the more unfortunate consequences of Multiculturalism. He suggest that Multiculturalism has contributed to a destructive relativism and individualism in the attitudes of many Canadians. Because of the need to extend legitimacy to a diversity of cultural viewpoints, Bibby suggests that we have lost sight of any overriding common vision which would serve as a basis for national unity and integration.

> To encourage individual mosaic fragments may well result in the production of individual mosaic fragments – and not much more. The multiculturalism assumption – that a positive sense of one's group will lead to tolerance and respect of other groups – has not received strong support, notes McGill University sociologist Morton Weinfeld. The evidence, he says, "suggests a kind of ethnocentric effect, so that greater preoccupation with one's own group makes one more distant from and antipathetic to others." [...] If we view Canadian society as a group of cultures that coexist like tiles in an art piece, we have nothing but parts beside parts. Socially, such a view translates into mosaic madness [...], Bibby, 1990:10;177.

Bibby is also concerned that those who see themselves as members of the cultural majority in Canada, now find it increasingly difficult to express opposition to Multiculturalism without being labelled as "racists", "sexists", or "bigots", of one kind or another.

> In keeping with the communication rules, if Natives feel they are being discriminated against when they are trying to obtain housing, they can call a news conference to register their concern. If a Jewish organization believes that anti-Semitism is on the increase, it can issue a press release. If women feel that they are experiencing discrimination in the workplace, they can hold a press conference. If Sikhs want to wear turbans in the workplace, they can turn to the media to express their concern over the opposition they encounter. However, the communication is all one-way. If the majorities involved do not agree with the claims of the minorities, they are labelled racists or bigots [...] Canadians do not allow majorities to speak out. And we don't encourage minorities and majorities to speak to each other (Bibby, Ibid:169-70).

For Bibby, and others like him (i.e., Zolf, 1982), Multiculturalism has left us without a common frame of reference; it has encouraged ethnic and cultural groups to pursue their own particular agendas without regard for the wider needs of the national collectivity. According to this view, Multiculturalism has encouraged the fragmentation of public life in Canada, and has made more difficult the task of creating national unity through consensus-building and compromise.

In many ways, this is a profoundly conservative critique of Multiculturalism, one which seeks to invoke the idea of a "national interest" over what is often seen to be the divisive interests of a highly relativistic and individualistic society. Conservative thinkers have, at least since the time of the French Revolution, stressed the importance of the social collectivity over its individual parts. And they have also emphasized the integrative functions performed by such traditional institutions as the church, the family, the community, and so on. There is, notwithstanding Bibby's efforts to remain evenhanded in his judgements, a strongly conservative sentiment expressed in this type of social criticism.

Not all criticisms of Multiculturalism have come from the political right, however. Some have originated from the very groups whose interests were supposedly served by Multiculturalism. Thus, some ethnic leaders and spokespersons have dismissed Multiculturalism as having very little relevance to the major problems presently confronting racial and ethnic minorities in Canada today. Instead of combating racial prejudice and discrimination in employment, housing, education, and other strategic areas of public life, some critics believe that Multiculturalism has remained preoccupied with the politically safer issues of preserving ethnic heritages, and fostering traditional ethnic identities. Instead of using the resources of Multiculturalism agencies to fund employment equity programs, organize campaigns against racial hatred, or for other aggressive programs for social justice and equality, it sometimes seems as though Multiculturalism has concentrated largely on funding Heritage Day events, ethnic dancing groups, and other cultural fringe activities which do little to challenge the institutional forms of racial and ethnic discrimination in our society.

> Although members of visible minorities appreciate government assistance in the multiculturalism area, they tend to see this as government fostering cultural patterns but not dealing with the key issues of multiracialism or discrimination. What they want are strong government measures not only to enhance their cultural origins but also to enhance their ability to integrate economically, de-

spite their cultural origins. Multiculturalism programs do little to assist in their economic integration or to confront racism (Abella, 1984:51).

This focus upon, what at least one politician of the left has described as "the singing and dancing syndrome"[14], has been accomplished at the expense of promoting full economic, social and political development for visible minorities. Whereas for conservatives, Multiculturalism has gone too far, for more radical critics it has not gone far enough.

> Despite the intention, there is little indication that racial prejudice has been less prevalent, or ethnic inequality less evident. The policy has failed to combat racism and discriminatory practices. Indeed, the persistence of ethnic inequality in the labour market is well documented by the report of the Royal Commission on Equality in Employment (1984). It is also interesting to note that there is no mention of the multicultural policy in the entire report – an omission that would imply the ineffectiveness of the policy to combat racism [...] the irony of multiculturalism is that it furnishes Canadian society with a great hope without having to change the fundamental structures of society. Multiculturalism is the failure of an illusion, not of a policy (Li, 1988:9).

RACE AND ETHNIC RELATIONS IN ORGANIZATIONAL THEORY

The Silence of Organizational Theory

When attempting to explain the traditional silence(s) of organizational theory towards the subjects of race and ethnicity, (as well as those of gender and class), it is necessary to examine both the ideological content of OT and the ethnocentric culture form which it has emerged.

One of the characteristics of most OT textbooks has been the focus on general principles. This focus has grown quite naturally out of the administrative and managerial interest which have underlaid the major traditions of organizational studies. Managers are, after all, primarily interested in learning a set of techniques which can be used to promote organizational effectiveness. The fewer the number of techniques to be learned, and the broader the range of application, the more efficient becomes the development and utilization of specialized managerial knowledge. One of the problems with this generalizing approach, however, is that it has tended to overlook many of the distinctive aspects of organizations which are rooted in particularities of their external or internal environments.

The systematic neglect of gender, race and ethnicity may be partly attributed to this generalizing approach which has until now, excluded these issues from mainstream organizational analysis. The image of the organization which appears in standard OT textbooks is an image from which all references to gender, race, ethnicity, class, nationality or history are largely absent. The models and theories developed in these texts are intended to be universal in their application, and to be used to analyze organizations in any part of the industrial world. However, because many of the general principles underlying modern organizational analysis have been developed in the United States, and based upon American cultural experiences, there is an important sense in which the much-touted universality of these models is open to question. All organizations are located within a larger society possessing its own distinctive history, culture, and social relations. No organization is free from the influences of this external environment, and many aspects of the internal environment of the organization are shaped by these external factors. What is often portrayed as a generalized model of organizational analysis, therefore, turns out in reality to be an American model, informed by the particular need and experiences of American managers[15].

In an important sense, therefore, the silences of OT have continued to reflect the traditional world view of the American corporate culture which has remained ethnocentric, androcentric and elitist in outlook. The consequence of this ethnocentrism for organizational studies has been to obscure the multicultural and multiracial reality of many organizations in Canada and the U.S., for much orthodox OT has been based upon what one critic (Rich, 1970:306) has called "white solipsism", which refers to the tendency to "think, imagine, and speak as if whiteness described the world". White solipsism, however, is "not the consciously held belief that one race is inherently superior to all others, but a tunnel vision which simply does not see non-White experience or existence as precious or significant" (ibid.). It is this ethnocentrism which has rendered ethnic minorities invisible in contemporary organizational studies, and which has overlooked the special problems that many members of these groups face in the modern organization world. The result, as several recent authors have suggested (e.g., Bell et al., 1992) has been to "whitewash" the modern organization by refusing to acknowledge the depth and breadth of institutional prejudice and discrimination against members of racial and ethnic minority groups.

> If one were to review much of the literature on organizations, one would as-
> sume that racism takes place somewhere else, outside of the workplace; or
> when the possibility is acknowledged at all, it is framed as an affirmative action
> issue. It is rarely acknowledged that race relations are reproduced in organiza-
> tional, behavioural and structural systems (ibid.:22).

In trying to understand why the topics of race and ethnicity have been so neglected in organizational studies, we sooner or later have to face the inescapable fact that the problem of institutional racism, which is generally widespread throughout North American society[16], is also present in OT and other organizational disciplines. Problems of race and ethnicity in organizations have been neglected for various reasons, but, in particular, due to the fact that the great majority of organizational researchers are White (males) and operate within a network of ideological factors which have served to reproduce the status quo in which other White males dominate organizations and their representation. The academic press, for instance, is a key factor in reinforcing ideological conformity. The editorial boards of scholarly publishing houses exercise considerable control over what is accepted for publication within their journals and textbooks, serving in effect as the legislators of what are acceptable research problems, methodologies, and standards of argumentation. They have acquired the status of "gatekeepers" of knowledge, letting in those who conform to the canons of orthodoxy, and refusing entry to those who don't (cf. Crane, 1967; Morgan, 1985; Jauch and Wall, 1989). Other ideological controls within academia include internal controls related to the certification process of new academics – the graduate programs, which shape, direct, and approve the research proposals and dissertations of graduate students.

The impact of these ideological controls in regard to race and ethnicity has been to reproduce colour-blind research that reflects the prevailing priorities of the North American corporate culture. A stark example can be seen in the comments of one distinguished contributor to a 1990 special issue of the Journal of Organizational Behaviour on race and ethnicity:

> I am unaware of a mainstream journal in organizational behaviour ever before
> devoting a special issue to the subject of race, authorizing a black scholar to be
> in charge of the issue, and publishing a complete set of papers by black authors
> (Alderfer, 1990:493).

The situation was, in the words of Alderfer, "an historic event" but one which took until the 1990s to happen. Until this point the great majority of journal articles and texts in organizational and management disciplines have had little or nothing to say on race and ethnicity (cf. America and Anderson, 1978; Davis and Watson, 1982; Dickens and Dickens, 1982; Fernandez, 1975; Cox and Nkomo, 1990). Certainly, there has been virtually nothing written from the perspective of non-White workers, or which has focused on minority workers as subjects in their own right (cf. Murphy, 1973).

It is only very recently that the silence on race and ethnicity has been broken by a new generation of minority group scholars whose work has inspired fresh attempts to include the experiences of ethnic and racial minorities in the tradition of organizational research. A number of these scholars are also women, and in their writings they have focused on the "double jeopardy" of racism and sexism faced by many minority women within the workplace (cf. Nkomo and Cox, 1989; Bell, 1990; Denton, 1990; Campbell, 1984). Nonetheless, it remains true that organizational theorists with an interest in pursing research into race and ethnicity face a number of institutional obstacles within their respective disciplines (Cox, 1990). Scholars, including minority group scholars, have been discouraged from pursuing these subjects for fear of being perceived as overly specialized in fields which have remained marginal to mainstream OT research. Similarly, as Cox (ibid.:10) also documents, some faculty members in OT departments have not hesitated to use what can only be described as outright intellectual harassment and intimidation to prevent their graduate students from selecting research topics on race and ethnicity. These pressures to marginalize and exclude racial and ethnic research have been exerted through a network of different control agencies within the academic community – through university hiring committees and, of course, through interpersonal contacts. All of these pressures have succeeded in defining race and ethnicity as taboo subjects in the mainstream tradition of organizational research.

> [C]ompared to most other topics related to organization management, work on racioethnicity is both more difficult to perform and more difficult to publish, at least in the leading academic journals. Much of this difficulty exists because American society has never really resolved problems of racioethnic relations and racioethnic heterogeneity, including those related to racism (Cox, ibid.:19).

The Influence of American Assimilation Theory

Although traditional research in OT has remained largely silent on the issues of race and ethnicity, this does not mean that no organizational research has been undertaken in these areas. As Alderfer and Thomas (1988) have shown, even during the earlier part of the twentieth century, the issues of race and ethnicity had already acquired a significance in several sectors of organizational life in the United States.

They certainly had significance for business organizations at a time when immigrants from all parts of Europe were coming to America in search of work and prosperity. The period of mass immigration which lasted well into the first quarter of the twentieth century produced a labour force with an increasingly ethnic and cultural heterogeneity. Interestingly enough, this ethnic transformation of the labour force was even recorded in the Hawthorne Studies of the Western Electric plant − studies which gave birth to the Human Relations School of Management Theory. Roethlisberger and Dickson (1939:6), for example, allude to the ethnic diversity of the work force in their sample of respondents:

> In 1927, when the studies commenced, the company employed approximately 29,000 workers, representing some 60 nationalities. About 75% [...] were American born. The Poles and Czechoslovakians were by far the largest foreign groups; there was a fair sprinkling of Germans and Italians.

Given this recognition of the importance of the ethnic work force, why was it, then, that the Human Relations researchers paid so little attention to ethnicity in the course of their research on the Western Electric plant? This passing reference to ethnicity was never expanded into a topic of research interest. The answer, as Alderfer and Thomas (op. cit.:27) suggest, lies in the ideological world-view held by the researchers, themselves, at this time. In common with many other Americans of the period, the leading researchers subscribed to a radical assimilationist vision of society, in which differences of race and ethnicity were perceived as temporary impediments to the eventual achievement of a democratic cultural uniformity and homogeneity throughout the United States. Such a view was essentially inimical to focusing on the differentia speciae of race and ethnicity. This is well illustrated in an autobiographical fragment from Roethlisberger's (1977:14-15) own self-portrait:

> I was an American − an isolationist by factors then unknown to me [...] who was not going to have anything to do with battles fought in Switzerland [...] or

with the Franco-Prussian War. This was America, where race, colour, creed, birth, heredity, nationality, family and so forth, did not count and where individual merit, skill, competence, knowledge, freedom, and so on did. I believed it with all my heart and in a crazy way, in spite of many subsequent experiences to the contrary, I still do.

Part of the silence on race and ethnicity, therefore, especially in studies of business organizations, may well derive from a disinclination to focus on these issues for ideological and political reasons. Organizations, after all, were expected to be melting pots for the American work force.

In other organizations, however, the strongly assimilationist creed of the times succeeded in motivating, rather than inhibiting, some of the earliest studies of ethnicity in American organizations. This was especially true of the military after President Harry Truman's 1948 executive order desegregating the armed forces. Samuel Stouffer's monumental study, *The American Soldier,* included a chapter on "Negro Soldiers", which illustrated in some detail the racial dynamics of the armed forces. Similarly, in educational organizations, studies of race played an important part in the legal and constitutional battles to desegregate the U.S. public school system. As Alderfer and Thomas (op. cit.:10) record, the research of Kenneth Clark (Clark and Clark, 1958), which examined the racial preferences of Black children for White over Black dolls, played an important role in influencing the Supreme Court decision to abolish the "separate but equal" doctrine of education in the United States, in the case of Brown versus Board of Education. Again, the motivating force behind the development and use of this type of racial research in the educational system was the strong assimilationist commitment to equality and integration which began in the 1950s – and later erupted into the Civil Rights movement of the 1960s.

Subsequent research, which has since been carried out in military, educational and, finally, also in business organizations in the United States, has continued to build upon this early legacy of assimilationism. Common to most of these assimilationist studies has been the assumption that for most organizational research, it is almost always the racial minority group which is problematized, rather than the organization, or majority culture. In most contemporary studies, race is typically defined as a "problem" which more and more organizations are having to deal with in the course of their day to day operations. Indeed, this perspective of race as a problem is apparent from much of the substantive research which has been undertaken on race and ethnicity in organizations. Thus, studies in the area of job satisfaction have invariably compared levels of satisfaction between Black and White workers, often with inconsistent, inconclusive or even tautological results, (see, for example, Jones, James, Bruni and Sell, 1977; Konar, 1981; Slocum and Stranser, 1972; Vecchio, 1980).

Earlier studies of race and ethnicity more typically focused on the evidence of discrimination in the occupational distribution of jobs. To what extent have Blacks remained overrepresented in lower socioeconomic jobs, (Franklin, 1968)? Or have there been systemic disparities between the recruitment and selection of Blacks and Whites in selected occupational areas, (Brown and Ford, 1977; Newman, 1978; Stone and Stone, 1987; Terpstra and Larsen, 1985).

More recently, a growing number of studies have investigated evidence of bias in the performance ratings of Black and White ratees. Several comprehensive literature reviews have appeared on this subject (Dipboye, 1985; Kraiger and Ford, 1985; Landy and Farr, 1980). While there appears to be some inconsistency between these findings, several of the more influential of these studies have reported rates that tend to receive higher ratings from raters of the same race, and that these effects were more pronounced in field studies than in laboratory ratings (see Kraiger and Ford, 1985).

By far the largest number of studies in the U.S., however, have concentrated on the legal and administrative aspects of how organizations could comply with the Civil Rights legislation – specifically Title VII Guidelines requiring them to develop affirmative action programs to increase minority representation. Much of this research has centred on the validity of various measures which have been designed to test the effectiveness of these programs (for example, Schmidt, Pearlman and Hunter, 1980; Arvey and Faley, 1988).

THE ETHNICITY PARADIGM

In a recent critical review of OT, Nkomo (1992) has argued that much current organizational research has remained dominated by what she calls the "ethnicity paradigm".

Derived in large part from the ideology of assimilationism, the ethnicity paradigm provides a framework for interpreting the significance of race and ethnic relations in organizations, and for focusing on the areas of priority in current organizational theory and research. According to Nkomo, however, the ethnicity paradigm has remained locked into an ethnocentric view of the world: a view in which minority individuals are expected to conform to, and to assimilate into, the organizational culture of the racial and ethnic majority – that is, of the White, Anglo-Saxon, (or in Canada, Anglo-Celtic) Protestant majority. This Eurocentric and latently racist view of minority individuals is constructed from several theoretical and methodological assumptions which are implicitly contained in the ethnicity paradigm:

1. Race and ethnicity are commonly perceived as essential properties of individuals – whether these are biological, cultural, or social psychological properties. Problems of race relations, therefore, are frequently related to some of these essential properties, and to the need to change those which are amenable to change (such as attitudes, motivation, work ethic, etc.). This essentialist view of race and ethnicity overlooks the extent to which racial categories have always been imposed on the politically weak by the politically powerful, and in this sense represent socially constructed categories which are often legacies of conquest, colonization, slavery or economic exploitation.

2. Studies of race and ethnicity in organizations typically focus on the individual rather than on the organization or culture of the racial majority. Because of their individualistic focus, most studies of race and ethnicity in organizations are primarily concerned with psychological or social psychological variables, but remain silent on the socio-historical dynamics of the capitalist system. The major emphasis of this kind of research, therefore, is how to get the minority individual to fit into the organization, or how to rid the majority individual of prejudiced attitudes. The legitimacy of the status quo is rarely challenged, and questions regarding the dominance of racial majorities are never asked.

This focus on the individual absolves the researcher from problematizing the dominant culture of the racial majority. Indeed, it is only non-Whites who are seen as having a racial status; the terms race or ethnic are never applied to members of the majority culture. The result of this individualistic focus has been to assume that the problems of racial discrimination, segmentation or exclusion in organizational life are reducible to problems of individual prejudice and intolerance. Traditionally, the roots of such prejudice have been sought in attributes of the individual – whether in terms of authoritarian personality, (Adorno et. al., 1950), or in terms of other cognitive processes, (Allport, 1954), but rarely in the social system itself, or in the structures of power and domination. Consequently, the solution to problems of racism is always understood to lie in the reform of individuals, rather than in the restructuring of organizations, or other significant parts of the social order. This tendency to psychologize the issues of race and ethnicity has been a characteristic of the ethnicity paradigm.

(3.) Inequality is accepted as a natural feature of industrial societies in general, and of organizations in particular. In common with the long-term tradition of OT, hierarchy is accepted as an inevitable feature of all large-scale organizations; the problem is to prevent a concentration, or overrepresentation, of visible minority members at the bottom of the organization. By accepting the inevitability of hierarchy and inequality, in society and in its institutions, the problem(s) of racial minorities are invariably defined in terms of: Why aren't they like us, and what will it take for them to become like us?

(4.) The model of assimilation which has traditionally been used to explain the successful integration of White ethnic groups (such as Italians, Poles, Jews, etc.) into the institutions of the majority culture is also seen as the appropriate model for bringing about the assimilation and integration of currently disadvantaged visible minority groups. In other words, the historical experiences of European immigrants in the U.S. (and Canada) are presumed to provide an appropriate framework for understanding the experiences and social patterns of non-White minorities. There is an unspoken assumption that the processes which worked to integrate European groups into the institutions of the majority culture will also work to integrate currently disadvantaged visible minority groups.

Notwithstanding the fact that several sociologists, (Blauner, 1972; Omi and Winant, 1986), have argued that because of their histories of conquest, colonialism, slavery, and other forms of unfreedom, the experiences of many non-White groups have differed significantly from those of traditional European immigrant groups, much of the research undertaken within the ethnicity paradigm has ignored this distinction. It has assumed that conclusions based on the experiences of White ethnic groups are generalizable to the case of non-White groups. As Nkomo, (ibid.:500) observes,

> [C]onspicuously absent from these articles is any suggestion or recognition of the different socio-historical experience of Afro-Americans or other racial minorities in the United States.

Taken together, these orienting assumptions have ensured that the prevailing paradigm for studying race and ethnicity in organizations — the ethnicity paradigm — has remained ethnocentric (that is, Eurocentric), and paternalistic in its view of race relations. It has typically defined racial status, itself, as a problem in need of a solution: Do racial and ethnic minorities have what it takes to succeed in organizations; or more concisely, why aren't they like us? Much of this work is often characterized by what has been labelled as the "deficit hypothesis" (Nkomo, ibid.:499): the assumption that in order to succeed in typical organizations, minority individuals need to overcome a deficit in "motivation", "education", "mentors", "human capital", and so on. Because of this tendency to problematize race, much current research within the ethnicity paradigm has focused on how to incorporate minority individuals into typical organizations by rectifying, or compensating for, any "deficits" in their cultural or psychological backgrounds.

What is conspicuously absent from these studies is any reference to the structures of power and domination which have resulted in the minoritization and marginalization of some racial and ethnic groups, and in the dominance of others. Similarly, most of these studies never examine how it is that the dominant values of organizational culture represent the attitudes and interests of the dominant ethnic group. These are some of the deafening silences of mainstream OT when it has turned its attention to the issues of race and ethnicity.

The Ethnicity Paradigm and Canadian Research

At first glance, it might seem reasonable to expect that the problems associated with the ethnicity paradigm had been avoided in the Canadian literature of organizational theory and research. After all, the ideology and policy of assimilationism has long been officially rejected in this country in favour of ethnic pluralism, or Multiculturalism, as it has come to be known.

However, the truth is that Canadian research has so far failed to take the lead in the study of race and ethnicity in organizations. Much traditional research on minority groups in Canada has focused on (White) ethnic groups to the virtual exclusion of (non-White) racial groups.

It has only been in the last decade or so that any serious academic attention has been paid to problems of racial prejudice and discrimination, and to the contentious issues of racial and ethnic inequality in Canada, (see, for example Li, 1988; Bolaria and Li, 1985; Ramcharan, 1982; Foster, 1991; McKague, 1991). For the most part, however, Canadian studies have paid remarkably little attention to the more vexatious questions of race and ethnic relations[17].

Notwithstanding the history of official Multiculturalism in Canada, organizational theory and research in this country has remained as much locked into the ethnicity paradigm as that in the U.S. There are several reasons for this:

1. In its own way, Canadian research has exhibited an overly individualistic definition of ethnicity. This is true even though Canadian studies have frequently included research on ethnic communities, and ethnic group relations. The focus of much of this research, however, has remained psychological or social psychological in nature: language retention, identity, intergenerational attitudes, etc., have all continued to be popular topics in the literature of Canadian research.

2. In common with assimilationist studies, most Canadian research has defined ethnicity in terms of some essential properties such as nationality (or homeland), language or religion. This essentialist view of ethnicity is similar in its results to that employed in assimilationist studies, and suffers from the same drawbacks and limitations as those already discussed in the previous section.

3. If assimilationist studies have tended to accept the inevitability of inequality in race and ethnic relations, this is even more so for multiculturalist research. In their celebration of difference and diversity, many Canadian scholars have turned their backs on the legacy of John Porter and have avoided asking troubling questions about ethnic inequality – either in organizations, or in society at large. This lack of any critical perspective, with its attendant blindness to the issues of power, conflict, and inequality, has rendered the Canadian tradition of ethnic studies particularly susceptible to government influence through direct funding for policy-oriented research.

4. Although the Canadian tradition of ethnic studies has normally eschewed the strong assimilationist undertones of much American research, in its own way, it has also remained ethnocentric (i.e., Eurocentric) in terms of its basic assumptions. Instead of preaching the sermon of assimilation, integration, and homogenization, Canadian scholars have accepted ethnic difference and diversity. However, the unspoken assumption of the multiculturalist view of society implies that ethnic diversity be necessarily contained within the framework of a standardized, civic culture: that of the ethnic majority. This is especially true of organization studies, in which the management of diversity is normally assumed to take place in the context of a typical corporate or business culture. Perhaps more significant is the fact that the acceptance of difference and diversity in multicultural studies is rarely linked to questions of equality. For clearly, any acceptance of difference and diversity in a system based on inequality can be little more than a sanctification of the status quo.

There has, therefore, been little significant difference between Canadian and American studies of race and ethnicity in organizations. The larger political climate of multiculturalism does not appear to have advanced the study of race or ethnicity in organizations.

In part, this may reflect the traditional reluctance of a corporate culture to acknowledge the importance of multicultural or multiracial differences in the workplace. On the other hand, as the sociologist Karl Peter (1981:57,59), has suggested, the ideology of multiculturalism, itself, has sometimes served to inhibit the study of race and ethnic relations, especially where the issues of power and inequality are involved.

> The denial of any economic and political significance to ethnic groups, which is the essence of the government's policy on Multiculturalism, has been adopted by Canadian sociologists and has largely prevented them from analyzing Multiculturalism in terms of power and politics [...] The reluctance of many leading liberal Canadian sociologists to deal with ethnicity in terms of power and politics, it seems, is proportionate to their commitment to the policies of bilingualism and Multiculturalism, and ultimately to the concept of Canadian unity as proposed by the Liberal government.

Beyond the Ethnicity Paradigm

Today, however, a growing number of researchers in Canada and in the United States have begun to employ a more multiculturalist approach to the study of race and ethnicity in organizations in order to distance themselves from earlier assimilationist studies. This has resulted in a crop of recent studies focusing on the management of diversity in the workplace, (see for example, Alderfer, 1991; Burke, 1991; Kirchmeyer and McLellan, 1991; Mighty, 1991a; Nkomo, 1992). This celebration of diversity marks a clear departure from earlier organizational studies which sought solutions to problems of race and ethnicity in the greater integration and homogenization of the workplace.

In a recent review of the literature on ethnic diversity in the workplace, Kirchmeyer and McLellan (1991) concluded that most organizations have attempted to assimilate minority individuals into the corporate culture of the majority group. This has typically been done through a process of "cultural homogenization", whereby "cultural differences are ignored and suppressed so that potentially valuable perspectives remain unexplored," (Kirchmeyer and

McLellan, ibid.:75). The consequence of these homogenization pressures can be very harmful to members of minority groups:

> Members of ethnic and racial minorities may be most vulnerable to organizational pressures to conform because they tend to have the least status [...] For these minorities, conforming to corporate values can also mean denying their own culture, and even turning against others of their own category, (Kirchmeyer and McLellan, ibid.:75).

Similar findings were also reported by Mighty (1991a), who suggested that many organizations in her study resorted to a form of "cultural imperialism", in which the dominant group would seek to homogenize non-dominant cultures in an effort to transform them into a single majority culture. According to Mighty, (ibid.:66), "In ethnocentric organizations the usual mode of maintaining stability is through the social influence process of conformity."

For the management of many organizations, therefore, the norms and values of the majority group are those which define the normal standards of the corporate culture, and any minority or divergent values are necessarily defined as aberrant or deviant. For minority members of organizations, however, the pressures of homogenization can be onerous in their psychological and cultural consequences. In reporting these results, Mighty (ibid.:69) observes that minority members of an organization who feel victimized on account of their racial or ethnic status may suffer from an "internalized oppression" which leads them to model their behaviour on the (idealized) behaviour of the majority culture, while simultaneously devaluing fellow minority members who continue to display minority cultural characteristics. In this way, minority individuals become alienated not only from their own ethnic groups, but – perhaps more ominously – from themselves.

These, and similar findings, have persuaded some researchers that the ethnocentric practices of many organizations are extremely harmful to minority individuals working within them. However, beyond the simple concern for the welfare and equity of minority employees, there is a growing body of evidence to suggest that the adoption of more multicultural management policies and workplace practices brings rewards, not just for minorities, but for the organization as a whole. Thus Burke (1991) has shown how more multiculturalist approaches to the management of workplace diversity may have a number of benefits for the organizations involved. At the very least, these new approaches help organizations to harness the full potential of their diverse workforces, but in addition to this, proper management of ethnic diversity can also provide an organization with a competitive edge, in an increasingly multicultural and international market (see Nelson, 1988). As well as these advantages, however, a more equitable treatment of racial and ethnic minorities in an organization may also bring benefits to members of the majority group:

> Interestingly, attempts to make organizations more supportive of the career aspirations of minorities may also have benefits for the white majority and the organization itself. The development of a more objective performance or potential appraisal system would benefit both; the development of a more comprehensive career management process would benefit both (Burke, 1991:120).

Besides these considerations, there are other instrumental benefits which have been shown to be associated with a more multicultural management of ethnic diversity in organizations. Kirchmeyer and McLellan, (op. cit.:77) have recorded that:

> In ethnically diverse workshops, an appreciation of various cultures not only heightens mutual understanding, but it can also facilitate the group's understanding.

At the same time, however, as Mighty (1991a) and Alderfer (1991) are at pains to point out, the benefits of racial and ethnic diversity in the workplace are only likely to be realized in a setting which encourages mutual respect between members of different groups. To achieve this, it is necessary for diverse groups, not only to respect each other's cultural differences, but also to occupy equal statuses within the organization. This is very important, as the status of minority groups within the traditional ethnocentric organization has always been institutionally inferior to that of the majority group. A long-term condition for the successful management of workplace diversity, therefore, is the disappearance of all forms of ethnic stratification within the organization.

Although the corporate cultures of most organizations in North America have remained resolutely ethnocentric (and androcentric), there is an increasing number of organizations today which have introduced more enlightened policies for the management of diversity. Mighty (op. cit.:68), records that Avon Products Inc., has implemented regular management sensitivity programs for dealing with issues of race and ethnicity which have resulted in a dramatic reduction in the turnover rate for minority employees. Similarly, the Municipality of Metropolitan Toronto has developed its "Kingswood Management Training Programme" to enable managers to respond more effectively to the problems of women, and of racial and ethnic minorities. Several other corporations, including Shoppers Drug Mart, Northern Telecom Canada, and the Canadian Imperial Bank of Commerce, now have programs which place Aboriginal peoples into entrepreneurial training internships for six months of the year. These, and other examples, serve to illustrate how many organizations have begun to see the light, and are attempting to turn the ethnic diversity of their respective workforces into an asset.

There can be little doubt that the new focus of some organizations on more effective management of ethnic diversity represents a definite advance over earlier practices. Any programs which increase interracial or intercultural sensitivity and respect among members of an organization are to be applauded, whether these are implemented by government agencies, or by private corporations. In this respect, it is clear that Multiculturalism has something to offer, both to the study of race and ethnicity in organizations, and to the design of new ways of managing workforce diversity. At the same time, however, we should not expect too much from this approach. As we have already suggested, Multiculturalism is also limited by inherent individualism, psychologism, and its acceptance of organizational hierarchy. The sudden appearance of management strategies for optimizing the advantages of workplace diversity owes as much to the need for greater labour productivity, and the need for competitive advantage in a global market, as it does to any profound regard for human rights.

While a fresh perspective on ethnic diversity may make it easier for some minority individuals to scale the corporate hierarchy, it in no way questions the need for hierarchy, nor does it point towards other, more humanized forms of corporate organization. Because they both take the present structures of power and domination as given, neither variants of the ethnicity paradigm provide a critical alternative to the status quo. For although Multiculturalism is an improvement over the Assimilation perspective, it still falls short of being a radical critique of race and ethnic relations in organizations. While it has made it easier for some minority individuals to move up the class system inside the organization, the existence of the class system itself is never open to question. Much as John Porter suggested, some three decades ago, Multiculturalism (or what he called "ethnic pluralism"), simply facilitates the growth of ethnic elites within their own communities, and within the organizations of a larger society. But as far as the conditions of most racial and ethnic minority individuals are con-cerned – especially the conditions of minority women – not much has changed.

WHAT DOES THE FUTURE HOLD?

Whenever we leave our office at the end of a particularly full day and beat a hasty retreat through the empty hallways and corridors of the deserted campus buildings, we encounter members of a community who are largely invisible during the day. Like the legendary Owl of Minerva, they only seem to emerge when the shades of night are falling. We are talking, of course, about the evening workforce of cleaners and janitors whose job it is to scrub the floors, polish the tables, empty the trash cans and ashtrays, long after the daytime population of staff and students have gone home. They are the graveyard shift, and together they form their own small nocturnal community.

It is a community largely made up of women, many of whom are from minority ethnic backgrounds. Some are visible minority women: West Indians, South Asians, Filipinos, Chileans, and other non-European nationalities. Oth-ers are from European countries. Many of these seem to be recent immigrants judging from their styles of dress and modes of speech. But within this com-munity of women the only men to occasionally be seen are the supervisors or foremen who periodically come to inspect the work that is done.

In one way or another, this scene – or one like it – is replayed every evening in the hospitals, airports, shopping malls and other large work organizations in our society. It is in places like these that women and ethnic minorities are em-ployed to perform some of the most menial and low-paid jobs in the labour market. These workers are also more likely to suffer the disadvantages of tem-porary, part-time and shift work, all of which comes without the security, op-portunity and benefits associated with permanent, full-time employment[18].

For most Canadians, these are the invisible workers in our society who may remain trapped at the lowest levels of the labour force, sometimes because of their lack of skills and education, but often because they are working-class women, or people of colour. In this respect, Canada is no different from many other Western societies where women and ethnic minorities are often em-ployed in what one writer (Bonacich, 1972), has called the "split labour mar-ket", to fill the lowest paying, least secure, most menial dead-end jobs that nobody else really wants. Today, this type of labour market segmentation has become a fact of life in many countries, and may be seen in such cases as North African workers in France; Turkish and Yugoslav workers in Germany; Italians in Switzerland; West Indians and Asians in Great Britain; and immigrant and visible minority workers here in Canada (cf. Castles and Kosack, 1973, for a review of the immigrant labour market).

Many of these minority workers, especially those who happen to be non-White women, have continued to face special problems of discrimination and exploitation in the workplace. This has been especially true for those workers who have remained trapped at the lowest ends of the occupational ladder, for it is here that the forces of sexism and racism combine to perpetuate the existence of a cheap labour force which has remained largely invisible to the larger society.

> One has only to look at the employment practices of police departments, fire departments, government services, universities, the media and private companies to see that visible minorities are consciously or unconsciously denied full participation in almost all Canadian institutions. Visible minorities are, in fact, the invisible members of our society (Equality Now, 1984:1).

Of course, not all minority workers end up at the lowest levels of the labour force. Some succeed in obtaining relatively well-paid, secure and prestigious jobs in public services or private corporations. However, many of these middle-class managers, bureaucrats and professionals have also faced special problems of discrimination and prejudice in their workplaces. But because little attention has been paid to these problems in mainstream studies of organizations, they also have remained largely invisible to the public eye.

It is only recently that OT and public policy have begun to address the special problems experienced by minorities within workplaces, and other organizational settings. In the past, members of disadvantaged minority groups have been excluded from many forms of employment, and today, they still face institutional discrimination and prejudice in many organizations. Not all of these barriers have been deliberate, however. Some, like the traditional height and weight requirements for certain jobs, often represent residual ethnocentric (and androcentric) standards established at a time when only White males were seen as suitable candidates for these jobs, and which have never been revised to take account of the changing composition of the labour force. Many of these institutional barriers can be removed once the needs and cultural sensitivities of minority groups have been recognized and accommodated. Although it has proven to be a controversial decision, the amendment of the RCMP dress code to permit the hiring of women, Sikhs and Aboriginals is just one example of how organizations can move with the times. If we are serious about offering equal access to employment for all members of our society, regardless of gender, ethnic or racial background, the institutional barriers which have traditionally excluded these groups must be removed.

It is not that individuals in the designated groups are inherently unable to achieve equality on their own, it is that the obstacles in their way are so formidable and self-perpetuating that they cannot be overcome without intervention. It is both intolerable and insensitive if we simply wait and hope that the barriers will disappear with time. Equality in employment will not happen unless we make it happen (Abella, 1984:254).

A recent survey of 1,200 adult Canadians conducted by Decima Research, between October 23-28, 1993 showed that 3 out of 4 Canadians reject the notion of cultural diversity, and think that ethnic minorities should try harder to fit into mainstream society. As well, 54 per cent of those surveyed believe that current immigration policy allows too many people of different races and cultures.

These indications of shifting public opinion may sometimes be used by unscrupulous politicians as an opportunity to campaign against the protection of minority rights. Recently in Alberta, for example, several senior politicians in the provincial conservative government have called for the repeal of the (provincial) Individual Rights Protection Act, as well as the (federal) Canadian Charter of Rights and Freedoms.

Today, however, the political climate has shifted away from the welfare liberalism of the 1960s, 1970s and 1980s, to the neo-conservatism of the 1990s. With this shift has come a weakening of popular and political support for minority rights, including such programs as Multiculturalism and employment equity. The prevailing preoccupation with the debt crisis has brought with it a backlash against many minority rights concerns and programs. The evidence of this backlash may be seen in negative public attitudes towards minorities, and in a weakening of political support for the protection of minority rights[19].

Notwithstanding these temporary setbacks, however, which are typical of troubled economic times, most of the evidence suggests that the struggles of ethnic and racial minorities for social justice and greater equality will continue to move ahead. The literature of OT has finally begun to acknowledge the presence of minorities in organizations, and to examine their special problems of institutional prejudice and discrimination.

With the demographic trend towards increasing ethnic and racial diversity in the workplace, the issue of minority rights is here to stay, and the effective management of this issue has become a matter for the operational effectiveness and welfare of the organization.

KEY TERMS

Americanization of organization research		*ethnic mosaic*
racism	*androcentrism*	*ethnocentrism*
tokenism	*assimilationism*	*glass ceiling*
vertical mosaic	*biculturality*	*institutionalized discrimination*
visible minorities	*discrimination*	*multiculturalism*
race relations	*ethnicity*	

REVIEW QUESTIONS

Q1. Briefly define each of the following terms, and say how an understanding of each can help us to understand organizations.

androcentrism
ethnocentrism
discrimination
racism

Assignment: Now turn to the glossary at the end of the book and compare your definitions.

Q2. What does the "Americanization of organizational research" refer to?

Assignment: First, read the introduction of any mainstream U.S. OT text and then compare it with the introduction of one of the few mainstream Canadian OT texts (e.g., Johns, 1988). What are the main similarities? What are the main differences? Secondly, read and compare any one of the Canadian accounts of race/ethnicity in organizations. Third, reread the section in this chapter on "The Influence of American Assimilation Theory". What is the main difference between mainstream accounts and accounts focused on race/ethnicity? How do U.S. and Canadian accounts differ? What general conclusions do you draw?

Q3. Define "institutionalized or systemic discrimination". What does this tell us about the design and processes or organizations in Canada? Identify four groups in Canada who have been the victims of institutionalized discrimination.

Assignment: In answering this question, read the first section of the Abella Commission Report on Equality in Employment (1984). Who are the four main disadvantaged groups focused upon by the Abella Commission? What groups does the term "visible minorities" refer to? Distinguish three visible minority from three invisible minority groups in Canada.

Q4. Briefly define each of the following terms and say what impact they are likely to have on "visible minority" persons in "majority settings":
      biculturality
      glass ceiling
      tokenism

Assignment: Now turn to the glossary at the end of the book and compare your definitions.

Q5. Who is in favour of, and who is opposed to, the policies of Multiculturalism in society, generally; and in the workplace, in particular?

Assignment: Make a list of all groups and individuals you know who support multiculturalist policies, and all those who oppose those who oppose them. On what basis do those different sides support or oppose those policies?

EXERCISE 6.1

This exercise is designed to make you think about the significance of race and ethnicity for an understanding of organizations. Do the tasks individually and then discuss your findings in small groups.

A. Obtain information on the composition of visible minority and Native peoples in your region (i.e., what percentage of the local population are Native and what percentage from non-White heritage).

> Your University/College, or public library will have Statistics Canada material that will help you with this exercise. As you do this exercise take notes on, (i) the level of difficulty you encountered on making the assessment, and (ii) what this tells you about the problem of assessing the impact of race/ethnicity in the workplace.

B. Compare and contrast the race/ethnic composition of two local organizations.

1. The class should meet in small groups to coordinate the division of labour for studying local organizations. A number of options are possible, (i) the group could agree to collectively study two organizations, or (ii) each group member could undertake to study one or two different organizations, or (iii) half the group members could study one organization while the other half studies a different organization.

2. Choose which organizations are to be studied. Organizations should be chosen according to the following criteria: (i) access – you should be able to have relative access to the organization (e.g., a church of which you are a member, a department store, a college, a political party to which you are affiliated), and (ii) public information – it should be relatively easy to obtain public information (e.g., corporate brochures, advertisements, etc.) on the organization, from the organization itself or from a public library.

3. Gather as much data on the ethnic composition – particularly the employment of visible minorities and Native peoples – of the organizations as possible, using observation, and other data collection. Focus upon the visible, and public image of the organization. Does it have visible minorities and/or Native people in its work force? At what levels are visible minorities and/or Native people employed? Do visible minorities and/or Native people feature in the public materials (e.g., advertising materials, brochures, etc.) of the organizations? To what extent are visible minorities and/or Native peoples in any obvious position of power and authority?

4. Now, rank the order of all the organizations studied in terms of the extent to which Native and visible minority peoples are evident (a) in the organization per se, (b) in the higher ranks of the organization, and (c) in the public image of the organization – with the best organization ranked #1 downward.

This exercise should be done over the course of a week (but longer may be taken if the class agrees).

C. Now, as a group discuss your findings and prepare a report for class discussion, focusing on the following questions:

1. (a) How many of the local organizations studied can be said to include a significant and representative number of Native and visible minority peoples at all levels?

(b) How would you define significant and representative, and why?

2. To what extent, in your estimate, is the employment of Native and visible

minority peoples representative of the percentage of those peoples in the local region?

3. In what types of jobs are Native and visible minority peoples most commonly found?

4. From you rank ordering, (a) which organizations are better and which worst in regard to the employment of Native and visible minority peoples? (b) how do you account for the differences between organizations?

5. What is your overall assessment of the contribution of local organizations to the maintenance and/or development of institutionalized racism?

D. As a class take group report-backs and then discuss the implications of the actual race/ethnicity composition of local organizations on how we should approach organizational research. Pay attention to one or more of the following topic areas – motivation, organizational culture, communication, organizational structure, leadership, organizational conflict.

FURTHER READING

Critiques of OT for its Neglect of Race and Ethnicity

JOURNAL OF ORGANIZATIONAL BEHAVIOUR, Vol.11, 1990.

Mills & Tancred (Eds.) 1992, chapters by Marta Calas (chapter 11), and by Ella Bell and Stella Nkomo (chapter 13).

E.L. Bell, T.C. Denton, & S.M. Nkomo (1992) WOMEN OF COLOR IN MANAGEMENT.

Analyses of Race/Ethnicity in Canadian Organizations

Carty, Linda (1991) BLACK WOMEN IN ACADEMIA.

Wallis, M. (1989) THE DYNAMICS OF RACE IN INSTITUTIONS.

Mighty, J. (1991) TRIPLE JEOPARDY: EMPLOYMENT EQUITY AND IMMIGRATION, VISIBLE MINORITY WOMEN.

Beattie, C. (1975) MINORITY MEN IN A MAJORITY SETTING.

✳ CANADIAN JOURNAL OF THE ADMINISTRATIVE SCIENCES ASSOCIATION OF CANADA, "Special Issue on Diversity", 8(2), 1991.

END NOTES

1. To avoid confusion in the mind of the reader, we have, right from the outset, defined some of the key concepts used in this chapter.

2. According to Hodgkinson (1985), by the year 2000, one in three of the overall U.S. population will be non-White. In Canada, projections on the percentage of visible minorities show an increase from 5.6 per cent of the total population in 1986 to over 9.6 per cent by 2001 (Samuel, 1988).

3. Blauner (1972)

4. Research data collected by Tony Simmons in Edmonton in the late 1980s, early 1990s.

5. Prime Minister Pierre Trudeau formally announced the policy of Multiculturalism on October 8th, 1971, in the House of Commons with the following statement:

   "A Policy of Multiculturalism within a bilingual framework commends itself to the government as the most suitable means of assuring the cultural freedom of all Canadians."

6. One of the more lyrical endorsements of the new policy was provided by the Liberal Senator, Paul Yuzuk, in 1975. It accurately portrays the sense of optimism that many politicians around this time felt towards the concept of Multiculturalism:

   "It is fortunate that Canadian governments have rejected the 'melting pot' theory with its colourless uniformity and have promoted a 'mosaic-type' of Canadian culture based on the voluntary integration of the best elements of the cultures of the component ethnic groups. The development of a composite Canadian culture, rich in variety, beauty and harmony, reflects the principle of 'unity in continuing diversity' and the democratic spirit of compromise inherent in the Canadian Confederation" (Anderson and Frideres, 1981:101).

7. Since the publication of the report of the special committee on the participation of visible minorities in Canadian society (Equality Now), in 1984, as well as The Royal Commission Report on Equality in Employment (Abella Report), also in 1984, several pieces of legislation have been passed, including the Employment Equity Act in 1986, and the Canadian Multiculturalism Act in 1988. Several years earlier, however, in 1982, the exclusion of visible minorities from the advertising industry had already been investigated by the Ontario Task Force on the Portrayal of Racial Diversity in Government Advertising and Communications.

8. In late August, 1991, Prime Minister Mulroney gave a mandate to a seven-member Royal Commission on Aboriginal Issues to deal with "an accumulation of literally centuries of injustices". The Commission is headed by Georges Erasmus, former national chief of the Assembly of First Nations, and Rene Dussault, a Justice of the Quebec Court of Appeal. Four of the seven members of the Commission are Indian, Inuit, or Métis; the first time that aboriginal people have played a dominant role on a Royal Commission.

9. A notable exception was John Porter (1975), who continued to believe that the policies of ethnic pluralism resulted

in the persistence of ethnic stratification and inequality. According to Porter, the best guarantee of ending ethnic inequality was to eliminate any notion of group rights, and emphasize the supremacy of individual rights and equality before the law. This, he believed, entailed a policy of individual assimilation into the majority culture.

10. The exception to this seems to be the persistence, and maybe even the strengthening of anti-semitism in some quarters. The well publicized trials of Jim Keegstra in Alberta and Ernst Zundel in Ontario, and the dismissal of Malcolm Ross in New Brunswick, as well as the activities of such groups as the Aryan Nations, are evidence of the fact that anti-semitism is far from dead in Canada.

11. A 1990 Angus Reid-Southam News Poll, for example, found that 59 per cent of Canadians want ethnic minorities to abandon their customs and languages and become "more like most Canadians". According to Reid, whose Winnipeg polling firm has conducted several polls for the federal immigration department, Canada is on the brink of a backlash against Multiculturalism. "What Canadian's are saying is that they're sick and tired of being asked to be tolerant", Reid told a meeting in Toronto in 1990 (Edmonton Journal, May 13th, 1990).

12. Discrimination against Sikhs seems to have really come to a head in 1991. In another turban-related incident, Mr. Ram Raghbir Singh Chanal, secretary of the Alberta wing of the Federal Liberal Party, was barred from entering the Red Deer Legion hall on his way to attend a speech by Ontario Liberal M.P. Sheila Copps on August 13th, 1991. Mr. Chanal was apparently also subjected to verbal abuse and told to remove his turban.

13. For a current review of recent criticisms of the theory and practice of Multiculturalism, see Abu-Laban et al, 1992.

14. In a speech to the National Association of Canadians of Origins in India, held in Edmonton in September 1987, Ray Martin – the leader of the Alberta NDP – told the convention that the Alberta Government's focus on the "singing and dancing syndrome" had obscured more important multicultural issues such as equal access to employment, and career advancement for new Canadians (Edmonton Journal, September 8th, 1987).

15. There are those who argue that "the logic of industrialization" has created general trends throughout industrial societies; that industrialization has rendered cultural differences obsolete (Galbraith, 1967).

16. This includes Mexico where deep-rooted racism discriminates against people the more Spanish, and the less like the gringos of the U.S., they appear to be.

17. Some of the more valuable studies of racial or ethnic inequality in Canada have been done by historians: see, for example, Avery (1979), Bradwin (1972), and Woodsworth [1909] (1972).

18. Similar observations have recently been made by another writer commenting upon racial segmentation within the Canadian workforce,

   "[O]ne may see Sikhs and South Asians working as taxi drivers and parking lot attendants, see South Asian and Latin American women and men cleaning not only the corporate floors but also the floors of airports and universities; however, seldom does one see them reading the news on prime-time television, keeping the peace and enforcing community laws, working in senior levels of government and industry, or receiving awards for their contributions to the fields of medicine, natural and social sciences, and community development. It is interesting to note that a Treasury Board survey in 1985 revealed that few visible minorities worked with the federal government; at that time, visible minorities constituted 1.7 per cent of federal employees (Public Service Commission of Canada, 1988:29)". (See, Depass, 1992:101)

19. Edmonton Journal December 14, 1993.

Knowledge and Power
in Organization Theory:
The Organizational World
and the Managerial Paradigm

This chapter sets out to explain why OT continues to be dominated by managerialist think-ing – arguing that mainstream OT should be viewed not so much as a paradigm but as a field of discourse. The chapter goes on to detail the rise of critical theories of organization and suggest ways forward in developing organizational research that can address the needs of persons in the new postmodernist, yet continually problematic, organizational world.

INTRODUCTION

The underlying purpose in writing this book has been to argue for a radical rethinking of Organization Theory. By "radical," however, we are not propos-ing that serious theoretical analysis be abandoned in favour of political sloganeering. What we are suggesting is that it is now time for Organization Theory to return to its intellectual roots to renew itself and to come to terms with the contemporary needs of organizational analysis. This, after all, is the original meaning of the word, "radical": a return to the roots in search of re-generation.[1]

To go back to its own roots, Organization Theory needs to re-establish its ties to the classic tradition of social theory, and to the general theories of soci-ety represented in this tradition. Indeed, this book has been written very much in the belief that it is neither possible nor desirable to divorce the study of organizations from the broader study of society. This is because all organizations are part of the history and culture of their respective societies and cannot meaningfully be analyzed in isolation from these larger influences.

Although the relationship of organizations to the history and culture of their respective societies may seem self-evident once stated in these terms, the fact remains that much mainstream work in Organization Theory has consistently overlooked the extent to which organizations – and organizational theorizing – are shaped by influences from the larger society.

To argue for the return of OT to its classical roots in more general theories of society, is, of course, to run counter to the direction in which OT has evolved over the past fifty years or so. In common with the general tendency for increasing specialization in academia – as in most other institutions of the modern world – the emergence of OT as an independent discipline, (alongside its sister disciplines of Organizational Behaviour, Organizational Psychology, and Organizational Development), has taken it farther and farther away from its root in classical social theory.

FROM PARADIGM TO DISCOURSE: UNDERSTANDING THE MANAGERIALIST DOMINANCE OF OT

Superficially, it may even appear as though the development of OT has followed the pattern of growth of other modern scientific disciplines. According, for example, to Thomas Kuhn (1962), an eminent historian of science, most of the modern sciences came into existence through a process of "scientific revolution," whereby a number of traditionally competing schools of thought were replaced by a single powerful scientific "paradigm" which succeeded in unifying a previously fragmented community of scholars around a common conceptual framework. This is how the modern sciences of chemistry and physics emerged from the rival schools of alchemy and natural philosophy. In each case, a powerful and new scientific paradigm – whether Daltonian atomic theory, or Newtonian mechanics – served to unite the community of scholars, and to render obsolete the traditional rivalries which had characterized the earlier pre-scientific schools of thought. Once the new paradigm was fully accepted by the scientific community, it began to function as a common framework for all scientific inquiry undertaken within the discipline. The adoption of this common framework for theory and research put an end to the earlier debates which had traditionally preoccupied the pre-scientific schools of thought. With the entrenchment of a single scientific paradigm, scientific enquiry entered a stage of "normal science," in which problem-solving research within a common conceptual framework replaced the more philosophical and fundamental debates of earlier, pre-scientific days.

In most disciplines, this period of normal science has lasted for as long as the prevailing paradigm has continued to provide an effective framework for solving the ongoing problems of research. Only when confronted by a growing number of "anomalies" which defy explanation through the procedures of normal science have scientific paradigms finally lost their credibility and legitimacy. At these times of "revolutionary crisis," a discredited paradigm has sometimes been displaced by a number of new and rival conceptual frameworks which may compete with each other for acceptance within the scientific community. This state of affairs has only been concluded with the emergence of a new paradigm which has reunited the scientific community around another common framework.

For some social scientists, Kuhn's theory of the growth of scientific knowledge has been accepted only as a description of the way in which modern sciences emerged from their pre-scientific origins. For others, however, Kuhn's theory has been interpreted as a prescription of the path that any discipline must follow to attain the status of a modern science. According to this latter, positivist view – positivist in the sense that it seeks to imitate the development of the natural sciences – it is only through the development of a single unifying paradigm of theory and research that any discipline can ever reach scientific maturity.

The fact that Kuhn, himself, rejected any suggestion that paradigms could be artificially imposed or "legislated" on scientific communities, and even questioned the applicability of his analysis to the social sciences, has not prevented positivist readings of Kuhn from being adopted by some social scientists. In these readings, the development of a single, dominant paradigm has always carried with it the promise of a "takeoff" into sustained scientific development, and to the eventual consensus of the scientific community around a unified set of theories and methods of social scientific research.

When we look back over the past several decades at the development of OT as an independent discipline of applied social science it is apparent that, until very recently, a dominant view of organizational analysis prevailed within the discipline. Whether this view has constituted a "paradigm" in the strict Kuhnian sense remains debatable, but there can be little doubt it has exercised a controlling influence within the discipline, and has become recognized as an orthodoxy by a majority within the community of organizational theorists. That orthodoxy has been termed "functionalist" by Burrell and Morgan (1989), who – using a Kuhnian-type approach – attempted to conceptualize the field of organizational analysis as being comprised of four main paradigms (or ways of viewing reality): a dominant, "functionalist" paradigm, and competing "interpretive," "radical humanist" and "radical structuralist paradigms." Burrell and Morgan's intention was to "expose" the dominant paradigm as but one way of viewing the world, one way of several potential ways of viewing reality and, in the process of exposing "functionalism" in this way, to weaken its dominance and open the field to new ideas. Morgan (1986) has taken the idea farther by attempting to expose views of organizations as a series of competing metaphors – each one of which is at least partially true, none of which is completely valid.[2] As useful as the exercise of exposure has proved to many radical scholars within the field of OT, the dominant, "functionalist" or managerialist approach – despite the protestations of some to the contrary[3] – still continues to hold sway like a dead hand on the discipline, a fact that needs to be explained as well as countered.

In many ways, it may be more useful to analyze the dominant view of OT as a (Foucauldian) field of discourse than as a (Kuhnian) paradigm. For in Foucault's analysis, the emergence of a dominant, or hegemonic field of discourse is inseparable from the institutionalized practices and relations of power and authority which serve to privilege some forms of knowledge over others. In other words, to understand how particular fields of discourse have come to constitute certain domains of knowledge it is always necessary to examine the institutions which are linked to these new ways of thinking and speaking about the social (or natural) world.

Organization Theory, as a field of discourse, is derived from a number of different intellectual traditions. Its origins, as we have already seen, date back to the schools of classical social theory, most notably to Weber's theory of bureaucracy, but also, as Gouldner (1954) has suggested, to the work of Saint-Simon and Comte. Later sociological writers such as Parsons, Selznick, Gouldner, Kanter and others, have continued to work within this sociological tradition of OT.

However, it is only with the rise of management theory at the turn of the century that the study of organizations began to acquire a distinctly administrative focus, one which has remained its hallmark until the present time. It was through the contribution of such "classical" management theorists as F.W. Taylor, and others, as well as the later contributions of Human Relations theorists, that a managerial perspective became firmly entrenched within organizational discourse.

When, after World War Two, OT finally emerged as an independent discipline, amalgamated from a number of different fields of discourse which included not only social systems theory (from sociology), but also decision theory (from mathematics), rational choice theory (from economics), and information theory (from psychology), it was the managerial perspective which served as a common point of reference, and as a framework for the assimilation and synthesis of these diverse traditions within a distinctive discourse of OT.

Organization Theory, therefore, emerged as a successor to the earlier schools of management theory and incorporated many of their insights into its fields of discourse. Its language and concepts were used by managers to legitimize farther their authority within the modern organization. Within the academic community, the dominant managerial perspective of OT became fully institutionalized through the proliferation of management schools, standard textbooks, disciplinary journals and professional associations. Notwithstanding the polyglot origins of modern OT, therefore, these powerful institutions of thought control have successfully combined to impart a dominant managerialist perspective to the discipline, one which has continued to provide a common problem-solving framework for ongoing theory and research. In this sense, we may say that in spite of its interdisciplinary origins and its diverse conceptual frameworks, OT is characterized by a highly orthodox approach to the study of organizations, and one which has remained distinguished by its managerialist orientation. This is the closest we can get to saying that OT has developed a "paradigm" which has served to give some unity and coherence to the field of organizational discourse, as well as some basis for intellectual consensus within the academic community of organization theorists.

More than anything else, the prevailing paradigm of OT has continued to assume that rational action within organizations is primarily, (if not exclusively), associated with the functions of management. This is an assumption which has helped to integrate such otherwise diverse theoretical schools as Scientific Management, Human Relations and neo-Weberian studies of bureaucracy, with more recent traditions of decision theory, rational choice theory, game theory and contingency theory. In earlier schools of management theory the assumption, that the only rational functions in the organization were those which were performed by managers, was generally stated openly and explicitly. For Scientific Management theorists, it was axiomatic that managers had a rational interest in maximizing the efficiency of work, while workers maintained an irrational interest in "soldiering." Similarly, Human Relations theorists also distinguished between what they saw as a "logic of efficiency" which informed the actions of managers within an organization, and a "logic of sentiment" which motivated the actions of workers. In this respect, as in many others, early management theorists were united in their belief that only managers fully identified with the formal goals of the organization, but workers were more typically motivated by their own self-interests. It is easy to see how these beliefs contributed to the general assumption that the rationality of the organization resided exclusively in the functions of management.

Later theorists, such as Chester Barnard, Herbert Simon and others, revised their conceptions and definitions of organizational rationality. Whereas for Taylor, rationality was manifested in the "scientific" reclassification of work tasks and in the redesign of work processes, later theorists located rationality in other dimensions of the organization: in communication structures, information processes, rational choice designs, and so on. Common to virtually all these traditions, however, is the basic assumption that organizations may be viewed, first and foremost, as instrumental tools, (variously conceptualized as "machines," "organic structures," "social systems," "cybernetic systems," etc.) for the accomplishment of rational goals, and that primary responsibility for the formulation and realization of these goals remains with a specialized group of rational decision-makers, i.e., managers.

It is only recently that contemporary critics of OT – especially feminist critics – have shown how this apparently objective, neutral and universalistic assumption of organizational analysis is based on a highly gendered view of the organization. For, as Kanter (1977) has suggested, the identification of "rationality" as the primary attribute of any organization also implies a corresponding rejection of such other attributes as "emotionality," "subjectivity," and so forth. In other words, the concept of "rationality" which has remained so central to most traditions of OT, is based on a strong identification with stereotypical masculine values, and an equally strong rejection of stereotypical feminine values. This "masculine ethic" of rationality has had lasting theoretical and practical consequences for the participation of women (and other so-called minorities) in organizational life.

At a theoretical level, it has centred organizational analysis around the masculinized ideals of rationality and hierarchy, and has overlooked the experiences and values of other groups which not conform to these ideals. At a practical level it has helped to typify the ideal manager according to heavily masculinized criteria, thereby legitimating the long-term exclusion of women from positions of management.

WHAT IS TO BE DONE? THE CHALLENGE AND LIMITATION OF RADICAL THEORIES OF ORGANIZATION

Karl Marx once wrote that, "Philosophers have only interpreted the world, the point is to change it." By this he was saying that it is not enough merely to analyze uncomfortable realities but that we need to find ways of challenging and changing those realities. The 'uncomfortable realities' that we have documented in this book include organizations that are dominated by white, able-bodied men that, more often than not, either exclude women and visible minorities or relegate them to the lower echelons, that have a morality which is guided more by the needs of profitability and efficiency than by social need and responsibility and that, all too often, are places and experiences which inhibit human growth, sociability, and the potential for warmth and creativity. The 'uncomfortable realities' also include the discipline of Organization Theory which, far from questioning the darker realities of organizations, more often than not reflect those realities – in the process contributing to and strengthening them.

So what is to be done? What is the role of radical OT in the process of change and, equally to the point, what is the role of change in the development of radical theories of organization? Organization Theory has, as we have argued in earlier parts of the book, tended to reflect much of the times in which it was located. Not as a simple mirroring of reality but, at one level, as an interpreter of aspects of reality: those aspects that serve a managerialist focus. At another level, OT has developed as a 'field of discourse' – a living element in the process of producing and reproducing managerialist views of reality. In the 1930s, which were characterized by mass unemployment, widespread poverty, and preparations for war, management control was the major emphasis in the theories and practice of organizations. Managers needed little more than the threat of unemployment to control their workforces. It was in the looming shadow of the Second World War that the key leadership study of Lewin, Lippitt, and White (1939) emerged, with its appropriate characterization of different leadership styles whose names – democratic, authoritarian and laissez faire – referenced the actual international political concerns of the time. The immediate postwar era was shaped by a number of forces including – particularly in North America – rising expectations, high levels of employment, rising educational standards, and a rapid shift from blue- to white-collar work. This had its impact on the new breed of professional manager who, by inclination – they too were part of the changing ways of seeing the world which emerged after 1945 – and by the force of the new circumstances sought different ways to achieve coordination and control. They turned to humanistic theories of motivation and leadership style to manage the work of the growing white-collar and professional workers whose ranks were growing rapidly. These forms of "hegemonic" control (Clegg, 1981) were applied in the white-collar sphere but traditional "technical forms of control" still seemed to hold sway in those blue-collar or more routinized white-collar work.

Over much of the postwar era the ghost of the Cold War has hung over organizational thinking and practices that have characterized industrial societies East and West. This was no idle fantasy. The Cold War was experienced in a number of institutional ways. It was a discursive practice; a set of institutionalized relationships that has shaped the way we saw the world. It was manifest in the proliferation of Cold War institutions (NATO, the Warsaw Pact, The Pentagon, the Red Army, the KGB, the CIA, etc.) which have dominated our lives till now. It was manifest in the McCarthyism in the West and Stalinism in the East that led to the purging of persons from (government, military, media, school, and trade union) organizations. It was manifest in the strengthening of conservative and bureaucratic forces both in the East and the West. It was manifest in funding priorities which focused on military and space development, espionage, arm's manufacture and other war preparations. It was manifest in the social, military and political links between the top managers of the large corporations and government bodies (from I.T.T.'s link to the 1974 coup in Chile – see Sampson, 1983, through to the so-called Irangate disclosures of the 1980s). It was manifest in the government policies of the U.S., (for example, the U.S. involvement in the Vietnam War, designed to protect U.S. corporations), and of the Soviet Union, (for example, their involvement in the Afghanistan War, designed to retain Soviet influence, or hegemony, in the region). And, no doubt, it was manifest in the multitudes of ordinary workplace practices (in particular management, industrial relations, the maintenance of hierarchical relations) that went to shape management thinking to the present time.

In the same way the Cold War has served as a framework – sometime background, often foreground – for the development of radical theories of organization. In the East, where the dead hand of Cold War orthodoxy excluded the possibility of alternative theories of organization, critiques of organization appeared in literary form – the books of Solzhenitsyn, for example, that attacked much of the institutions of oppression (the Gulags, the KGB, etc.). In the West, George Orwell's *1984*, Ken Kesey's *One Flew Over the Cuckoo's Nest,* and Margaret Atwood's *Handmaid's Tale*, have carried on a similar tradition.

It was a sharp reaction against the Cold War that led many persons – East and West – to protest on the streets throughout much of the late 1960s and well through the '70s. The year of 1968 was in many ways pivotal. In Paris during May of that year workers and students were barricading the streets, and a nationwide strike and series of sit-ins threatened radical change. In Vietnam the National Liberation Front was planning a key military offensive – the Tet Offensive – against the U.S. forces in their country, and in Czechoslovakia the people were celebrating a 'Prague Spring' under a communist leader – Alexander Dubcek – who promised, "Socialism with a Human Face." (Six years later Edward Heath, the Conservative Prime Minister of Britain, was promising "Capitalism with a Human Face'")

As we know, the 'May '68' events ended in defeat for the French Left, and the Czechoslovak Spring was crushed under the weight of Soviet tanks. Only the Tet Offensive achieved a measure of success in embarrassing the U.S. military and helping to push them further on the road towards political defeat. Ironically, this era was also marked by a "thaw" in the Cold War, and the development of a coherent body of radical theories of organization. In the East — still under great danger — a limited number of challenging works appeared (cf. Djilas, 1982). In the West a number of radical critiques appeared, such as that of Ivan Illich (1973) and David Dickson (1977) which challenged the whole notion of organization and called for a radical restructuring of key social institutions (e.g., the schools) and of work. These were joined by a series of books and key articles (within the organizations and management literatures) — which owed much to the traditional Marxist perspective — including Allen (1975), Clegg (1975), Benson (1977), Hydebrand (1977), and Clegg and Dunkerley (1977). In some ways these works reflected the growing schism in the traditional Marxist Left between those who saw the need for a radical restructuring of society and those argued for a new type of 'non-organizational thinking'. Interestingly, these works were joined by a new orthodoxy in the work of Althusser (1979) who provided a new framework for the old Marxist concept of organization, with its notion that the economy is 'in the last analysis' determinate. They were also joined by new, feminist writers who were beginning to challenge sexist character of organizations (cf. Acker and Van Houten, 1974; Kanter, 1977).

By the end of the 1970s the work of Burrell and Morgan (1979) and Clegg and Durkerley (1980) signified a new level of analysis in the development of radical organization theories. Burrell and Morgan set out, in summarizing developments of several schools of radical and alternative thought, to challenge the prevalent managerialist orthodoxy of the time to 'educate' new generations of organizational analysts in the possibilities of alternative ways of viewing organizational analysis. Where Burrell and Morgan stopped short of explicitly encouraging the development of a radical theory of organization, Clegg and Dunkerley (1980) set out to provide radical educators with a text that would present the radical alternative to conservative theories of organization. Clegg and Dunkerley's text had a considerable initial impact on the field of organization studies but it is the Burrell and Morgan work that has had the greater impact. This is due to Burrell and Morgan's open-ended approach — suggesting that each of four major paradigms has something to offer: this appeals to those who see a need for change in the 'ethos' of management but not a radical change in the character of organizations and organizational control. Ironically, it is on the development of interpretive and radical humanist approaches to organization that Burrell and Morgan seem to have had the most impact, a factor no doubt encouraged by Morgan's (1986) next book which offered managers a smorgasbord of 'images of organization' from which to chose. It is likely that the potential of Clegg and Dunkerley's work was inhibited by subsequent events in the development of the Cold War. While Clegg and Dunkerley's work is by no means an apologia for the Soviets the general demise of East European communism – from glasnost to the fall of the Berlin Wall – seems to have thrown much of the broad left forces into a kind of doldrums, where they have remained for the past three or four years.

In an atmosphere of near euphoria where the conservative anti-Communist forces are loudly proclaiming victory in the Cold War, the Left has become introspective. While the large multinational companies are moving into Eastern Europe with undue haste, people on the Left are halfheartedly debating 'the future of Socialism'; for the time being socialist thinking has disappeared as a force within radical organizational thinking. So too have some of the more radical elements of so-called Radical Humanism. The Cold War framework, against which East Europeans rebelled, has been rapidly transformed into a drive for the development of 'market economies', losing much of its focus on a rethinking about the structure of society and its central institutional forms.

Over the same period, feminism has continued to have a strong and growing presence within organization theory. An increasing number of works over the last two decades have challenged the male domination of organizations and the gender-blindness of organization theory (Mills and Tancred, 1992). The growing strength of feminist theory has been due to three factors, (i) the fact that it was relatively untroubled by the Cold War – in as much as many of the Cold War institutions and practices could be translated as manifestations of a type of male-associated organizational behaviour (ii) the changing character of the workforce and the increasing numbers of women in the labour force in general, and in management in particular and (iii) because a significant element of feminist theory has been co-opted and adapted to mainstream OT, in the form of much of what is called "women-in-management approaches". Such approaches set out to replace the gender of persons in management positions rather than challenging the nature of the positions themselves. The existence of a strong and growing body of women-in-management theory has not been a bad thing. It has almost certainly helped to strengthen those organizational discourses which question the gendered character of institutions and it has helped to keep alive a broad discourse in which more radical feminists are able to raise issues and to continue to question.

It is only now – after years of Black struggle, with the changing demographics of North America, and with the development of the notion of the 'global economy'– that we are getting Black, or people of colour, critiques of OT, but as yet these approaches appear to be centred on getting more Blacks into existing forms of management – again, an important contribution to the development of a broad discourse in which racial issues can be raised and debated.

And what of the future? A vital feature of the current debate about radical organization theory is a growing interest in postmodernist and post-structuralist theory. We can see this as very much a reflection of our time: Postmodernism questions not only the rationale behind much of traditional institutional thinking (questioning notions of progress, rationality, objectivity, etc.), but also any potential 'truth claims' (e.g., philosophies of change based on ideas of truth, or 'the right way forward,' etc.) which set out to change the world by replacing existing power structures with new ones. These approaches tend to be highly introspective and focus on the relationship between organization and different forms of subjectivity. Postmodernism currently has a growing following across a broad cross-section of OT theorists – uniting previously socialist theorists with those who, in other times, may have been attracted to humanist managerialism, interpretive approaches and the tamer versions of radical humanism.

Today, postmodernism is providing a rich and challenging debate within the discourse of OT, but it is a debate which seems destined to be short-lived in a field that traditionally seeks clear answers, and in the face of potential changes in the organizational world. Within postmodernism there appears to be two main trends regarding the development of opposition and change. One trend – the main tendency – focuses largely on critique by explaining current organizational discourse, frowning upon any attempt to go beyond explanation, to strategies for change. The other tendency – exemplified by Burrell (1984) and Ferguson (1984) – argues that postmodernism is impotent if it acts as a break on challenges to existing forms of oppression. This approach takes the difficult but necessary road of arguing for the development of alternative discourses, discourses which question their own truths as part of a wider agenda of challenging discourses of oppression.

In the period ahead the world is being reformed into new power blocs – this time among competing capitalist entities. Thus, we see the consolidation of the European Common Market (EEC), with the Maastricht Treaty, and the consolidation of the North American Free Trade Agreement (NAFTA) with the inclusion of Mexico in the pact. Some of the more developed South East Asia countries (Thailand, Singapore, Korea) are already operating as an informal trading bloc. Many of the former East European countries seem intent on eventually joining the EEC. In these circumstances, those who question the notion of modernity might find themselves swamped by the creation of new subjectivities in which people sink into old ways of thinking and rivalries and resort to traditional forms of organizational control.

Of course, it is not that simple. The world is also troubled by many new questions and much new questioning. Some of it is negative as in the rise of neo-Nazism in Germany, or ethnic rivalries in the former territory of Yugoslavia. Some of it is a renewal of old capitalist values of entrepreneurship – as in the wave of interest sweeping Eastern Europe in entrepreneurial skills and values. Much of it is potentially positive – as in the widespread questioning of and opposition to bureaucracy throughout Eastern Europe, as in the questioning across Canada of the Free Trade Agreement, and in the Danish and French people's questioning of the Maastricht agreement.[4] It is a time when new discourses, new frameworks of thinking and organizing are developing. Radical theories of organization have a crucial role to play not only in providing a critique of existing organizational frameworks but in developing a discourse of opposition and change. This must be a self-critical discourse which seeks to avoid replacing – à la *Animal Farm* – one group of truths with a new set of (oppressive) truths. We need to see radical OT as a process of change, rather than a prescription for change – a journey rather than a destination, a permanent revolution in which our vision is a constant striving for change rather than a blueprint for change. That is the challenge of radical organization theory.

END NOTES

1. The need for a radical rethinking of O.T. has been expressed by a number of recent authors, for example:

   "The second key word in our definition is radical, which is derived from the Latin word "radix", meaning root. Radical redesign means getting to the roots of things [...] (Hammer and Champy, 1993:33).

2. Burrell and Morgan (1979) have since been taken to task for failing to include feminist ways of viewing the world as part of the paradigmatic landscape of organizational analysis (see Hearn & Parkin, 1983; Mills and Murgatroyd, 1991)

3. See Lex Donaldson (1986) who, believing that the functionalist orthodoxy was under threat, felt compelled to write 'in defence of organization theory'.

4. In 1992 a referendum in Denmark voted 'No' to the Maastricht Treaty. A similar referendum in France later in the year resulted in the slimmest margin for a 'Yes' vote. The Maastricht Treaty – agreed by the heads of the EEC countries in the city of Maastricht in December 1991 – proposed greater institutional and economic union of the EEC countries – towards the ideas of a supranational state.

Glossary of Terms

Americanization of organizational research – the tendency of most mainstream texts in OT and OB to uncritically adopt American organizational models and principles, and the generalization of these ideas over different cultures and societies. With few exceptions, (see Das, 1990), most OB and OT texts used in Canadian universities have made little if any reference to such specifically Canadian policies as Bilingualism, or Multiculturalism. For a much earlier protest over the neglect (and distortion) of Canadian reality in Americanized research, see John Seeley (1967).

Androcentricism – male-centred; a way of viewing the world exclusively from the perspective of men.

Assimilationism – the doctrine, first popularized in the United States, which emphasized the desirability and the inevitability of the process whereby overseas immigrants relinquished their own cultures in favour of that of the host country – America. In popular parlance, American society became seen as a huge "melting pot" which stripped immigrants of their original cultural identities (sometimes over a period of several generations) before transforming them into standardized (or fully homogenized) American citizens.

Besides attaining the status of an unofficial national doctrine in the U.S., assimilationism also influenced the work of a generation of early American race relations researchers, most notably, Robert Ezra Park (1950). In Canada, however, although the doctrine of assimilationism was initially supported by many powerful groups, it has long been rejected in favour of the policy of cultural pluralism, or what in the 1970s became known as the policy of Multiculturalism.

Authoritarian personality – a term devised by Adorno et al. (1950) to describe a person with a set of authoritarian characteristics. In some "potentially fascist" people there are a number of characteristics which form an authoritarian pattern or syndrome. The defining characteristics of the syndrome are a fear of strangeness and an emotional and ideological dependence on authority. The authoritarian personality is someone who fears strangeness and persons who are culturally, ethnically, politically, and/or religiously different from themselves. The authoritarian personality is manifest in anti-Semitic, ethnocentric, and politically conservative behaviour.

Authority – the social power that a person or social group believes to be legitimate. The important point here is the stress on legitimacy of the power exercised. In other words those who recognize the *authority* believe that it is justified and proper, and for these reasons the exercise of this authority tends to be effective in achieving its aims. It is directly opposed to the exercise of social power which relies on the coercive consequences of noncompliance for its effectiveness. (definition taken from Weeks, 1978: 13).

Bio-power – a term developed by Foucault to describe the relationship between power, knowledge and the body. Foucault contends that we live in a world which concerns itself with understanding and controlling the human body. Many organizations have come into being whose purpose is to collect data on the body and its functions; in the process there has been developed an understanding of the body which ultimately controls the way we view life. Medicine, education, public health and prisons, for example, all contribute to the way we view "*normalcy*" and this has a controlling influence – or bio-power – over the way we think and act.

Budgeting – this refers to one of the universal principles of management identified by the early American management theorist, Luther Gullick (1937). Gullick defined as "budgeting" those activities which related to the financial planning, accounting and control of the fiscal life of the organization. Today, budgeting is widely acknowledged to be one of the key elements in the practice of management. Without budgetary control, no manager can exercise real authority within an organization.

Bureaucracy – to many people, the term, "bureaucracy" has become synonymous with "red tape", over-regulation, wastage and general organizational inefficiency. To the sociologist, however, the term has a more technical (and a more neutral) meaning. It can best be defined as "a large, complex, formal organization which is organized through an elaborate division of labour, under an hierarchical structure of authority and which operates according to explicit rules and procedures". The actual word "bureaucracy" means "rule by officials, or office holders", and is often associated with the use of written files as part of the apparatus of administration. Although large organizations have existed for over a thousand years (for example, the Roman Catholic Church), the first writer to study the modern bureaucratic organization was the sociologist Max Weber, who described the typical characteristics of the bureaucracy.

Bureaucratic systems of control – according to Richard Edwards (1979), the bureaucratic system is the most recent system of managerial control to emerge in the modern workplace. Unlike earlier systems of workplace control, which relied on direct supervision or on the technical control of the workplace through technological means, bureaucratic systems of control regulate the workplace through company rules and policies. Bureaucratic forms of control, therefore, include collective agreements, job descriptions and designations, wage and salary scales, work rules, and so on.

Calculability – one of the characteristics of bureaucratic organizations is their tendency to subject all activities to precise measurement and calculation. Whether this involves a government caseworker calculating an applicant's eligibility for social assistance payments, or the worker in a fast-food industry who is obliged to carefully measure levels of coffee dispensed to customers, all bureaucracies try to ensure that their activities are subject to strict calculation and measurement.

Charismatic authority – this is a term used by the sociologist Max Weber to describe the type of authority which is based upon some extraordinary or outstanding personal qualities of a leader, or authority figure. Examples of charismatic authority vary from those of religious prophets (Jesus, Mohammed, Buddha, etc.), to political or demagogic figures (Hitler, Mao-Tse Tung, etc.). In each of these cases, however, it was the individual qualities of the charismatic leader that formed the basis of his (or her) authority. Although the word, "charisma" originally meant "magical" (in Greek), it has more commonly been used in a theological sense to refer to "the gift of grace".

Class – refers to a group of people with a shared relationship to social and economic aspects of society. For Marx, "ownership of the means of production" (by which he meant whether or not a person was a business owner) was the most important defining characteristic of class. The two main classes in capitalist society are the owning class and the working class (those who do not own a business and who need to work to earn a living). Marx believed that these two classes stand in an antagonistic relationship to one another, leading to economic conflict which will eventually result in the revolutionary transformation of society. For Max Weber, on the other hand, "life chances" (by which he meant the ability to advance socially due to income, skills, market assets, and/or property) is the defining characteristic of class. Nowadays, many sociologists take account of both "life chances" and a person's relationship to "the means of production" to attempt to predict future events.

Classical approach – the classical approach to any field of study is usually associated with those writers who have attained recognition in the area, and whose works are commonly acknowledged to have an enduring and permanent value within the field. The classical approach is often synonymous, therefore, with the established tradition, or the accepted wisdom, within an academic or professional discipline. The classical approach to the study of bureaucracy, for example, normally includes such writers as Marx, Weber and Michels; while the classical approach to management studies normally includes such writers as F. W. Taylor and Henri Fayol, among others.

Commanding – refers to one of the key activities involved in the practice of management which was first identified by the French management theorist, Henri Fayol, and later elaborated more fully by the American management theorist, Luther Gullick. "Commanding", or "directing", refers to the practice of setting goals, and of decision making within an organization.

Confessional practices – a term developed by Foucault to refer to the influence of psychological and psychoanalytical practices on notions of the self. Foucault contends that certain practices within society exert a powerful influence on the way we come to view our self and the selves of others. Take, for example, the influence of psychology on the legal system – in particular, modern notions of guilt and innocence. Psychological explanations of human growth and development have helped to shape the widespread belief that a person is not fully responsible for their actions: if it can be proven that a person had a bad upbringing the law is likely to be more lenient on the person charged with a crime. (See also disciplinary practices)

Consensus view of management – this expression refers to a conception of management which views the organization as a set of mutually interrelated parts linked together by strong underlying common interests. The manager, according to this view, is seen as a catalyst for bringing together the different physical and human resources in order to achieve the commonly desired goals of the organization. Because of its overemphasis on shared interests and commonly held goals, the consensus view overlooks, to a large extent, the existence of opposed interest groups, as well as conflict, power and inequality within the organization.

Controlling – this refers to another of the key activities involved in the practice of management, which was also identified by the French management theorist, Henri Fayol. It also refers to the regulation of all aspects of work processes within the organization.

Coordinating – this refers to another of the key activities involved in the process of management, originally identified by the French management theorist, Henri Fayol and later more fully elaborated by the American management theorist Luther Gullick. According to Gullick, coordination refers to the integration of the different parts of the organization in an effort to ensure the fulfillment of organizational goals.

Corporate culture – this refers to the prevailing set of values which are typically reflected in the managerial practice of most large corporations. Among other things, the corporate culture of many large organizations has been characterized by strong personal ambition, aggressive competition, and an all pervading individualism. While these values have traditionally been represented as desirable and necessary for the efficient performance of managers, more recent critics (especially feminists) have suggested that these values have more to do with patriarchal attitudes than with corporate efficiency. Indeed, even the most central values of the bureaucratic organization, those of rationality and hierarchy (inherited from the time of Max Weber), have been seen by some writers as no more than the institutionalization of patriarchal attitudes and practices. (See Ferguson, 1984; Morgan, 1988; Kanter, 1977).

Decisional roles – this concept was introduced by Henry Mintzberg (1975) in his efforts to distinguish between the variety of roles performed by managers in the everyday practices of management. Decisional roles refer to those activities which relate to the efficient deployment of resources within the organization.

Deskilling – this concept is often associated with the work of Harry Braverman (1974) who was one of the earliest labour process theorists to question the optimistic conclusions of the post-industrialism thesis. Unlike many theorists of the late 1960s, Braverman did not believe that the new technologies of industry would necessarily eliminate the need for unskilled labour nor bring about the expansion of a new highly skilled middle class. Instead, Braverman suggested that the new technologies have often been used by managers to strip workers of their traditional craft skills and to cheapen the value of their labour power in the workplace.

Directing – see **Commanding**

Disciplinary practices – a term used by Foucault to refer to those practices concerned with knowledge and control of the body. Medicine, education, public health, prisons, schools and many other organizations have developed sets of practices which combine to control how we view the world and how we behave as a result. The school system, for example, involves a series of practices which require that as children we attend school at certain ages, and during specified periods of time. The school system also helps to create the viewpoint that being schooled is the mark of a "normal" person: as a reaction against the disciplinary nature of schools Illich (1973) has suggested that we "deschool" society. (See also bio-power)

Discourse – refers to a set of ideas and viewpoints, experienced in and through a series of communications, which influence the behaviour and thinking of the persons involved. Organizing, for example, is a discourse that is reproduced daily through sets of practices. From religion to sport, from physical activity to music, whenever we want to achieve something in the modern world we usually think of organization. We rarely stop to think whether an activity is best left unorganized. Organizing is a powerful discourse which influences the way we think.

Discrimination – refers to the process or processes whereby some individuals are deprived of equal access to rights and opportunities generally available to others. Individuals who face discrimination in such areas as employment, housing or educational opportunities are frequently members of particular minority groups (whether racial/ethnic, women, physically handicapped, etc.,).

Division of labour – refers to the specialization of tasks within the process of production. Popularized by Adam Smith during the eighteenth century in his economic writings, the term originally indicated the breakdown of the production process into a series of separate and distinct technical tasks. However, the term was later used by Emile Durkheim in a broader sense to describe the social division of labour: that is, the specialization of different occupational groups in any given society.

Dominance – a personality characteristic which involves a striving to exert control over others. In some persons – due to the effects of socialization – this can be experienced as a need to be dominated.

Efficiency – the concept of efficiency implies the selection of the most appropriate means in order to achieve certain predetermined ends. In organizational terms, efficiency implies the effective utilization and allocation of physical and human resources for the achievement of organizational goals. The standard measurement of efficiency in most organizations (in both private and public sectors), are those of productivity and profitability.

Ethnic mosaic – refers to the pattern of social relations in a society whereby different ethnic groups maintain their distinctive ethnic identities and their separate cultural heritages. In Canada, (unlike the U.S., which still espouses the goal of assimilating all ethnic groups into the dominant North American culture), the maintenance of ethnic diversity has been officially supported by the Federal Government's policy of Multiculturalism.

Ethnicity – refers to the social categorization of persons according to their cultural background. Factors taken into account can include a person's national, cultural, and language heritage. The term is utilized by some people to build pride in their heritage (e.g., as in the various heritage and cultural celebrations that take place throughout Canada's provinces). In recent years the term has been used by some as a political weapon: to proclaim White supremacy (e.g., such people never use the term "ethnic" to describe their own White, Anglo-Saxon heritage); to create an ethnic hierarchy of peoples (e.g., references to "ethnic food" or "ethnic people"); and, to attack people of colour (e.g., references to Black people as "ethnics").

Ethnocentricism – refers to the tendency of many, if not most, individuals to centre their beliefs and attitudes around the cultural values and practices of their own particular ethnic group. In practice, this usually means that the values and practices of one's own group are seen as superior to those of other groups, or that elements of one's own culture have universal validity across all cultures. Unlike a fully developed racist ideology, however, the biases of ethnocentrism are usually implicit and taken-for-granted.

Femininity – characteristics associated with *being a woman*; culturally specific notions of what physical and behavioural features constitute females. What is seen as feminine changes over time and depends on a number of factors, including female resistance to patriarchal rules. In Victorian Britain, for example, it was not considered "feminine" for a woman to have the vote. In today's Britain some people still consider it unfeminine for women to go out to work. Notions of femininity vary not only with time but with context. In Northern Holland, for example, the working woman is a fact of life, but in Maastricht, in the South of Holland, it is still regarded as unfeminine.

Formalization – refers to the process by which informal social relations are gradually replaced by social relations governed by explicit rules and regulations oriented towards the realization of officially defined goals. In organizational terms, the modern bureaucracy, with its highly specialized division of labour and differential allocation of authority represents a high level of formalization.

Gender – culturally shaped characteristics associated with being a man or a woman. Gender is often confused with sex. While sex refers to a person's biological constitution (i.e., specifically the genitalia) gender refers to socially constructed understandings of what it means to be a man or a woman. The biological features that a person is born with serve only as a basis for categorization as male or female. The characteristics of manhood and of womanhood are dependent on cultural notions and have to be learned. People spend most of their lives learning what it is to be masculine or feminine, to be a *real man* or a *real woman*. Historically notions of gender have been constructed in male-dominated contexts and as a result are made up of a series of discriminatory ideas. For example, the notion that men are "strong" and women are "weak" is a culturally devised idea which has been used in a number of discriminatory ways, including preventing women from gaining the vote or serving in the armed forces, or being employed in a range of occupations. (See also femininity, masculinity)

Glass ceiling – concept invented by Morrison et al (1987) to describe a situation where companies' statements encourage women to enter senior management but their practices prevent them from doing so. Thus, women can see the top of the management ladder but a seemingly invisible ceiling prevents them from climbing above the middle rungs.

Goal displacement – a term used to describe how a commitment to the goals of particular sectors of an organization may sometimes become more important to the individuals and groups within these sectors than the larger goals of the entire organization. Thus, competition between officials from different departments may result in their losing sight of, or displacing, the more central goals of the organization. This problem was first clearly articulated by Robert Merton (1940), in his discussion of "bureaucratic ritualism".

Hierarchy – virtually all large organizations are characterized by a differential allocation of authority, status and prestige. Which is to say that all large organizations are based upon a principle of inequality: those at the top have more authority and prestige than those at the lower levels. Most organization theorists have traditionally assumed that hierarchy is a necessary condition of organizational efficiency. Today, however, opinions are changing on this issue. Some theorists may believe that hierarchy in bureaucracies contributes to poor communication, poor motivation and reduced efficiency. Others have argued that the principle of hierarchy simply reflects an entrenchment of patriarchal attitudes.

Identity – the psychological experience of sameness over time. Through various processes of socialization and other experiences a person comes to believe that they are a certain, and unique, person. This belief plays an important part in the way a person orients his or her actions.

George Herbert Mead argues that the self – a crucial aspect of identity – is socially constructed, that we develop a sense of self through interaction with others. Mead contends that we acquire a sense of self through social contexts involving the organized attitudes of others (the "Me") and our reflections on those attitudes (the "I"). Mead's view suggests that the self is never finally formed but is always to some degree in a state of flux and mediation. Leonard (1984) argues that Mead's theory lacks an understanding of the concrete situations in which identities are formed; contexts in which people are not equal in their power and ability to shape how other persons are viewed. For the large majority of working people, for example, the self is developed in contexts in which the "I" is confronted by more powerful symbols and actors.

Some theorists argue that as we develop into adults we acquire a fixed and unchangeable identity; Flax (1990), for example, refers to the "core identity" which we have acquired by the age of three years. Postmodernist theorists, on the other hand, argue that people develop "multiple identities" which depend on the person's location in, and experience, of a number of social discourses (cf. Dreyfus & Rabinow 1982).

Impersonality – this term describes the kind of social relations which typically exist between members of a bureaucracy and their clients. Impersonality implies, on the one hand, that all clients are treated alike without preference or favouritism; on the other hand, impersonality may also imply a lack of personal feeling or empathy with the other person. Although impersonality has often been seen as a necessary condition for efficiency and equity in bureaucratic transactions, it has been recognized as a problem in interpersonal relations.

Informational roles – this concept was introduced by Henry Mintzberg (1975) in his effort to distinguish between the variety of roles performed by managers in the everyday practice of management. Informational roles refer to those activities which relate to the communication of ideas (both their transmission and their receipt) within the organization.

Institutionalized, (structural, or systemic) discrimination – refers to indirect discrimination that occurs as a by-product of the normal functioning of bureaucratic organizations. In this sense, institutionalized discrimination may often be unintended, and often results from the entrenchment of selection criteria, or other job-related qualifications, which have failed to keep up with the changing composition of the workforce in particular, and of society in general. Examples would be physical requirements for jobs which may well exclude some ethnic groups, as well as women. (For a useful discussion of institutionalized discrimination in Canada, see Abella, 1984).

Instrumental reason – a term developed by Max Weber to characterize modern thinking based on means and ends calculations. According to Weber, the success of bureaucracy as an enduring and widespread form of organization is due, in large part, to instrumental reasoning. People accept bureaucratic rules and authority because it accords with their own way of measuring the world; people are motivated to act by judging whether what they will put into a situation will be balanced by what they get out of it. Bureaucracies offer employees a system in which they can advance according to the effort and commitment of the employee and not at the whim of the employer or by dint of personality. Ferguson (1984) and Morgan (1988) challenge this perception and argue that

patriarchal discourse intervenes to inhibit the advancement of female employees of bureaucracies. Martin (1990) questions whether instrumental reason can
be said to be characteristic of both men <u>and</u> women; arguing that it is more
likely a part of male thinking.

Interpersonal roles – this concept was introduced by Henry Mintzberg (1975) in his
effort to distinguish between the variety of roles performed by managers in the
everyday practice of management. Interpersonal roles refer to those activities
associated with the leadership functions of management, whether these are
understood in ritualized, symbolic, or in wholly practical terms.

Life instincts/Eros – a term developed by Freud who argued that people are born
with a drive for species survival. The drive has two main elements: (i) self-preservation, and (ii) sexual instincts. In other words, we act in certain ways because of an unconscious striving to ensure the survival of humankind. The
problem is, according to Freud, that this striving is shaped by family and social
influences which can lead to personality disorders.

Managerial revolution – a term developed by James Burnham (1960) to refer to the
twentieth century rise and development of professional managers as a new, and
powerful class in the day-to-day running and control of organizations.

Managerial viewpoint – see **Managerialist**

Managerialist – an analysis of organizations which takes the needs and the perspectives of management as its starting point.

Masculinity – characteristics associated with *being a man*; culturally specific notions of
what physical and behavioural features constitute males and maleness. What is
seen as masculine changes over time and depends on a number of factors. In
eighteenth century Britain, for example, it was considered masculine in some
quarters to wear long hair and brightly coloured clothing. It was quite the
opposite in the Britain of the mid-twentieth century. Notions of masculinity
vary not only with time but with context. In the U.S., for example, there are
some communities which view masculinity as the ability to cry (*new age man*)
while in other communities the ability to avoid crying is viewed as a sign of
manhood.

Mirroring – a psychoanalytic term referring to the process where the actions of certain others becomes reflected (or mirrored) in the thoughts and behaviour of a

person. Kets de Vries (1989a, 1989b, 1990) argues that an unreflective and psychologically weak person is in danger of over identifying with a strong other; he contends that, in the workplace, mirroring is facilitated by excessive dependency between executives and subordinates. Organizational success often depends on a mirroring of appropriate behaviour and, in such situations, subordinates can come to identify excessively with the leader. This can lead to situations of moral uncertainty and corruption as employees attempt to mirror, rather than reflect upon, executive decisions. In a patriarchal world, mirroring helps to reproduce discriminatory practices against women.

Multiculturalism – refers to the official policy of ethnic pluralism in Canada which was introduced in October 1971 by the Liberal Government of Prime Minister Trudeau. This policy has supported the right of ethnic groups in Canada to preserve their ethnic identities and cultural heritages, and has provided government funding for this purpose. Recently, however, Multiculturalism has come under attack from a number of directions. Some groups and individuals have argued that Multiculturalism policies should no longer be financed through public funds. Others have suggested that Multiculturalism has eroded our sense of national identity and national unity (Bibby, 1990); still others have argued that Multiculturalism has not gone far enough in combating racial prejudice and discrimination. Multiculturalism has become a divisive issue in Canadian politics.

Narcissism – a Freudian term for the psychological condition of having an exaggerated love of self; it involves the development of an idealized and unrealistic image of self, which becomes the object of the person's love.

Organizing – refers to another of the key activities involved in the practice of management. Originally identified by the French management theorist, Henri Fayol, it was later elaborated more fully by the American management theorist, Luther Gullick. According to Gullick, planning refers to the process of identifying tasks and how to complete them in order to fulfil the goals of the organization.

Planning – refers to another of the key activities involved in the practice of management. Originally identified by the French management theorist, Henri Fayol, it was later elaborated more fully by the American management theorist, Luther Gullick. According to Gullick, organizing refers to the establishment of a formal structure in an organization, and to the implementation of an efficient division of labour in the workplace.

Power – the control which a person has over other people; the ability of a person to exact compliance or obedience of other individuals to his or her will. Persons in positions of authority have power by dint of the fact that they hold legitimate office; people usually comply with the will of an office holder because it is assumed that they have legitimately attained the post and therefore have a certain level of competency. But not all people with power are in positions of authority. The unofficial trade-union organizer, the charismatic rabble-rouser, and the well-respected member of a social group can also exercise power due to their character or attributes. It used to be argued that power corrupts and absolute power corrupts absolutely, but Kanter (1979) argues that *a lack* of (organizational) power can be more corrupting. For example, the person with no organizational autonomy or discretion often resorts to the rules in dealing with problems.

    Postmodernist writers of recent years argue that power is "decentred" in that we all contribute to practices and discourses which bestow different elements of power (and powerlessness) on each of us. The U.S. airline industry of the 1960s, for example, restricted the recruitment of flight attendants to *pretty*, young, White females. This practice originated from top management in the business, but was also supported by a travelling public which accepted the practice as "normal", and by the tens of thousands of female applicants who attempted to join the business. The problem with the postmodernist version of power, however, is that it underestimates the range of power involved in any given context. Clearly, airline executives were powerful in the creation of sexist recruitment practices and in their maintenance. Other actors helped to support those practices, but individually would have found it difficult to have changed them. It took a concerted action on the part of the modern women's liberation movement before some of the airlines' sexist practices were changed.

Psychic prison – a metaphor developed by Gareth Morgan (1986) to characterize the way that people can experience organizations as confining and dominating; people can actually become imprisoned or confined by the images, ideas, thoughts, and actions to which organizational processes give rise.

Race – the categorization of persons – usually according to skin colour and ethnic origin – into subspecies of humanity. The development of the concept of race is bound up with the development of imperialism and this is reflected in its usage, which suggests that some peoples are biologically inferior to others. The concept, which owes more to belief and political use than to biological fact, has for centuries been invoked to discriminate against and suppress people of colour. (See also ethnicity)

Race relations – this refers to the pattern of social relations existing between members of different visible minority groups and the dominant (i.e., White) groups in society. The state of race relations between different groups may be variously defined as harmonious, antagonistic, etc., depending upon a number of different factors. The greatest threat to the existence of harmonious race relations is often the presence of sharp inequalities of power and/or wealth, especially when differences in socioeconomic status are reinforced by differences in racial or ethnic background.

Racism – refers to a set of beliefs which are based on the assumption that differences in racial or ethnic background correspond to differences in social, cultural, intellectual or even moral development. Implicit in this assumption is the belief that some "races" have a higher potential for development than others; in other words, that some "races" are superior to others in terms of their innate abilities. Racism can also be expressed as a set of practices which are consistent with the above beliefs. Unlike ethnocentric beliefs, therefore, which are often held naively without conscious reflection, racist beliefs are often codified into self-conscious ideological frameworks. The historical function of racist beliefs and practices has typically been that of denying to certain minority groups equal access to strategic resources (such as employment, housing, education, voting rights, etc.,) while protecting and rationalizing privileges enjoyed by a dominant group (or groups).

Rational-legal authority – this is the term used by Max Weber to describe the type of authority which is based upon a system of explicitly defined rules and regulations in which authority derives from the status of the office held rather than from any personal or traditional qualities of the individual. Bureaucratic organizations represent the most complete example of a system of rational-legal authority. Authority within a bureaucratic system may either come from appointment (as in private corporations) or from election (as in many public bodies).

Reporting – refers to another of the key activities involved in the practice of management. Originally identified by the American management theorist, Luther Gullick, reporting refers to the processes of information gathering, storage and retrieval through such activities as research, inspection and record keeping.

Repression – in psychoanalytical theory this refers to the psyche's main defence mechanism which acts unconsciously to exclude from memory unpleasant experiences: the ego pushes unwanted memories into the unconsciousness. According to psychoanalysts, repressed thoughts, memories and experiences not only continue to exert an influence on thoughts and behaviour but, because they are repressed, can be the major cause of thoughts and actions.

Rigidity – refers to the fact that bureaucracies can sometimes appear inflexible and inefficient when dealing with unusual, exceptional or atypical cases. This is because bureaucracies are established to process large amounts of information, and large numbers of people, as efficiently as possible. When confronted with unusual cases which cannot be processed according to standard procedures, those who administer the rules and regulations within bureaucracies can sometimes appear to be rigid, insensitive and singularly unimaginative.

Routinization – refers to the process whereby regularly recurrent patterns of social interaction acquire the status of relatively stable and objective elements of social structure. All social structure, including organizational relations, is based upon the routinization of particular forms of social interaction.

Scientific Management – refers to the movement established early in the twentieth century by the American management theorist, F. W. Taylor. Scientific Management, or Taylorism, comprised a system of principles and practices which rapidly transformed workplace relations during the opening decades of the twentieth century. Central to Taylorism was the idea that increased workplace efficiency depended upon a greater divisions of labour, and on the systematic analysis and redesign of jobs. Taylor believed that every work process could be analysed systematically and broken down into its constituent parts, thus reducing each worker's job to a simple, single task. He also believed that the planning and conception of work should remain the sole responsibility of management, while the actual performance and execution of work tasks remained the responsibility of workers.

Taylor's ideas led to a revolution in workplace relations, enabling managers to acquire a new monopoly of knowledge and control over most industrial work processes, and also enabling them to progressively replace higher-waged skilled workers with lower-waged unskilled workers. In historical terms, therefore, Scientific Management directly contributed to the cheapening and to the deskilling of the modern industrial labour force (See Braverman, 1974).

Sexual preference – refers to a person's choice of sexual orientation, from a range of sexual possibilities that include heterosexuality, homosexuality and bisexuality. The term was developed in recent years as a reaction against heterosexist assumptions and terms which labelled non-heterosexual orientation "abnormal". The term sexual preference, as opposed to earlier terms (e.g., sexual deviancy), suggests choice rather than biological abnormality; *sexual preference* suggests that all forms of sexual orientation are equally acceptable.

Simple control – according to Richard Edwards (1979), the earliest system of managerial control to emerge in the modern workplace was that of 'simple control'. Largely associated with small owner-operated firms, this form of control was characterized by highly personalized and paternalistic systems of supervision where the workplace was small, and the bosses were close and powerful.

Specialization – refers to the division of labour which has accompanied the growth of large bureaucratic organizations in the modern world. Modern organizations are characterized by the elaborate division of occupational roles into separate and distinct spheres of competence and responsibility. Functional specialization and structural differentiation have become the hallmarks of the modern bureaucracy.

Staffing – refers to all aspects of personal and human resource management including the recruitment, evaluation, promotion and dismissal of employees within an organization.

Standardization – refers to the tendency for the modern bureaucracy to reduce many of its activities to simple, easily reproducible tasks which help to fulfil the goals of the organization. This standardization of functions is one aspect of what Max Weber termed the growing "rationalization" of organizations in the modern world.

Subjectivity – a person's sense of self as a person; a set of understandings about what constitutes the human subject. In early times it was generally believed that people were ordained to occupy a certain status or position in life: people spoke, for example, of *the divine right of kings*. This influenced how people viewed themselves and humanity in general. In South Africa, how people understand themselves and others was shaped by the policy of Apartheid; a person's subjectivity was constructed out of a society that was sharply divided along racial lines. Today, subjectivity is being shaped differently in a South Africa rocked by economic and political crises.

Systematic soldiering – this is the term used by F. W. Taylor, and other managers and business people of his generation, to designate the way many workers deliberately regulated the pace of their work, and often restricted their productivity and output. For Taylor and his associates, the tendency for workers to produce below their optimal speeds constituted a major "problem" for the efficient organization and supervision of work. Taylor's system of Scientific Management was designed to strip workers of any effective control over their work processes, and to return this control exclusively to managers.

Systemic discrimination – a term developed by the Abella Commission (1984) to characterize forms of discrimination which arise out of the ways in which organizations are structured. (See also *Institutionalized discrimination*)

Technical control – according to Richard Edwards (1979), the emergence of systems of technical control in the workplace corresponds to the growth of big business and to the introduction of new forms of technology. With the installation of assembly lines, workers became subject to the control of the new machinery which directed not only their pace of work, but also their rates of pay. Under these new conditions, the role of management became more related to the monitoring and evaluation of work, than to its initiation and direction.

Time and motion studies – refer to those studies undertaken by management researchers and consultants, such as F. W. Taylor and his followers, which were designed to increase the efficiency of work. Time and motion "experts" were primarily interested in clocking speeds at which workers completed their assigned work tasks, and in exploring ways in which these tasks could be performed more efficiently by redesigning them for greater specialization.

Tokenism – refers to the practice of hiring a single, or small number of, individual(s) from underrepresented minority or disadvantaged groups (often racial, ethnic, gender, or physically challenged), as evidence of any lack of institutional discrimination against these groups. Rather than demonstrating any serious commitment to employment equity, however, tokenism usually implies the "showcasing", or "window-dressing" of a few minority individuals as a minimal way of fulfilling moral, political or even legal obligations for fair employment practices.

Traditional authority – is a term used by Max Weber to describe the type of authority which is based upon a system of long-lasting beliefs and practices passed down from one generation to the next. Such authority derives its legitimacy from the continuity which links it to previous generations, as in the customary status accorded to hereditary chiefs in traditional societies, or in the institution of the monarchy in modern societies.

Uniformity – refers to the tendency of the modern bureaucracy to impose a common format on many of its products and services. Large bureaucracies have often tended to discourage diversity or variety in the mass production of goods and services. Uniformity has often been seen as a logical consequence of technical efficiency.

Universalist tradition – is a term normally used to describe the tradition of management studies which emerged at the beginning of this century, and was associated with the work of the French management theorist, Henri Fayol, among others. Many of these early theorists began their careers as engineers, which accounts for their tendency to view organizations much as they viewed machines. Because of this, universalist theorists focused almost exclusively on the formal structure and design of organizations, and in their writings, they sought to discover a universal set of management principles which could be applied to any organization. Their general aim was to develop a universal "science" of management.

Vertical mosaic – is a term that was introduced by the Canadian sociologist, John Porter (1965), to describe the degree of ethnic inequality in Canadian society. From his research, Porter found that ethnicity had traditionally played an important role in determining the occupational and socioeconomic status of early immigrants upon their arrival in Canada. He concluded that the historical legacy of ethnic stratification had contributed to the low rates of social mobility, and to the lack of any genuine equality of opportunity in Canadian society.

Visible minorities – is a term which has replaced that of "racial minority" as a way of describing non-White people, or people of colour, in multicultural societies. Visible minorities refer to those communities who come from other than a European ethnic background.

Bibliography

Abu-Laban, Yasmun and Stasiulis, Daiva, 1992, "Ethnic pluralism under seige: popular partisan opposition to 'multiculturalism,'" *Canadian Public Policy*, 18(4):365-386.

Acker, J., and D.R. van Houten, 1974, "Differential recruitment and control: the sex structuring of organizations," *Administrative Science Quarterly*, 9(2): 152-163.

Abella, Judge Rosalie Silberman, 1984, *Equity in Employment. A Royal Commission Report*, Ottawa: Ministry of Supply and Services Canada.

Adorno, T.W. and E. Frankel-Brunswik, 1983, *The Authoritarian Personality*, New York: Norton.

Agócs, C., 1989, "Walking On The Glass Ceiling: Tokenism in Senior Management." Paper presented to the annual meeting of the Canadian Sociology and Anthropology Association, Université Laval, Quebec, June 4.

Aird, A.R., P. Nowack, and J.W. Westcott, 1989, *Road to the Top: The Chief Executive Officer in Canada*, Toronto: Doubleday.

Alderfer, C.P., 1991, "Changing Race Relations in Organizations: A Critique of the Contact Hypothesis," *Canadian Journal of Administrative Studies*, 8(2):80-89.

Alderfer, C.P., and D.A. Thomas, 1988, "The significance of race and ethnicity for understanding organizational behaviour," in *International Review of Industrial and Organizational Psychology*, Vol.2, edited by C.L. Cooper and I.T. Robertson, pp.1-41, New York: Wiley.

Allen, V., 1975, *Social Analysis*, London: Longman.

Allport, G., 1954, *The Nature of Prejudice*, New York: Doubleday.

Alvesson, M., 1987, *Organization Theory and Technocratic Consciousness*, Berlin: Walter de Gruyter.

American, R.F., and R. Anderson, 1978, *Moving Ahead: Black Managers in American Business*, New York: McGraw-Hill.

Anderson, A.B., and J.S. Frideres, 1981, *Ethnicity in Canada: Theoretical Perspectives*, Toronto: Butterworths.

Argyris, C., 1987, *Personality and organization*, New York: Garland Publishing.

Armstrong, M., 1990, *Management Processes and Functions*, Institute of Personnel Management, Exeter: Short Run Press.

Arvey, R.D., and R.H. Faley, 1988, *Fairness in Selecting Employees*, Reading, MA.: Addison-Wesley.

Astley, W.G., and A.H. Van de Ven, 1983, "Central perspectives and debates in organizational theory," *Administrative Science Quarterly*, 28, pp.245-73.

Avery, Donald, 1979, *Dangerous Foreigners: Immigrant Workers and Labour Radicalism in Canada, 1896-1932*, Toronto: McClelland and Stewart.

Bahro, R., 1978, *The Alternative In Eastern Europe*, London: New Left Books.

Bannerji, H., L. Carty, K. Dehli, S. Heald, and K. McKenna, 1991, *Unsettling Relations. The University as a Site of Feminist Struggles*, Toronto: Women's Press.

Barnard, C., 1939, *The Functions of the Executive*, Cambridge, MA: Harvard University Press.

Berle, A. Jr., and G. Means, 1933, *The Modern Corporation and Private Property*, New York: MacMillan.

Beattie, C., 1975, *Minority Men in a Majority Setting*, Toronto: McClelland and Stewart.

Beatty, C., 1991, "Stress in Professional and Managerial Women." Paper presented to the Current Canadian Research on Women in Management conference, Winnipeg, May 5-7.

Bell, E.L., 1989, "The Mammy and the Snow Queen." Paper presented at Research in Women in Management conference, Kingston, Ont., September.

✳ Bell, E.L., 1990, "The bi-cultural life experience of career-oriented black women," *Journal of Organizational Behaviour*, 11:459-477.

✳ Bell, E.L., T.C. Denton, and S.M. Nkomo, 1992, "Women of Color in Management: Towards An Inclusive Analysis," in *Women and Work, Vol. VI., Women in Management: Trends, Issues, and Challenges*, edited by L. Larwood and B. Gutek (eds) Newbury Park, CA.: Sage.

Bell, E.L. and S.M. Nkomo, 1992, "Re-Visioning Women Manager's Lives," in *Gendering Organizational Analysis*, edited by A.J. Mills and P. Tancred, pp. 235-247, Newbury Park, CA.: Sage.

Bendix, R., 1949, *Higher Civil Servants in American Society*, Boulder, CO.: University of Colorado Press.

Bennis, W., 1966, "The Coming Death of Bureaucracy," *Think*, Nov-Dec: 30-35.

Benson, J.K., 1977, "Organizations – A Dialectical View," *Administrative Science Quarterly*, 22, 1-21.

Benson, S.P., 1988, *Counter Cultures, Saleswomen, Managers and Customers in American Department Stores 1890-1940*, Urbana and Chicago: University of Illinois Press.

Beynon, H., and R.M. Blackburn, 1972, *Perceptions of Work*, Cambridge: Cambridge University Press.

Blackburn, Robin, ed., 1991, *After the Fall: The Failure of Communism and the Future of Socialism*, London: Verso.

Blau, P., 1955, *The Dynamics of Bureaucracy*, Chicago: University of Chicago Press.

Blauner, R., 1967, *Alienation and Freedom*, Chicago: The University of Chicago Press.

Blauner, R., 1972, "Colonized and Immigrant Minorities," in *Racial Oppression in America*, New York: Harper and Row.

Blustein, D.L., L.E. Devenis, and B.A. Kidney, 1989, "Relationship between the identity formation process and career development," *Journal of Counselling Psychology*, Vol.36, No.2, pp.196-202.

Bolaria, B.S., and P. Li, 1985, *Racial Oppression in Canada*, Toronto: Garamond Press.

Bonacich, E., 1972, "A theory of ethnic antagonism: the split labor market," *American Sociological Review*, 37:547-559.

Borisoff, D., and L. Merrill, 1985, *The Power to Communicate. Gender Differences as Barriers*, Prospect Heights, Ill.: Waveland Press.

Bradbury, B., 1979, "The Family Economy and Work in an Industrializing City: Montreal in the 1870s," *Canadian Historical Association Papers*, pp. 71-96.

Bradshaw-Campball, P., 1991, "Canadian Women on Boards: Excellence In A Box." Paper presented at the Current Canadian Research on Women in Management conference, Winnipeg, May 5-7.

Brandwin, Edmund, 1972, *The Bunkhouse Man: A Study of Work and Pay in the Camps of Canada, 1903-1914*, University of Toronto Press.

Braverman, H., 1974, *Labor and Monopoly Capital: the Degradation of Work in the Twentieth Century*, New York: Monthly Review Press.

Breton, R., 1964, "Institutional Completeness of Ethnic Communities and the Personal Relations of Immigrants," *American Journal of Sociology*, 70: 193-205.

Brindley, J. E., and P. Frick, 1990, *Gender Differences in Management. A Study of Professional Staff in Registrars' Offices in Canadian Universities*, Athabasca University.

Brown, H.A. and Ford, D.L. Jr., 1977 "An exploratory analysis of discrimination in the employment of Black MBA graduates," *Journal of Applied Psychology*, 62:50-56.

Burawoy, M., 1979, *Manufacturing Consent*, Chicago: University of Chicago Press.

Burawoy, M., 1985, *The Politics of Production*, London: Verso.

✳ Burke, R.J., 1991 "Managing an increasingly diverse workforce: experiences of minority managers and professionals in Canada," *Canadian Journal of Administrative Sciences*, 8(2):108-120.

Burke, R. and C. McKeen, 1988, "Mentor Relationships in Organizations: Issues, Strategies and Prospects for Women" in proceedings of the Women in Management Research Symposium, Mount Saint Vincent University, Halifax, N.S., April 27-29.

Burnham, J., 1960, *The Managerial Revolution*, Westport, CT.: Greenwood Publishing.

Burnham, Patrick, 1988, *Killing Time, Losing Ground: Experiences of Unemployment*, Toronto: Wall and Thompson.

Burrell, G., 1984, "Sex and Organizational Analysis," *Organization Studies*, 5/2, pp.97-118.

Burrell, G., 1988, "Modernism, Post-Modernism and Organizational Analysis 2: The Contribution of Michel Foucault," *Organization Studies*, 9/2, pp.221-235.

Burrell, G., and G. Morgan, 1979, *Sociological Paradigms and Organizational Analysis*, London: Heinemann.

Calas, M.B., 1988, "An/Other Silent Voice: Organization Theory and Research on Hispanic Populations." Paper presented at the national meeting of the Academy of Management, Anaheim, August.

Calas, M.B., 1991, "Re-Writing Gender Into Organizational Theorizing: Directions From Feminist Perspectives," in M.I. Reed and M.D. Hughes (eds) *New*

Directions in Organizational Research and Analysis, London: Sage.

Calas, M.B., 1992, "An/Other Silent Voice? Representing 'Hispanic Woman' in Organizational Texts," in *Gendering Organizational Analysis*, edited by A.J. Mills and P. Tancred, pp.201-221, Newbury Park, CA.: Sage.

Calas, M.B. and L. Smircich, 1992, "Using the 'F' word: Feminist Theories and the Social Consequences of Organizational Research," in *Gendering Organizational Analysis*, edited by A.J. Mills and P. Tancred, pp.222-234, Newbury Park, CA.: Sage.

Caley, D., 1988, "Part Moon, Part Travelling Salesman: Conversations With Ivan Illich." Montreal: CBC Transcripts.

Campell, B.M., 1984, "If you can't go home again, where can you go? The isolation of the black executive," *Savvy* (December issue: 67-74).

Camphell, Maria, 1973, *Halfbreed*, Goodread Biographies, Halifax: Formac Publishing Co. Ltd.

Canada, 1974, Green Paper on Immigration and Population. Canadian Immigration and Population Study.

Canada, 1984, *Equality Now*, Minutes of the Proceeding and Evidence of the Special Committee on Participation of Visible Minorities in Canadian Society.

Canada, 1969, Royal Commission on Bilingualism and Biculturalism, Book IV, *The Cultural Contributions of Other Ethnic Groups*.

Carey, A., 1967, *The Hawthorne Studies: A Radical Critique*, American Sociological Review, 32:403-416.

Carlsson, S., 1951, *Executive Behaviour: a study of the workload and the working methods of managing directors*, Stockholm: Strombergs.

Carroll, S.J., and D.J. Gillen, 1987, "Are the classical management functions useful in describing managerial work?" *Academy of Management Review*, 12 (1): 38-51.

Carty, L., 1991, "Black Women in Academia: A Statement From The Periphery," in *Unsettling Relations*, edited by Bannerji et al, pp.13-44, Toronto: Women's Press.

Castles, S., and G. Kosak, 1973, *Immigrant Workers and the Class Structure in Western Europe*, Oxford: Oxford University Press.

Cava, R., 1988, *Escaping the Pink Collar Ghetto, How Women Can Advance in Business*, Toronto: Key Porter Books.

Chandler, A.D., 1977, *The Visible Hand: the Managerial Revolution in American Business*, Cambridge, MA.: Harvard University Press.

Chandler, A.D., 1984, "The emergence of managerial capitalism," *Business History Review*, 58 (Winter): 473-503.

Chapman, B., 1961, "Facts of Organized Life." *Manchester Guardian Weekly*, Jan 26 edtn.

Clark, D.L., 1985, "Emerging Paradigms in Organizational Theory," in *Organizational Theory and Inquiry: The Paradigm Revolution*, edited by Y. Lincoln, Beverley Hills, CA.: Sage.

Clark, K.B., and M.P. Clark, 1958, "Racial identification and preference in negro children," in *Readings in Social Psychology*, edited by E. Macoby and T.M. Newcomb, New York: Holt, Rinehart and Winston.

Clegg, S.R., 1975, *Power, Rule and Domination: A Critical and Empirical Understanding* of Power in Sociological Theory and Organizational Life, London: Routledge and Kegan Paul.

Clegg, S.R., 1981, "Organization and Control," Administrative Science Quarterly, 26, pp.545-562.

Clegg, S.R., 1989, Frameworks of Power, London: Sage.

Clegg, S.R., 1990, Modern Organizations, London: Sage.

Clegg, S.R., and D. Dunkerley, 1980, Organization, Class and Control, London: RKP.

Coch, L. and J.R.P. French, 1948, "Overcoming resistance to change," Human Relations, I, pp.512-532.

Cockburn, C., 1985, Machinery of Dominance, London: Pluto Press.

Collinson, D.L., 1988, "Engineering Humour: Masculinity, Joking and Conflict in Shopfloor Relations," Organization Studies, 9(2), pp.181-99.

Collinson, D.L., and Margaret Collinson, 1989, "Sexuality in the Workplace: The Domination of Men's Sexuality," in The Sexuality of Organization, edited by J. Hearn, D.L. Sheppard, P. Tancred-Sherrif, and G. Burrell, pp, 91-109, London: Sage.

Collinson, D.L., D. Knights, and M. Collinson, 1990, Managing To Discriminate, London: Routledge.

Conklin, D., and P.Bergman (eds), 1990, Pay Equity in Ontario: a manager's guide, London, Ont.: National Centre for Management Research and Development.

Cooper, K.C., 1985, Stop It Now. How Targets and Managers Can End Sexual Harassment, St.Louis: Total Communications Press.

Corliss, R., 1993, "Hollywood's Summer: Just Kidding," Time magazine, Vol.141, No.26, June 28th, pp.62-65.

Coser, Lewis A., et al, 1985, Books: The culture and commerce of publishing, Chicago: University of Chicago Press.

Cox, M.G., 1986, "Enter the Stranger: Unanticipated Effects of Communication on the Success of an Organizational Newcomer," in Organization – Communication. Emerging Perspectives, edited by L. Thayer, pp.34-50, Norwood, NJ.: Ablex Publishing Corp.

✳ Cox, T. Jr., 1990, "Problems with organizational research on race and ethnicity issues," Journal of Applied Behavioural Sciences, 26: 5-23.

Cox, T., S. Lobel, and P. McLeod, 1991, "Effects of ethnic group cultural differences on cooperative versus competitive behaviour in a group task," Academy of Management Journal, 34:827-847.

Cox, T. Jr., and S. Nkomo, 1990, "Invisible men and women: a status report on race as a variable in organization behavior research," Journal of Organizational Behavior, 11: 419-431.

Crane, D., 1967, "The Gatekeepers of Science: Some Factors Affecting the Selection of Articles for Scientific Journals," American Sociologist, 2:195-201.

Crean, S., 1985, Newsworthy. The Lives of Media Women, Halifax, NS.: Formac Publishing Co.

Crozier, M., 1964, The Bureaucratic Phenomenon, London: Tavistock.

Cullen, D., 1992, "Sex and Gender on the Path to Feminism and Self-Actualization." Paper presented at the annual meeting of the Administrative Sciences Association of Canada (ASAC), Quebec, June.

Cuneo, C.J., 1990, *Pay Equity. The Labour-Feminst Challenge*, p.13, Toronto: Oxford University Press.

Cunningham, M., with F. Schumer, 1985, *Powerplay. What Really Happened at Bendix*, Toronto: Ballantine Books.

Daft, R., 1989, *Organization Theory and Design*, Third Edition, St.Paul, MN.: West.

Dahrendorf, R., 1959, *Class and Class Conflict in Industrial Society*, Stanford University Press.

Dagg, A. Innis and P.J. Thompson, 1988, *MisEducation: Women and Canadian Universities*, Toronto: OISE Press.

Dale, E., 1978, *Management: theory and practice*, Toronto: McGraw Hill.

Darroch, A.G., 1979, "Another Look at Ethnicity, Stratification and Social Mobility in Canada," *Canadian Journal of Sociology*, 4:1-25.

Das, H., 1990, *Organization Theory with Canadian Applications*, Gage Educational Publishers.

Davidson, M.J., and C.L. Cooper, 1983, *Stress and the Woman Manager*, Oxford: Blackwell.

Davies, S. 1990, "Inserting Gender in Burawoy's Theory of the Labour Process," *Work, Employment & Society*, 4/3, pp.391-406.

Davis, G., and G. Watson, 1982, *Black Life in Corporate America: Swimming in the Mainstream*, New York: Doubleday.

Deal, T.E., and A.A. Kennedy, 1982, *Corporate Cultures*, Reading, MA.: Addison-Wesley.

✳ Denton, T.C., 1990, "Bonding and supportive relationships among black professional women: rituals of restoration," *Journal of Organizational Behavior*, 11:447-457.

DePass, Cecille, 1992 "Centering on changing communities: the colours of the south in the Canadian vertical mosaic," *Canadian Ethnic Studies*, 24(3).

Dickens, F., and J.B. Dickens, 1982, *The Black Manager*, New York: Amacom.

Dickson, D., 1977, *The Politics of Alternative Technology*, New York: Universe.

Dipboye, R.L., 1985, "Some neglected variables in research on discrimination on appraisals," *Academy of Management Review*, 10:116-127.

DiTomaso, N., 1989, "Sexuality in the Workplace: Discrimination and Harassment," in *The Sexuality of Organization*, edited by J. Hearn, D.L. Sheppard, P. Tancred-Sherrif, and G. Burrell, pp. 71-90, London: Sage.

Djilas, M., 1982, *The New Class*, San Diego, CA.: Harvest Books.

Donnelly, J.H. Jr., J.L. Gibson, and J.M. Ivancevich, 1990, *Fundamentals of Management*, Illinois: BPI-Irwin.

Dreyfus, H.L., and P. Rabinow, 1982, *Michel Foucault: Beyond Structuralism and Hermeneutics*, Brighton: Harvester.

Driedger, Leo, 1987, *Ethnic Canada: Identities and Inequalities*, Toronto: Copp, Clark Pittman.

Drucker, P., 1986, *The Practice of Management*, New York: Harper.

Due Billing, Y. and Allvesson, M., 1994, *Gender, Managers, and Organizations*, Berlin: de Gruyter.

Edwards, R., 1979, *Contested Terrain: The Transformation of the Workplace in the Twentieth Century*, New York: Basic Books.

Etzioni, A., [ed], 1961, *Complex Organizations: A Sociological Reader*, Austin, Tx.: Holt, Rinehart and Winston.

Fayol, H., 1949, *General Industrial Management*, London: Pitman.

Feffer, John, 1992, *Shockwaves: Eastern Europe After the Revolutions*, Montreal: Black Rose Books.

Feldberg, R., and E.N. Glenn, 1984, "Male and female: job versus gender models in the sociology of work," in *Women and the Public Sphere*, edited by J. Siltanen and M. Stanworth, pp.23-36, London: Hutchinson.

Ferguson, K.E., 1984, *The Feminist Case Against Bureaucracy*, Philadelphia: Temple University Press.

Fernandez, J., 1975, *Black Managers in White Corporations*, New York: John Wiley.

Fernandez, J.P., 1981, *Racism and Sexism in Corporate Life*, Lexington: D.C. Heath.

Feyeraband, P., 1978, *Against Method*, London: Verso.

Fischer, F., and C. Siriani [eds], 1984, *Critical Studies in Organization and Bureaucracy*, Philadelphia, PA.: Temple University Press.

Flax, J., 1990, *Thinking Fragments, Psychoanalysis, Feminism, & Post-Modernism in the Contemporary West*, Berkeley: University of California Press.

Foster, Cecil, 1991, *Distorted Mirror: Canada's Racist Face*, Toronto: Harper Collins.

Foster, D., 1980, *The Management Quadrille*, London: Pitman Publishing Ltd.

Foucault, M., 1975, *The Birth of the Clinic*, New York: Vintage.

Foucault, M., 1977, "What Is an Author?" in *M. Foucault, Language, Counter-memory, Practice*, edited by D.F. Bouchard, Ithaca, N.Y.: Cornell University Press.

Foucault, M., 1979, *Discipline & Punish, The Birth of the Prison*, New York: Vintage.

Foucault, M., 1980, *Power/Knowledge: Selected Interviews and Other Writings 1972-77*, ed. Colin Gordon, New York: Pantheon.

Fox, B.J., and J. Fox, 1987, "Occupational gender segregation of the Canadian labour force, 1931-1981," *Canadian Review of Sociology and Anthropology*, 23(3), pp.374-397.

Franklin, R., 1968, "A framework for the analysis of inter-urban negro-white economic differentials," *Industrial and Labour Relations Review*, 2:209-223.

French, J.R.P., J. Israel, and D. Aas, 1960, "An experiment on participation in a Norwegian factory," *Human Relations*, 13, pp. 3-19.

Frost, P.J., V.E. Mitchell, and W.R. Nord, 1990, *Managerial Reality: Balancing Technique, Practice and Values*, Glenville, Ill.: Scott, Foresman – Little Brown Education.

Fukuyama, F., 1989, "The End of History?", *The National Interest*, Summer Issue.

Galbraith, J.K., 1967, *The New Industrial State*, New York: Houton Mifflin Co.

Galnoor, Itzhak, ed., 1977, *Government Secrecy in Democracies*, New York: Harper and Row.

Gemmill, G., and L.Z. Schaible, 1990, "Split vision, split vitality: the psychodynamics of female/male role differentiation within the organization." Paper presented at the meeting of Academy of Management, San Francisco.

Gerloff, E.A., 1985, *Organizational Theory and Design*, New York: McGraw-Hill.

Gilligan, C., 1982, *In a Different Voice: Psychological Theory and Women's Development*, Cambridge, MA.: Harvard University Press.

Glassman, R.M., W.H.Jr. Swatos, and P. Rosen [eds] 1987, "Bureaucracy Against Democracy and Socialism," *Contributions in Sociology #65*, Greenwood Press.

Goldman, P., 1978, "Sociologists and the Study of Bureaucracy: A Critique of Ideology and Practice," *The Insurgent Sociologist*, 3 (Winter): 21.

Gouldner, A.W., 1954, *Patterns of Industrial Bureaucracy*, Glenco, Ill.: Free Press.

Gram, H., 1986, *An Introduction to Management*, Toronto: Holt, Rinehart and Winston of Canada.

Grant, J., and P. Tancred-Sheriff, 1986, "A feminist perspective on state bureaucracy," in *Gendering Organizational Analysis*, edited by A.J. Mills and P. Tancred, Newberry Park, CA.: Sage.

Gross, B., 1980, *Friendly Fascism: the New Face of Power in America*, New York: M. Evans.

Gullick, L., 1937, "Notes on the theory of organizations," in *Papers on the Science of Administration*, edited by L. Gullick and L. Urwick, New York: Columbia University Press.

Guppy, N., 1989, "Pay equity in Canadian universities, 1972-73 and 1985-86," *The Canadian Review of Sociology and Anthropology*, 26:5, pp.743-758.

Gutek, B., 1985, *Sex and the Workplace*, San Francisco, CA.: Jossey-Bass.

Gutek, B., and A. Cohen, 1992, "Sex Ratios, Sex Role Spillover, and Sex at Work: a Comparison of Men's and Women's Experiences" in *Gendering Organizational Analysis*, edited by A.J. Mills and P. Tancred, pp.133-150, Newbury Park, CA.: Sage.

Gutek, B, and L. Larwood (eds), 1987, *Women's Career Development*, Newbury Park, CA.: Sage.

Halberstam, D., 1986, *The Reckoning*, New York: Morrow and Co.

Hall, M., 1989, "Private Experiences in the Public Domain: Lesbians in Organizations," in *The Sexuality of Organization*, edited by J. Hearn, D.L. Sheppard, P. Tancred-Sherrif, and G. Burrell, pp, 125-38, London: Sage.

Hammer, M. and J.C. Hampy, 1993 *Re-engineering The Corporation: A Manifesto For Business Revolution*, New York: Harper Collins Publishers.

Handelman, D., and E. Leyton, 1978, *Bureaucracy and World View: Studies in the Logic of Official Interpretation*, Institute of Social and Economic Research, Memorial University of Newfoundland.

Harriman, A., 1985, *Women/Men, Management*, New York: Praeger.

Harris, C., 1991, "Configurations of racism: the civil service, 1945-1960," *Race and Class*, 33:1-30.

Harrison, R., and R. Lee, 1986, " Love at Work," *Personnel Management*, Jan., pp. 20-24.

Hartman, C. and P. Vilanova, eds., 1992, *Paradigms Lost: The Post Cold War Era*, London: Pluto Press.

Hatton, M.J., 1990, *Corporations & Directors*, Toronto: Thompson.

Heap, J.L., 1974, *Everybody's Canada: the Vertical Mosaic Reviewed and Re-examined*, Toronto: Burns and MacEachern Ltd.

Hearn, J., 1985, "Men's Sexuality at Work," in *The Sexuality of Men*, edited by A. Metcalf and M. Humphries, pp.110-28. London: Pluto Press.

Hearn, J. and W. Parkin, 1987, *'Sex' at 'Work': The Power and Paradox of Organizational Sexuality*, Brighton: Wheatsheaf.

Hearn, J. and P.W. Parkin, 1991, "Women, Men and Leadership: a Critical Review of Assumptions, Practices, and Change in the Industrialized Nations," in N.J. Adler and D. Izraeli (eds) *Women in Management Worldwide*, pp.17-40. New York: M.E. Sharpe.

Hearn, J., D.L. Sheppard, P. Tancred-Sherrif, and G. Burrell [eds], 1989, *The Sexuality of Organization*, London: Sage.

Hegeous, A., 1976, *Socialism and Bureaucracy*, Boston, MA: Allison and Busby.

Held, D., 1980, *Introduction to Critical Theory. Horkheimer to Habermas*, London: Hutchinson.

Hathorn, H.B., et al., 1967, *A survey of the contemporary Indians of Canada: A report of economic, political and educational needs and policies, Vols. 1 & 2*, Ottawa: Queen's Printer.

Henry, F., and E. Ginzberg, 1985, *Who gets the work: A test of social discrimination in Employment*, Toronto: Urban Alliance on Race Relations and Social Planning Council of Metropolitan Toronto.

Hodge, B.J., and W.P. Anthony, 1991, *Organization Theory: A Strategic Approach*, Needham Heights, MA.: Allyn and Bacon.

Hodgkinson, H.L., 1985, *Demographics of Education*, Washington, D.C.: Institute of Educational Leadership.

Hoffman, E., 1988, *The Right To Be Human. A Biography of Abraham Maslow*, Los Angeles, CA.: Jeremy P. Tarcher.

Hofstede, G., 1984, *Culture's Consequences. International Differences in Work-Related Values*, Beverly Hills, CA.: Sage.

Hood, J.N., and C.S. Koberg. (In press), "Patterns and Consequences of Differen-

tial Assimilation and Acculturation for Women in Business Organizations," *Academy of Management Review*.

Huxley, A., 1950, *Brave New World*, London: Chatto and Windus.

Iacocca, L. with W. Novak, 1984, *Iacocca – An Autobiography*, New York: Bantam.

Illich, I., 1981, *Deschooling Society*, Harmondsworth: Penguin.

Irons, E., and G.W. Moore, 1985, *Black Managers in the Banking Industry*, New York: Praeger Publishers.

Irvine, J., I. Miles and J. Evans, 1979, *Demystifying Social Statistics*, London: Pluto Press.

Isajiw, W.W., 1981, *Ethnic Identity Retention*, University of Toronto Centre for Urban and Community Studies.

Jameson, F., 1989, "Marxism and Post-modernism," *New Left Review*, 176, pp. 31-45.

Jauch, L.R. and J.L. Wall, 1989, "What they do when they get your manuscript: a survey of Academy of Management reviewer practices," *Academy of Management*, 32: 157-173.

Johns, G., 1988, *Organizational Behaviour. Understanding Life at Work*, Second Edition, Glenview, Ill.: Scott, Foresman and Company.

Jones, A.P., L.R. James, J.R. Bruni, and S.B. Shell, 1977, "Black-white differences in work environment perceptions and job satisfaction and its correlates," *Personnel Psychology*, 30:5-16.

Kanter, R.M., 1979, *Men and Women of the Corporation*, New York: Basic Books.

Kerr, S., J. Tolliver, and D. Petree, 1977, "Manuscript characteristics which influence acceptance for management and social science journals," *Academy of Management Journal*, 20: 132–141.

Kets de Vries, M.F.R. [ed], 1984, *The Irrational Executive*, New York: International Universities Press.

Kets de Vries, M.F.R., 1989a, "The leader as mirror: clinical reflections," *Human Relations*, Vol.42, No.7, pp.607–623.

Kets de Vries, M.F.R., 1989b, "Leaders who self-destruct: the causes and cures," *Organizational Dynamics*, pp.5–17a.

Kets de Vries, M.F.R., 1989c, "Alexithymia in organizational life: the organization man revisited," *Human Relations*, Vol.42, No.12, pp.1079–1093.

Kets de Vries, M.F.R., 1990, "Leaders on the couch: the case of Roberto Calvi." Paper presented at the symposium of the Clinical Approaches to the Study of Managerial and Organizational Dynamics, Montreal.

Kets de Vries, M.F.R. and D. Miller, 1984, *The Neurotic Organization*, San Francisco: Jossey-Bass.

Kirby, S. and K. McKenna, 1989, *Experience, Research, Social Change. Methods From the Margins*, Toronto: Garamond.

Kirchmeyer, C. and J. McLellan, 1991, "Capitalizing on ethnic diversity: an approach to managing the diverse workgroups of the 1990s," *Canadian Journal of Administrative Studies*, 8(2):72–79.

Knights, D., and H. Willmott, 1985, "Power and identity in theory and practice," *The Sociological Review*, pp.22–46.

Knights, D., and D.L. Collinson, 1987, "Disciplining The Shop-floor: A Comparison of the Disciplinary Effects of Managerial Psychology And Financial Accounting," *Accounting, Organizations and Society*, Vol.12, No.5, pp.457–477.

Knights, D., 1989, "Subjectivity, Power and the Labour Process," in *Labour Process Theory*, edited by D. Knights and H. Willmott, pp.297–335, London: Macmillan.

Knights, D. and G. Morgan, 1991, "Organization Theory, Consumption and the Service Sector." Paper presented at the Towards a New Theory of Organizations Conference, University of Keele, April 3–5.

Knox, D., 1990, *Living Sociology*, St.Paul, MN.: West Publishers.

Kohut, Heinz, 1971, *The Analysis of the Self*, New York: International Universities Press.

Konar, E., 1981, "Explaining racial differences in job satisfaction: a re-examination of the data," *Journal of Applied Psychology*, 66:522–524.

Krahn, H.J. and G.S.Lowe, 1988, *Work, Industry and Canadian Society*, Toronto: Nelson Canada.

Kraiger, K. and J. Ford, 1985, "A meta-analysis of rated race effects in performance ratings," *Journal of Applied Psychology*, 70:56–65.

Kranz, H., 1976, *The Participatory Bureaucracy: Women and Minorities in a More Representative Public Service*, Lexington, MA.: Lexington Books.

Kuhn, T., 1962, *The Structure of Scientific Revolutions*, Chicago: University of Chicago Press.

Lakatos, I., 1972, "History of Science and its Rational Reconstructions," in *Boston Studies in the Philosophy of Science*, Volume 8, edited by R.C. Buck and R.S. Cohen, pp.91–135, Boston: Reidel Publishing House.

Lamphere, L., 1985, "Bringing the Family to Work: Women's Culture On The Shop

Floor," *Feminist Studies*, 11, no.3, pp.519-540, Fall.

Landy, F.J. and S.L. Farr, 1980 "Performance Rating," *Psychological Bulletin*, 87:72-107.

Lasch, C., 1983, *The Culture of Narcissism*, New York: Warner Books.

Lautard, H., and D. Loree, 1984, "Ethnic Stratification in Canada," *Canadian Journal of Sociology*, 9: 333-343.

Lawrence, P., 1984, *Management in Action*, London: Routledge and Kegan Paul.

Leavitt, H.J., 1986, *Corporate Pathfinders*, Illinois: Dow Jones Irwin.

Lee, M.D., 1991, "Women's Involvement in Professional Careers and Family Life: Themes and Variations." Paper presented at Current Canadian Research on Women in Management conference, Winnipeg, May 5-7.

Leonard, P., 1984, *Personality and Ideology*, London: MacMillan.

Lewin, K., R. Lippitt, and R.K. White, 1978, "Patterns of Aggressive Behaviour in Experimentally Created Social Climates," in *Organization Theory*, edited by D.S. Pugh, pp.230-260, Harmondsworth: Penguin.

Li, P., 1988, *Ethnic Inequality in a Class Society*, Toronto: Wall and Thompson.

Lincoln, Y., 1985, *Organizational Theory and Inquiry: The Paradigm Revolution*, Beverley Hills, CA.: Sage.

Lipset, S.M., 1950, *Agrarian Socialism: The Cooperative Commonwealth Federation of Saskatchewan: A Study in Political Sociology*, Berkeley, CA.: University of California Press.

Lipset, S.M., 1950, "Bureaucracy and Social Reform," in *Complex Organizations: A Sociological Reader*, edited by A. Etzioni, Austin, TX.: Holt, Rinehart and Winston.

Littrel, W.B., G. Sjoberg, and L.A. Zurcher [eds] 1983, *Bureaucracy as a Social Problem*, Greenwich, CT.: JAI Press.

Livingstone, D.W., and M. Luxton, 1989, "Gender consciousness at work: modifications of the male breadwinner norm among steelworkers and their spouses," *The Canadian Review of Sociology and Anthropology*, 26(2), pp.240-75.

Livingstone, J.S., 1971, "Myth of the well educated manager," *Harvard Business Review*, 49, (Jan-Feb): 79-89.

Locke, E.A., 1982, "The ideas of Frederick W. Taylor: An Evaluation," *Academy of Management Review*, 7, (1): 14-24.

Love, J.F., 1986, *McDonald's: Behind the Arches*, Toronto: Bantam.

Lowe, G.S., 1987, *Women in the Administrative Revolution*, Toronto and Buffalo: University of Toronto Press.

Lowe, G.S., and H.C. Northcott, 1986, *Under Pressure. A Study of Job Stress*, Toronto: Garamond Press.

Lukacs, G., 1971, *History and Class Consciousness*, translated by Rodney Livingstone, Cambridge, MA.: MIT Press.

Maier, M., 1991, "The Dysfunctions of 'Corporate Masculinity': Gender and Diversity Issues in Organizational Development," *The Journal of Management in Practice*, Summer/Fall Issue.

March, J.G., and H.A. Simon, 1958, *Organizations*, New York: Wiley.

Marcuse, H., 1941, "Some social implications of modern technology," *SPSS*, vol. 9.

Marcuse, H., 1970, *One Dimensional Man*, London: Sphere.

Marshall, H., and M. Wetherall, 1989, "Talking about career and gender identities: a discourse analysis perspective," in *The Social Identity of Women*, edited by S. Skevington and D. Baker, pp.106-129, London: Sage.

Martin, J., 1990a, "Rethinking Weber: A Feminist Search for Alternatives to Bureaucracy." Paper presented at the annual meeting of the Academy of Management, San Francisco, Aug.10-15.

Martin, J., 1990b, "Deconstructing Organizational Taboos: The Suppression of Gender Conflict in Organization," *Organization Science*, Vol.1, No.4, pp.339-359, November.

Marx, K., 1967, *Economic and Philosophic Manuscripts of 1844*, Moscow: Progress Publishers.

Marx, K., 1959, *Capital*, Vol.3, Moscow: Progress Publishers.

Marx Memorial Library, 1992, "Post Modernism", *Marx Memorial Library Bulletin*, Issue No.117.

Maslow, A., 1943, "A theory of human motivation," *Psychological Review*, vol.50, no.4, pp. 370-96.

Mayo, E., 1933, *The Human Problems of an Industrial Civilization*, New York: Macmillan.

McCarrey, M., 1988, "Work and personal values for Canadian anglophones and francophones," *Canadian Psychology*, 29:69-83.

McKague, Ormond (ed.), 1991, *Racism in Canada*, Saskatoon: Fifth House.

Media Watch, 1982, *Sex Role Stereotyping: A Content Analysis of Radio and Television Programs and Advertisements*, Vancouver: Media Watch.

Meissner, M., 1986, "The Reproduction of Women's Domination," in *Organization-*

Communication: Emerging Perspectives, edited by L. Thayer, pp. 51-67, Norwood, NJ.: Ablex.

Metcalfe, H., and R. Urwick, 1941, *Dynamic Administration, The Collected Papers of Mary Parker Follett*, New York: Harper and Brothers.

Michels, R., 1949, *Political Parties*, New York: Free Press.

Miewald, R., 1970, "The Greatly Exaggerated Death of Bureaucracy," *California Management Journal*, (Winter): 65-69.

Mighty, J., 1991, "Triple Jeopardy: Employment Equity and Immigration, Visible Minority Women." Paper presented at the Women-in-Management session of the Administrative Science Association of Canada Annual Meeting, Niagara, Ontario, June.

Mighty, J., 1991a, "Valuing workforce diversity: a model of organizational change," *Canadian Journal of Administrative Sciences*, 8:64-70.

Mikalachki, A., D.R. Mikalachki, and R. Burke, 1992, *Gender Issues in Management*, Toronto: McGraw-Hill Ryerson.

Mills, A.J., 1988a, "Organizational Acculturation and Gender Discrimination," in P.K. Kresl (ed) *Women and the Workplace*, Ottawa: International Council for Canadian Studies, pp.1-22.

Mills, A.J., 1988b, "Organization, Gender and Culture," *Organization Studies*, 9/3, pp. 351-369.

Mills, A.J., 1989, "Gender, Sexuality and Organization Theory," in *Sexuality and the Organization*, edited by J. Hearn, D. Sheppard, P. Tancred-Sheriff, and G. Burrell, London: Sage, pp. 29-44.

Mills, A.J., 1991, "Organizational Discourse

and the Gendering of Identity." Paper presented to the New Theories of Organization conference, Keele University, April 3-5.

Mills, A.J., and P. Chiaramonte, 1991, "Organization as Gendered Communication Act," *Canadian Journal of Communications*, Winter, 16/4.

Mills, A.J., and S.J. Murgatroyd, 1991, *Organizational Rules: A Framework for Understanding Action*, Milton Keynes: Open University Press.

Mills, A.J., and P. Tancred [eds], 1992, *Gendering Organizational Analysis*, Newbury Park, CA.: Sage.

Mills, A.J., 1994, "Organizational Sexuality," Contribution to *Encyclopedia of Women and Work*, edited by K.M. Borman and P. Dubeck, New York: Garland Publishing Inc.

Mintzberg, H., 1973, *The Nature of Managerial Work*, New York: Harper and Row.

Mintzberg, H., 1975, "The Manager's Job: Folklore and Fact," *Harvard Business Review*, 53, (4): 49-61.

Mitchell, J., 1975, *Psychoanalysis and Feminism*, New York:n Vintage Books.

Mockler, R.J., 1971, "Situational theory of management," *Harvard Business Review*, 49, (May-June): 146-151.

Morgan, G., [ed], 1983, *Beyond Method: Strategies for Social Research*, Beverly Hills, CA.: Sage.

Morgan, G., 1985, "Journals and the control of knowledge: a critical perspective," in *Publishing in the Organizational Sciences*, edited by L.L. Cummings and P.J. Frost, Homewood, IL.: Richard D. Irwin.

Morgan, G., 1986, *Images of Organization*, London: Sage.

Morgan, G., and D. Knights, 1990, "Consumption and the Sociology of Organizations." Paper presented at the Critical Approaches To Organizations session at the Canadian Sociology and Anthropology Association annual meeting, University of Victoria, May 26-30.

Morgan, N., 1988, *The Equality Game. Women in the Federal Public Service (1908-1987)*, Ottawa: Canadian Advisory Council on the Status of Women.

Morrison, A., R. White, and E. Van Velsor, 1987, *Breaking the Glass Ceiling*, Reading, MA.: Addison Wesley.

Mouzelis, N., 1967, *Organization and Bureaucracy: An Analysis of Modern Theories*, New York: Aldine de Gruyter.

Mumby, D.K. and L.L. Putnam, 1992, "The politics of emotion: a feminist reading of bounded rationality," *Academy of Management Review*, 17(3):465-486.

Mumby, D.K., and L.L. Putnam, 1990, "Bounded Rationality as an Organizational Construct: A Feminist Critique." Paper presented at the annual meeting of the Academy of Management, San Francisco, Aug. 10-15.

Murphy, C.J., 1973, "The invisibility of Black workers in organizational behavior," *Journal of Social and Behavioral Sciences*, Summer-Fall, 1-12.

Nahem, J., 1981, *Psychology and Psychiatry Today. A Marxist View*, New York: International Publishers.

Naidoo, J.C., and R.G. Edwards, 1991, "Combatting racism involving visible minorities," *Canadian Social Work Review*, 8(2):211-236.

Nelton, S., 1988 "Meet our new workforce," *Business Week*, 14-21.

Newman, J.M., 1978, "Discrimination in recruitment: an empirical analysis," *Industrial and Labour Relations Review*, 32:15-23.

Newson, J., and H. Buchbinder, 1988, *The University Means Business*, Toronto: Garamond Press.

Nichols, T., and H. Beynon, 1977, *Living with Capitalism*, London: Routledge and Kegan Paul.

Nkomo, S., 1992, "The emperor has no clothes: rewriting 'race in organizations'," *Academy of Management Review*, 17(3):487-513.

Nkomo, S., 1988, "Unchartered Journey: Minority Women in Management." Paper presented at the national meeting of the Academy of Management, Anaheim, CA, August.

Nkomo, S., and T.H. Cox Jr., 1989, "Gender differences in the upward mobility of Black managers: double whamming or double advantage?", *Sex Roles*, 21:825-839.

Oakley, A., 1972, *Sex, Gender and Society*, London: Temple Smith.

Ogmundson, R., 1990, "Perspectives on the class and ethnic origins of Canadian elites: A critique of Porter, Clement et al.," *Canadian Journal of Sociology*, XX: 165-177.

Omi, M. and H. Winant, 1986, *Race Formation in the United States: From the 1960s to the 1980s*, New York: Routledge and Kegan Paul.

Orwell, G., 1949, *Nineteen Eighty Four*, London: Secker and Warburg.

Ouchi, W., 1990 (Selections, Interview, Spring, p.38)

Parker, M., and J. Hassard (eds), 1993, *Postmodernity and Organizations*, London: Sage.

Parkinson, C.N., 1957, *Parkinson's Law*, Boston: Houghton and Miffin.

Pearson, J. Cornelia, 1985, *Gender and Communication*, Iowa: Wm. C. Brown.

Peitchinis, S.G., 1989, *Women at Work*, Toronto: McClelland and Stewart.

Perrow, C., 1982, "The Short and Glorious History of Organization Theory," in *Readings and Organizations*, edited by J. Gibson et al., Texas: Business Publications, Inc.

Perrow, C., 1984, *Normal Accidents*, New York: Basic Books.

Peter, L.J., and R. Hull, 1969, *The Peter Principle*, New York: W. Morrow.

✳Peter, K., 1981, "The Myth of Multiculturalism and Other Political Fables," in *Ethnicity, Power and Politics in Canada*, edited by J. Dahlie and T. Fernando, Toronto: Methuen.

Pfeffer, J., A. Leong, and K. Strehl, 1977, "Paradigm development and particularism: journal publication in three scientific disciplines," *Social Forces*, 55: 938-51.

Pineo, P., 1976, "Social mobility in Canada: the current picture," *Sociological Focus*, 9: 109-123.

Pollert, A., 1981, *Girls, Wives, Factory Lives*, London: Macmillan.

Ponting, R., 1986, *Arduous Journey: Canadian Indians and Decolonization*, Toronto: McClelland and Stewart.

Ponting, R., 1980, *Out of Irrelevance: A Socio-Political Introduction to Indian Affairs in Canada*, Toronto: Butterworths.

Porter, J., 1965, *The Vertical Mosaic*, Toronto: University of Toronto Press.

Porter, J., 1975, "Ethnic Pluralism in Canadian Perspective," in *Ethnicity*, edited by N. Glazer and D.P. Moynihan,

Cambridge, MA.: Harvard University Press.

Pugh, D.S., D.J. Hickson, and C.R. Hinings, [eds], 1983, *Writers on Organizations*, Harmondsworth: Penguin.

Pugh, T., 1987, "North Battleford's Gainers Plants: Sweet or Sour?", *Canadian Dimension*, Vol.21, No.3., May/June.

Pugh, T., 1987, "Gainers at the Trough: Taxpayers and Farmers Take All The Risks," *Canadian Dimension*, Vol.21, No.3, May/June.

Pusey, M., 1987, *Jurgen Habermas*, London: Tavistock.

Putnam, L., 1982, "In Search of Gender: A Critique of Communication and Sex-Roles Research," *Women's Studies in Communication*, 5, pp.1-9.

Putnam, L., 1983, "The Interpretive Perspective. An Alternative to Functionalism," in *Communication and Organizations. An Interpretive Approach*, edited by L.L. Putnam and M.E. Pacanowsky, Beverly Hills: Sage.

Putnam, L., and G. Fairhurst, 1985, "Women and Organizational Communication: Research Directions and New Perspectives," *Women and Language*, Vol.IX, No.1/2, pp.2-6.

Quinn, R.E., 1977, "Coping with Cupid: The Formation, Impact, and Management of Romantic Relationships in Organizations," *Administrative Science Quarterly*, 22, pp.30-45.

Rakow, L.F., 1986, "Rethinking gender research in communication," *Journal of Communication*, 36/4, Autumn: 11-24.

Ramcharan, S., 1982, *Racism: Non-Whites in Canada*, Toronto: Butterworths.

Ranke-Heinemann, U., 1990, *Eunuches For The Kingdom Of Heaven: Women, Sexuality, and the Catholic Church*, New York: Doubleday.

Reinharz, S., 1988, "Feminist Distrust: Problems of Context and Content in Sociological Work," in *The Self in Social Inquiry*, edited by D.N. Berg and K.K. Smith, Newbury Park, CA: Sage.

Reiter, E., 1991, *Making Fast Food: From the Frying Pan into the Fryer*, McGill-Queen's University Press.

Reiter, E., 1986, "Life in a Fast-Food Factory," in *On the Job: Confronting the Labor Process in Canada*, edited by C. Herron and R. Storey, McGill-Queen's University Press.

Reitz, J.G., 1980, *Survival of Ethnic Groups*, Toronto: McGraw-Hill Ryerson.

Rich, A., 1979, "Disloyal to Civilization: Feminism, Racism, Gynephobia," in *Lies, Secrets and Silence*, New York: Norton.

Rinehart, J., 1987, *The Tyranny of Work*, Harcourt Brace Jovanovich.

Robertson, I.T., and C.L. Cooper, 1986, *Human Behavior in Organizations*, London: Pitman.

Robbins, S.P., 1989, *Organizational Behavior, Concepts, Controversies, and Applications*, Fourth Edition, Englewood Cliffs, N.J.: Prentice-Hall.

Robbins, S.P., 1990, *Organizational Theory: Structure, Design, and Applications*, Third Edition, Englewood Cliffs, N.J.: Prentice-Hall.

Roethlisberger, F.J., and W.J. Dickson, 1939, *Management and the Worker*, Cambridge, MA.: Harvard University Press.

Roethlisberger, F.J., 1977, *The Elusive Phenomena: An Autobiographical Account of My Work in the Field of Organizational

Behavior at the Harvard Business School, Cambridge, MA.: Harvard University Press.

Rose, M., 1975, *Industrial Behaviour,* Harmondsworth: Penguin.

Rowney, J., and A.R. Cahoon, 1988, "Individual and Organizational Characteristics Of Women in Managerial Leadership Roles," in Proceedings of the Women in Management Research Forum, Mount Saint Vincent University, Halifax, N.S., April 27-29.

Samuel, T.J., 1988, "Immigration and visible minorities in the year 2001," *Canadian Ethnic Studies,* (20)2.

Satzewich, V., and P. Li, 1987, "Immigrant labour in Canada: the cost and benefits of ethnic origin in the job market," *Canadian Journal of Sociology,* 12: 229-41.

Sayles, L., 1964, *Managerial Behaviour,* New York: McGraw-Hill.

Schein, E., 1980, *Organizational Psychology,* Englewood Cliffs, N.J.: Prentice-Hall.

Schein, E., 1985, *Organizational Culture and Leadership,* London: Jossey-Bass.

Schein, V.E., 1989, "Sex Role Stereotypes and Requisite Management Characteristics Past, Present and Future," *National Centre for Management Research and Development,* Working Paper No. NC 89-26, Nov.

Schermerhorn, J.R., J.G. Hunt, and R.N. Osborn, 1986, *Managing Organizational Behaviour,* Third Edition, New York: John Wiley.

Schmidt, F.L., K. Pearlman, and J. Hunter, 1980, "The validity and fairness of employment and educational tests for Hispanic Americans: a review and analysis," *Personnel Psychology,* 33:705-724.

Schneider, B.E., 1982, "Consciousness about Sexual Harassment among Heterosexual and Lesbian Women Workers," *Journal of Social Issues,* Vol.38, No.4, pp.75-98.

Schneider, B.E., 1984, "The Office Affair: Myth and Reality for Heterosexual and Lesbian Women Workers," *Sociological Perspectives,* Vol.27, No.4, pp.443-64.

Seeley, John R., 1967, *The Americanization of the Unconscious,* Int. Science Press.

Selznick, P., 1949, *T.V.A. and the Grass Roots: A Study in the Sociology of Formal Organizations,* Berkley: University of California Press.

Shawcross, W., 1979, *Sideshow: Kissinger, Nixon and the Destruction of Cambodia,* New York: Simon and Schuster.

Sheff, D., 1993, *Game Over,* New York: Random House.

Sheppard, D.L., 1989, "Organizations, Power and Sexuality: The Image and Self-Image of Women Managers," in *The Sexuality of Organization,* edited by J. Hearn, D.L. Sheppard, P. Tancred-Sherrif, and G. Burrell, pp.139-57, London: Sage.

Sheriff, P., and E.J. Campbell, 1992, "Room For Women: A Case Study in the Sociology of Organizations," in *Gendering Organizational Analysis,* edited by A.J. Mills and P. Tancred, pp.31-45, Newbury Park, CA.: Sage.

Silverman, D., 1970, *The Theory of Organizations,* New York: Basic Books.

Sjoberg, G., 1983, "Afterword," in *Bureaucracy As A Social Problem,* edited by W.B. Littrell, G. Sjoberg, and L.A. Zurcher, Greenwich, CT.: JAI Press.

Slocum, J. Jr., and R. Strawser, 1972, "Racial differences in job attitudes," *Journal of Applied Psychology,* 56:28-32.

Smircich, L., 1983, "Concepts of Culture

and Organizational Analysis," *Administrative Science Quarterly*, 28, pp.339-358.

Smircich, L., 1985, "Is the Concept of Culture a Paradigm for Understanding Organizations and Ourselves?," in *Organizational Culture*, edited by P.J. Frost, L.F. Moore, M.R. Louis, C.C. Lundberg, and J. Martin, pp.55-72, Beverly Hills, CA.: Sage.

Squire, C., 1989, *Significant Differences – Feminism In Psychology*, London: Routledge.

Stanley, L., and S. Wise, 1983, *Breaking Out: Feminist Consciousness and Feminist Research*, London: Routledge and Kegan Paul.

Statistics Canada, 1989, *Work Injuries 1986-1988*, Ottawa.

Statistics Canada, 1990 (Dec.), *Earnings of Men and Women 1989*, Ottawa.

Stewart, M., 1967, *Managers and their Jobs*, London: Macmillan.

Stewart, T.A., "New Ways to Exercise Power", *Fortune Magazine*, Nov. 6, 1989, pp.52-64.

Stone, D.L., and E.F. Stone, 1987, "Effects of missing application-blank information on personnel selection decisions: Do privacy protection strategies bias the outcome?", *Journal of Applied Psychology*, 72:452-456.

Tancred-Sheriff, P., 1989, "Gender, Sexuality and the Labour Process," in *The Sexuality of Organization*, edited by J. Hearn, D.L. Sheppard, P. Tancred-Sherrif, and G. Burrell, pp. 44-55, London: Sage.

Task Force on Sex-Role Stereotyping in the Broadcast Media, 1982, *Images of Women*, Hull, Que.: Canadian Government Publishing Centre.

Taylor, F.W., 1911, *Principles of Scientific Management*, New York: Harper and Row.

Tepperman, L., 1975, *Social Mobility in Canada*, Toronto: McGraw-Hill Ryerson.

Terkel, S., 1974, *Working*, Pantheon.

Terpstra, D. and M. Larse, 1985, "A note on job type and applicant race as determinants of hiring decisions," *Journal of Occupational Psychology*, 53(3): 117-119.

Thompson, P., 1991, "Fatal Distraction, Post-Modernism and Organizational Analysis." Paper presented at the Towards a New Theory of Organizations conference, University of Keele, UK, April.

Thompson, V., 1961, *Modern Organizations*, New York: Knopf.

Toffler, A., 1981, *The Third Wave*, Glasgow: Pan.

Vecchio, R., 1980 "Worker alienation as a moderator of the job quality – job satisfaction relationship: the case of racial differences," *Academy of Management Journal*, 23:479-486.

Wall, J., 1986, *Bosses*, Lexington, MA.: D.C. Heath.

Wallis, M., 1989, "The Dynamics of Race in Institutions." Paper presented at the Canadian Sociology and Anthropology Association annual meeting, Quebec City, June.

Walter, G.A., 1983, "Psyche and Symbol," in *Organizational Symbolism*, edited by L.R. Pondy, P.J. Frost, G. Morgan, and T. Dandridge, pp.257-271, Greenwich, CT.: JAI Press.

Weaver, S., 1981, *Making Canadian Indian Policy: The Hidden Agenda, 1968-1970*, Toronto: University of Toronto Press.

Weber, M., 1947, *The Theory of Social and Economic Organization*, translated by A.R. Henderson and Talcott Parsons, London: Free Press.

Weber, M., 1948, *From Max Weber: Essays in Sociology*, translated, edited, and with an introduction by H.H. Gerth and C.Wright Mills, London: RKP.

Weeks, D., 1978, *A Glossary of Sociological Concepts*, Milton Keynes: The Open University Press.

Weiss, R.M., 1986, *Managerial Ideology and The Social Control of Deviance in Organizations*, New York: Praeger.

Wetherall, M., H. Stiven, and J. Potter, 1987, "Unequal Egalitarianism: A Preliminary Study of Discourses Concerning Gender and Employment Opportunities," British Journal of Social Psychology, 26, pp.59-71.

Williamson, O.E., 1975, *Markets and Hierarchies: Analysis and Antitrust Implications – A Study in the Economics of Internal Organization*, New York: Free Press.

Woodsworth, James, (1909) 1972, *Strangers Within Our Gates*, Toronto: University of Toronto Press.

Wren, D.A., 1979, *The Evolution of Management Thought*, New York: Ronald Press.

Wren, D.A., and D. Voich Jr., 1984, *Management: Process, Structure and Behaviour*, New York: John Wiley.

Zaleznik, A., 1989, *The Managerial Mystique*, New York: Harper and Row.

Zavella, P., 1985, "Abnormal intimacy – The varying networks of Chicana cannery workers," *Feminist Studies*, 11(3), pp.541-57.

Zolf, L., 1982, "How multiculturalism corrupts," *Maclean's*, 15 November.

Index

Abella Commission 51, 134, 144, 169,
    186,188
aboriginal peoples 10, 13, 156
Acker , J. 139, 140, 141, 148, 204
actionalist approach to organizations, 11-12
Adorno, T. 101, 106, 177
advertising 155,158,159,187
Afghanistan War 203
Agocs, C. 146
Alderfer, C. 172,173,174, 180,182
alienation 116, 140
Allen, V. 141, 204
Althusser, L. 204
Alvesson, M. 82
America, R.F. 172
Amway 82
Anderson, R. 172
androcentric 82, 170, 183,185
anti-Semitism 172
Argyris, C. 107, 110
Ash, Mary Kay 82
assimilationism 155, 164, 175, 176, 178
atomization 7, 104
Atwood, M. 203
authoritarian 8, 41, 42, 47, 73, 102, 105,
    106, 109, 202
authoritarian personality 104, 174
authority 22, 30, 34, 47, 48, 49, 51, 58, 62,
    65, 70, 100, 105, 135, 139, 147, 198, 199
    rational-legal authority 37, 38

bankruptcy 8
Barnard, C. 42, 69, 200
barriers to change 142-3, 146, 159, 167, 186
Beattie, C. 51, 158
Bell, E. 13, 121, 147, 171, 172
Bennis, W. 47
Benson, J.K. 112, 204
Benson, S.P. 145
Bergman, P. 6
Beynon, H. 141
Bibby, R. 167-8
bilingualism 161, 180
Black Loyalists 157
Black struggle 206
Blackburn, R.M. 141
Blauner, R. 140, 175
Blustein, D.L. 120
body, the 113, 114
Bolaria, B.S. 51, 179
Bonacich, E. 185
borderline personality disorders 115-116
Borisoff, D. 143
bounded rationality 141
Boyne, 114
Bradshaw-Campball, P. 134
Braverman, H. 56, 69, 75
Brindley, J. 146
Britain 3, 80, 160,165, 185, 203
British Airways 78
budgeting 78

bureaucracy 7, 29-56, 102, 103-4, 140, 198, 200, 207
   bureaucratic control 62, 67, 68
   bureaucratic forces 203
   bureaucratic institutions 36, 117
   bureaucratic principles of organization. 34, 50
   bureaucratic regimes. 33
   bureaucratic rules 35, 44, 102
   bureaucratization 7, 102
   bureaucrats 30, 36, 42, 43, 44, 45, 102, 185
   corporate bureaucracies 34
   government bureaucracies 6, 30, 31, 34, 35, 46, 47, 51
   ideal-typical bureaucracy 41, 43
   iron cage of bureaucracy 7, 47
   pre-industrial bureaucracies 43
   rational-legal bureaucracy 37
   state bureaucracy 8, 33, 36, 47
Burger King 76
Burke, R. 146, 180, 182
Burowoy, M. 65, 141
Burrell, G. 11, 12,110,112,137, 198, 205, 206
Cahoon, A.R. 146
Calas, M. 13, 147
calculability 104
Cambodia 46
Campbell, E.J. 141, 149
Campbell, B.M.172
Canada 3, 6, 30, 34, 44, 80, 134, 146, 155, 157, 158, 160, 161, 162, 163, 164, 165, 166, 167, 168, 176, 179, 180, 185, 207
   Canada Employment and Immigration Commission, 44, 157, 160
   Canadian Broadcasting Corporation 156
   citizenship 33, 160
   Crown corporations 134
   Department of Immigration 31
   Department of Indian and Northern Development, 30, 34, 210
   Parliament 6
   Public Service 51, 134
Canadian Pacific 31, 210
capitalism 7, 8, 36, 63, 102, 106, 110, 111, 112
Caribbean 210
Carlsson, S. 79, 80
Castles, S. 185
Catholic Church, the 147
Cava, R. 143
CCF provincial government in Saskatchewan 46
centralization 29, 34, 47
chambers of commerce 32
Chandler, A. 63, 64
Chiaramonte, P. 143
Chinese Immigration (Exclusion) Act 157
churches 6, 32, 37
CIA 202
Citizen's Forum on National Unity 166
Civil Rights movement 174
civil servants 29, 30, 46
civil service 36, 50
Clark, D.L. 48
class 2, 4, 9, 17, 18, 32, 36, 44, 46, 48, 49, 57, 63, 64, 68, 82, 100, 101, 113, 164, 165, 169, 185
   ruling class 36
classical schools of management theory 68, 79
Clegg, S. 98, 137, 202, 204, 205
Coch, L. 137
Cockburn, C. 140, 145
Cohen, A. 135, 147
Cold War, the 203-4, 205
Collinson, D. 114, 133, 147
Collison, M. 114, 133, 147
colonization 6, 157, 176
commanding 77, 84
communication styles 143
Communism 36, 46, 114, 205
Comte, A. 198

confessional practices 113, 119
Conklin, D. 4
contingency theory 71, 74, 76, 200
control 10, 20, 32, 35, 36, 42, 63, 65, 66,
    73, 75, 84, 96, 105, 108, 113, 114, 116,
    148, 204, 207
    bureaucratic control 67
    hegemonic control 202
    simple control 65
    technical control 66, 100, 202
Cooper, C.L. 107, 148
Cooper, K.C. 147
coordinating 59-60, 77, 78, 79, 104, 202
Corliss, R. 103
corporate culture 82, 83, 170, 172, 181, 183
corporate take-overs 33
coup d'etat (Chile, 1974) 203
Cox, M.G. 143
Cox, T. 172, 173
craft guilds 6
Crane, D. 171
Crean, S. 135
critical approach to organizations 2, 4, 5, 9-
    10, 20, 95, 101
Crozier, M. 141
Cullen, D. 110
Cuneo, C. 134
Czechoslovak Spring 203
Daft, R. 15, 16, 100
Dagg, A. 137, 138
Dahrendorf, R. 63
Dale, E. 60, 70, 78
Darroch, A.G. 212
Davidson, M. 148
Davies, S. 141, 147
Deal, T.E. 82
decision making 132
degradation of work 75, 80
democracy 32, 47, 49
democratic style of leadership 174, 202
democratic work climates 140
Denton, T. 172

deskilling 57, 69, 73, 75, 146
Dickens, F. 172
Dickson, D. 204
Dickson, W.J. 98, 173
directing 66, 77, 84
disciplinary practices 212
discrimination 10, 17, 18, 49, 50, 51, 95,
    138, 142, 144, 145, 157, 159, 160, 162,
    166, 168, 169, 171, 179, 185, 187, 188
DiTomaso, N. 4, 135, 147
division of labour 6, 43, 74, 77
Djilas, M. 204
domination 22, 47, 104, 108, 109, 177, 178,
    183, 205
Donnelly, J.H. 70
Dreyfus, H.L. 114
Drucker, P. 72
Dubchek, Alexander 203
Due Billing, Y. 82
Dunkerley, D. 98, 202, 204, 205
Dupont, Alfred 62, 73
Durkheim, E. 7, 8, 98, 101
Heath, Edward 203
Edwards, R. 59, 62, 65, 66, 67
efficiency 12, 14, 18, 29, 35, 37, 42, 43, 63,
    68, 70, 74, 75, 96, 103, 200, 201
employment equity 131, 142, 143, 149, 162,
    168, 186
entrepreneurs 62, 63, 80, 113
ethnic stratification 183
environment 34
    environmental disasters 9
    environmental pollution 8
ethnicity 2, 3, 15, 32, 45, 48, 52, 121, 122,
    155, 157, 160, 161, 163, 164, 165, 169,
    170, 171, 172, 173, 176, 178, 180, 181,
    183, 187, 188, 190
    ethnic mosaic 164
ethnocentrism 82, 167, 170, 171, 178, 179,
    181, 182, 186
European Common Market 207
Fayol, H. 69, 73, 74, 77, 79, 81

Feldberg, R. 141
femininity 97, 109, 117, 120, 134, 148, 201
feminism
    feminist organizational analysis 11, 12,
        13, 83, 98, 140, 144, 145, 148, 201
    feminist psychoanalytical perspective 117,
        119
    feminist organizations 21
    feminist theory 95, 119, 120, 206
Feminist Review, 21
Ferguson, K. E. 50, 141, 206
Fernandez, J. 172
financial planning 78
Flax, J. 22, 23, 113, 114, 119
flight attendants 147
Follett, Mary Parker141
Ford Motor Company 34, 65
Ford II, Henry 62, 118
Ford, Henry 62, 63, 118
formalization 35, 103
Fortune Magazine 70
Foucault, M. 113, 114, 116, 198
Fox, B.J. 4
Fox, J. 4
Francophones 51, 158, 161, 163
Frankfurt School 101
French Canadians 158
French, J.R.P. 140
Freud, Sigmund 98, 99, 106, 107
Frick, P. 137
Fromm, E. 101
Frost, P. 59, 78
Gemmill, G. 118
gender 1, 2, 3, 4, 15, 16, 18, 22, 32, 45, 49,
    52, 84, 101, 107, 118, 119, 122, 133,
    136, 137, 140, 141, 142, 143, 144, 146,
    147, 149, 169, 170
    gender identity 119, 120
    gendered character of organizations, 122,
        206
gender focussed approach 146
General Motors 31, 73

Gerloff, E.A. 82
Gibson, J.L. 70
Gillen, D.J. 81
Gilligan, C. 110
Ginzberg, E. 159
glasnost 34, 112, 205
glass ceiling, the 146
Glenn, E.N. 141
Gouldner, A. 42, 198
Gram, H. 11
Grant, J. 21
Gross, B. 33
Gulf War (1991), the 5
Gullick, L. 77, 78
Gutek, B. 135, 146, 147
Halberstam, D. 5
Hall, M. 136, 147
Harrison, D. 133
Hatton, M. 6
Hawthorn Report 163
Hawthorne Studies, the 11, 18, 42, 99, 138,
    163
Heap, J.L. 165
Hearn, J. 133, 146, 147, 148
Held, D. 104, 105, 106
Henry, F. 159
heterosexuality 13, 97, 133, 135
hierarchy 6, 7, 34, 38, 41, 51, 62, 83, 97,
    109, 177, 201
hierarchy of needs theory 107–109
historical materialism 111
Hoffman, E. 108, 109, 110
Hofstede, G. 144
homophobic 13
homosexuality 135, 136, 147
Hood, J. 145
Hoover, J.Edgar 118
Horkheimer, Max 101, 105
hospitals 6, 14, 33, 132, 184
Hudson Bay Company 34, 39
Human Relations school 11, 42, 72, 99,
    142, 173, 199

humanist theories of organization 12, 72, 75, 95, 98, 106, 107, 205, 206
Hunt, J.G. 100
Huxley, Aldus 32
Hydebrand, W. 204
I.T.T 203
Iacocca, L. 82, 118
IBM 67
identity 29, 95, 112, 118, 119, 120, 142, 148
ideology 52, 61, 110, 121, 163, 176, 178, 180
Illich, I. 18, 19, 20, 112, 204
immigrants 31, 45, 51, 158, 159, 160, 165, 166
    chinese immigrants 51
    non-white immigrants 160
Imperial Oil 31
Indian Act, the 158
Industrial Revolution, the 6, 65
informal work groups 42
informational roles 80
Institute of Social Research 101
instrumental reason 103, 104
interpersonal roles 80
interpretive approaches to organizations (see also actionalist approach) 12, 205, 206
Irangate 203
Italians 158
Ivancevich, J.M. 70
Japanese Canadians 157
Jauch, L.R. 171
Johns, G. 15, 16, 17, 69
Kanter, R.M. 4, 51, 198, 201, 204
Kennedy, A.A. 82
Kentucky Fried Chicken 76
Kets de Vries, M. 107, 117, 118
KGB 202, 203
Kidney, B.A. 119
Kirby, S. 149
Knights, D. 114
Koberg, C.S. 145
Kohut, H. 116

Kosack, G. 185
Kovel, J. 116
Kroc, Ray 82
Kuhn, T. 196, 197, 198
labour market segmentation 185
labour power 102
labour process 65, 66, 74, 143, 145
Lamphere, L. 145
Larwood, L. 146
Lasch, C. 107, 115, 116, 117
Lautard, H. 165
Lawrence, P. 45, 80
leadership style 99, 202
Leavitt, H. 82
Lee 133
Lenin, V.I. 36
Leonard, P. 4, 75, 110, 111, 112
Lewin, K. 141, 202
Li, P. 51, 166, 179
libido 105, 106
Lippitt, R. 141, 202
Lipset, S.M. 42, 46
Livingstone, D.W. 148
Locke, E. A. 73
Loree, D. 165
Lowe, G. 4, 145
Luxton, M. 148
Maastricht agreement, the 207
Maier, M. 147, 148
managerialist viewpoint 11, 57, 98, 195, 196, 198, 199, 202, 204
managers 11, 16, 35, 42, 58-66, 68, 69, 70, 74, 75, 76, 77, 79-83, 85, 98, 99, 104, 107, 145, 169, 170, 183, 185, 199, 200, 203, 205
managerial revolution, the 61, 63, 64, 66
Marcuse, H. 100, 104
Marshall, H. 120
Martin, J. 140, 145
Marx , K. 7, 8, 101, 102, 104, 110, 112, 141
Marxists 8, 95, 98, 104, 110, 141, 204
Mary Kay Cosmetics 82

masculinity 97, 109, 118, 131, 133, 134

Maslow, A. 107–110

mass communication 158

mass unemployment, 8, 202

May '68' events (France)203

Mayo, E. 42

MBA 3

McCarthyism 203

McDonalds 37, 76

McKeen, C. 146

McKenna, K. 149

Mead, G.H. 110–111

Meissner, M. 143

mentors 17, 146, 178

Merrill, L. 143

Merton, R.K. 42, 44

Michels, R. 36, 47

Miewald, R. 47

Mighty, J. 13, 121, 181, 183

Mills, A.J. 11, 82, 117, 145, 147, 150,

Mintzberg, H. 60, 79, 80, 81

mirroring, 118, 202

Mitchell, V.E. 59, 78

modes of production 12

monopolies 33

Morgan, Gareth 11, 12, 101, 112, 114, 141, 171, 198, 205

Morgan, Glenn 114

Morgan, Nicole 12, 141, 145

Morrison, A. 146

motivation 18, 99, 100, 107, 112, 176, 178, 190, 202

multi-culturalism 3, 5, 155, 161, 164, 167, 168, 169, 179, 180, 182, 184, 186

Mumby, D.K. 141

Murgatroyd, S. 11, 117, 147

Murphy, C.J. 172

Nahem, J. 118

narcissism 106, 107, 115, 116, 117, 118

narcissistic organizational culture 117

National Liberation Front (Vietnam) 203

NATO 46, 202

Nazi Germany 106, 158

Nazis 106

neo-Nazism in Europe 106, 207

neurosis 99, 106, 107, 115, 116, 118

Nintendo 103

Nixon administration, the 46

Nkomo, S. 13, 121, 172, 176, 178, 180

Nord, W. 59, 78

North American Free Trade Agreement 207

Northcote Parkinson, C. 45

Nova Scotia 157

nurses 147

Offical Languagues Act 161

Official Secrets Act, the 46

opportunity structure 51

Organization Theory 2, 3, 10, 13, 15, 23, 32, 34, 36, 40, 41, 42, 48, 49, 52, 58, 61, 68, 69, 97–98, 122, 141, 155, 157, 169, 170, 176, 178, 179, 190, 196, 198, 199, 201, 202, 205, 206, 207

Organizational Behaviour 2, 3, 9, 10, 15, 97–98, 100, 107, 172, 196, 205

organizational change 10, 76

organizational crisis 5

organizational culture 2, 18, 82, 83, 98, 117, 118, 143, 144, 145, 176

organizational pathways 143, 146

organizational power 10, 12, 97, 101, 114, 131, 135, 136

organizational rules 104

organizational structure 2, 18, 23, 64, 98, 103, 110

Orwell, George 32, 203

Osborn, R.N. 100

Ouchi, W. 3

Pareto, V. 98

Parkin, W. 146, 147, 148

Parsons, T. 198

patriarchy 13, 105

    patriarchal authority 116

    patriarchal dominance 82

    patriarchal structures 83

pay inequities 4, 134
Pearson, J.C. 143
Peitchinis, S.G. 134, 142
Pentagon, the 202
people of colour 17, 83, 185
perestroika 34
Perrow, C. 5, 9
personality 29,98, 101, 102, 106, 107, 110,
    111, 112, 115, 120, 121, 122, 156
Peter, K. 180
phenomenological approaches to organiza-
    tions 107
Pineo, P.C. 165
planning 19, 34, 74, 76, 77, 78, 79, 84
Polaroid 67
Pollert. A. 145, 147
Ponting, R. 30
Porter, J. 51, 159, 165, 184
postmodernism 22, 115
Potter 120
power 10, 12, 16, 17, 18, 22, 30, 31, 33, 36,
    42, 48, 50, 60, 66, 67, 69, 70, 83, 97,
    100, 101, 102, 104, 105, 113, 114, 115,
    122, 133, 135, 136, 146, 147, 177, 180,
    195, 198
power blocs 207
power structures 122, 135, 198
prisons 6, 101
profits 62, 70, 103
psychic prison 95, 101
psychoanalytic theories of organization 107,
    118
Putnam, L. 141, 143
Quebec 131, 158
Quebec sovereignty 161
Quinn, R.E. 133
race 1, 3, 4, 48, 57, 101, 119, 122, 138, 155-
    190
Rabinow, P. 114
racism 4, 121, 138, 159, 160, 169, 171, 173
    institutional racism 162, 171
    racial discrimination 138, 169

race relations 155
radical humanist approaches to organization
    12, 122
radical structuralist perspectives on organiza-
    tions 12, 122, 198
Ramcharan, S. 51, 166, 179
Ranke-Heinemann, U. 147
rationality 31, 37, 40, 43, 50, 104, 141, 200,
    201
Rattansi 114
RCMP 166, 186
recession 8, 166
Red Army 202
registered Indians 30
Reich, W. 101, 105, 106
Reinharz, S. 13, 14
repressed sexuality 106
repressed urges 106
Revenue Canada 34
Robbins, S. 9, 15, 16
Robertson, I. 107
Roethlisberger, F. 98, 173, 174
Rose, M. 11, 98, 99
routinization 35
Rowney, J. 146
Royal Commission on Biculturalism and
    Bilingualism 161
Royal Commission on Equality in Employ-
    ment 3, 169
rules 20, 35, 37, 40, 44, 49, 102, 104, 118,
    145, 167
    impersonal rules 37
    technical rules 104
    written rules 39
Russian Revolution (1917) 8
Saint-Simon 198
Sampson, A. 203
Satzwich, V. 166
Schaible, L.Z. 118
Schein, E. 18, 19
Schein, V. 19
Schermerhorn, J.R. 100

Schneider, B.E. 136, 147

schools 6, 14, 20, 113, 122, 204

Scientific Management 11, 42, 57, 66, 70, 71, 72, 73, 75, 76, 98, 141, 200

self, the 29, 62, 101, 103, 107, 110, 111, 112, 114, 116, 117, 119, 120, 122, 149

   core self 119

   gendered self 119, 122, 149

   racial self 120

   self centeredness 106

   self control 114

   self esteem 4, 116, 117, 122

   self-image 116

   self-knowledge 112, 114, 116, 122

   self-perpetuation 45, 149

   self-preservation instincts 103

   self-sufficiency 32,

   self-respect 30

self-actualization 108

Selznick, P. 42, 44, 198

sex 10, 16, 17, 105, 118, 133, 136, 138, 141, 146, 148

   sex based power differentials 118, 139

   sex characteristics 16

   sexual discrimination 17, 49, 118, 138, 142, 144

   sex-role stereotypes 16, 17, 135, 146

sex differences approach 146

sexual harassment 4, 16, 118, 135, 142, 147

sexual preference 118, 135, 136, 147

sexuality 49, 104, 105, 108, 109, 113, 117, 118, 133, 135, 136, 139, 146, 147

   genital sexuality 105

Shawcross, W. 46

Sheppard, D. 146, 147

Sikhs 168, 186

Silverman, D. 141

Simon, H. 141, 200

Sjborg, G. 50

Smircich, L. 12, 144

socialism 8, 36, 205

   socialist governments 7, 8

socialist societies 33, 34, 36

Solzhenitsyn, Alexander 203

specialization 35, 38, 60, 64, 103, 104, 110, 170, 196, 200

Squire, C. 118

staffing 77, 78

Stalinism 102, 103

standardization 35, 47, 76, 78

Stanley, L. 149

Statistics Canada 134, 160

Stelco 31

Stewart, M. 80

Stiven, H. 120

stress 4, 50, 116

Supreme Court (US) 174

systematic soldiering 74

   Tancred[Sheriff] 52, 145, 146, 205

Task Force on Sex-Role Stereotyping 135

Taylor, F.W. 41, 69, 73, 74, 75, 76, 98, 199, 200

Taylorism 2, 75

Tepperman, L. 165

Thomas, D.A. 173, 174

Thompson, P. 115

Thompson, P.J. 115

Thompson, V. 42

time and motion studies 75

Toronto 159, 183

trade unions 6, 15, 21, 32, 145

Trudeau, Pierre 161

Truman, Harry 174

Ukrainians 158

U.S.S.R 34

uniformity 41

United Nations 5

universalist approach to organization 41, 51, 73, 74, 201

universities 6, 14, 37, 45, 48, 137, 138

Urwick, L. 69

U.S. 3, 21, 44, 50, 70, 146, 203

U.S. Commission on Admission to Graduate Management Education 3 use-time 111

Van Houten, D. 138, 139, 140

vertical mosaic 51, 164

Vietnam War 203

visible minorities 3, 51, 72, 156, 158, 159,
160, 162, 169, 177, 184, 185, 201

Voich, D. 59, 78

Wall, J. 171

Wallis, M. 4, 147

Walter, G.A. 116, 117

Ward, Max 82

Wardair 82

Warsaw Pact 202

Watson, G. 172

Webb, Sidney 60

Weber, M. 7, 8, 36, 37, 38, 41, 43, 47, 51,
102, 103, 107, 200

Wetherall, M. 120, 121

White, R.K. 141, 202

Willmott, H.114

Wise, S. 149

women 3, 10, 13, 16, 17, 18, 21, 48, 50, 51,
68, 69, 76, 97, 98, 107, 109, 118, 119,
121, 122, 134, 135, 138, 139, 140, 141,
143, 145, 146, 147, 148, 149, 160, 167,
172, 183, 184, 185, 186
black women 21, 121, 147
gay women 135
white women 21, 135
women of color 121, 138
women in the federal bureaucracy 50

women in management 134, 142, 146, 186,
206

women workers 68, 119, 135, 143, 146

women's movement 13, 145

working class 10, 17, 18, 36, 122

Wren, D.A. 59, 62, 70, 71, 78

MARQUIS

PRINTED BY THE WORKERS OF
IMPRIMERIE D'ÉDITION MARQUIS
IN NOVEMBER 1994
MONTMAGNY (QUÉBEC)